Don't Deny My Name

Don't Deny My Name

Words and Music
and the Black Intellectual Tradition

by Lorenzo Thomas

Edited and with an Introduction by Aldon Lynn Nielsen

THE UNIVERSITY OF MICHIGAN PRESS

ANN ARBOR

Copyright © 2008 by Lorenzo Thomas
All rights reserved
Published in the United States of America by
The University of Michigan Press
Manufactured in the United States of America
⊚ Printed on acid-free paper

2011   2010   2009   2008   4   3   2   1

A CIP catalog record for this book is available from the British Library.

Library of Congress Cataloging-in-Publication Data

Thomas, Lorenzo, 1944–2005.
    Don't deny my name : words and music and the black intellectual
tradition / by Lorenzo Thomas ; edited and with an Introduction by
Aldon Lynn Nielsen.
       p.   cm.
    Includes bibliographical references and index.
    ISBN-13: 978-0-472-09892-7 (cloth : alk. paper)
    ISBN-10: 0-472-09892-6 (cloth : alk. paper)
    ISBN-13: 978-0-472-06892-0 (pbk. : alk. paper)
    ISBN-10: 0-472-06892-X (pbk. : alk. paper)
    1. African Americans—Music—History and criticism.   2. Blues
(Music)—History and criticism.   3. Jazz—History and criticism.
4. Black arts movement—History.   I. Nielsen, Aldon Lynn.   II. Title.
ML3479.T56   2008
781.64089'96073—dc22   2007045154

Acknowledgments

Grateful acknowledgment is owed to Luzmilda Thomas and Donald H. Ford for permission to examine documents held by the Eric and Sadie Dolphy Trust.

The editor wishes to thank Cecilio Thomas for his dedication to the legacy of Lorenzo Thomas. Karen Luik has been of invaluable assistance in making this project possible. Julius Lobo assisted in researching many of the sources that were left incomplete at the time of the author's death and helped in the preparation of the final manuscript. A particular note of thanks goes to LeAnn Fields and all of the staff at the University of Michigan Press for bringing Lorenzo Thomas's last prose work to an eager audience. Some portions of this book were originally delivered as talks or lectures, or appeared in slightly different form in pamphlets, papers and other venues. The editor appreciates that early support for this enterprise and acknowledges the good taste and editorial wisdom of those who have gone before.

Contents

Introduction
by Aldon Lynn Nielsen

"We did them a fortune," wrote Lorenzo Thomas. "We did / them a favor just being / Ourselves inside of them."[1]

That's how I first knew him, reading him as his words crossed the horizon into me. It was, just as he'd said, a favor, a fortune, a fortune you had to keep reading as it turned in your hand. Lorenzo's words became a talisman I held against the confusion, and there is, as always, confusion. You had to step carefully in those times; it helped if you had a good time step. Lorenzo's poems had that knack, that way of getting inside your time, of making you step differently.

It was later that I met Lorenzo Thomas, introduced, of course, by another poet, Charles Bernstein. Lorenzo came to be a friend and a generous supporter of the work I was trying to do, following along, humbly stumbling, in the territories traversed by his timely steps. We came to be something of a tag team on the odd circuit of conference life we both traveled as wandering scribes and scholars. I thought often of those learned bards who fell into step with one another on the road to Timbuktu. I would have liked to have traveled the paths of Mali with Lorenzo.

We wound up in Boulder instead. My wife, Anna Everett, and I more than once made a point of arriving in Boulder when we knew Lorenzo would be there. We'd have dinner, spread a blanket on the ground outside Naropa, and watch the Fourth of July fireworks from the lawn. The fireworks always burned brighter, in keener demarcations measured to the meters of Lorenzo's voice. I was thinking of that on the Fourth of July, 2005, when word reached me that Lorenzo had at last achieved escape velocity, followed that arc of ascent, traveling the space ways.

The first poem of a chapbook Lorenzo published just a year before his passing closes on a question that could serve as summary of everything he ever wrote: "But which way is redemption?"[2] It was a favor he did us just by asking that question. He did us a favor by being, and each of us is better for having been beside him, for having fallen into step with him on the journey toward whatever imaginable redemption. He did us a fortune, and because of him we are the more fortunate travelers.

And, as one last fortune, he left us yet more books. In the weeks before his death, Lorenzo sent an email to me and to his brother, Cecilio, whose artworks accompanied several of Lorenzo's volumes of verse. Lorenzo asked the two of us to serve as his literary executors. It was not a request I had anticipated, and I rushed to assure Lorenzo that he should be doing me that service long before it would become necessary for me to live up to the task he had bequeathed me. Only days later I received the phone call from Houston telling me of Lorenzo's end. I sat down and read "God Sends Love Disguised as Ordinary People," and then the whole of "Euphemysticism," but then I circled back inevitably to "Fit Music" and "Walking Vicksburg Blues." "History is still ephemera," that last begins. And then:

> I walked along the dark lonely
> Road
> I walked beside the fields of Dudley Pillow
> I walked in Mississippi and Louisiana
> And felt the negro terror of a moonless night
> Baptized in more history than I wanted[3]

But none of us has to walk that lonesome valley, in the lengthening shadow of our own histories, by himself, no matter what that song says. There are always other songs, and you can sing them. "I went to the valley," Paul Robeson used to sing:

> I didn't go to stay.
> But my soul got happy
> and I stayed all day.

That's how it was to be with Lorenzo's songs. Whether the "Progressive Reggae" of one of his poems or the "Morning Raga" of another; whether the "Country Song" of *Dancing on Main Street*, the urban soul of that same collection's "Low Rider" or even the British Invasion blues of "Please, Don't Let Me Be Misunderstood." That poem, whose title could be the title of all books of poetry of all times and all places, says everything poets in America find at their fingertips:

> You vex me so
> Impatient sigh,
> Land whose liberation waits
> In my own breath[4]

It was the breath that came with difficulty in Lorenzo's final times. The land he sang of, the land of the blues, waited breathlessly, attending him. He intended it. The blues tends to be that way.

Much was left pending in July 2005, including the texts of two books Lorenzo had submitted to the University of Michigan Press. One of them, this one, had already passed through that initial stage of peer reviewing so familiar to those of us in the academy. I know this because my eyes were among those peering in review at that first draft. No doubt Lorenzo would have added to this collection. He left notes to himself, and to us, here and there throughout the text, pointing toward things he wanted to look up, to find out, address himself to. In the end, I felt it would be unseemly to add words to this text that were not Lorenzo's own, to make of myself an interstitial coauthor, and I so staved off the temptation to fill in the gaps. Instead, while I have edited for errors and elisions, tracked down those tantalizing but unsourced quotations, this is wholly Lorenzo Thomas's book. And it is a blues book.

Some years ago, one of the many conferences at which both Lorenzo and I spoke was a sixtieth birthday tribute to Amiri Baraka hosted at the Schomburg library in Harlem. Typically for the world of poetry, the financing for this event hadn't fallen into place in time for Baraka's actual birthday, and he had already hit sixty-one by the time we all convened to honor those first six decades. It was a deeply emotional event for me, as it brought me together with so many long-term friends, such as Billy Joe Harris, Kalamu ya Salaam, and Lorenzo Thomas, to mount a series of explorations of the works and career of Baraka, who had been one of my teachers when I was a graduate student. Each of us took up a different segment of Baraka's enormous body of work, saying a few words to set a critical frame and then sitting down to a conversation with Baraka on the Schomburg's stage. Lorenzo Thomas drew Baraka's landmark writings on music as his lot, and I couldn't help recalling his talk that day as I reread this book on words, music, and the black intellectual tradition. Lorenzo began by pointing to the obvious, that before *Blues People* there had not been a book-length study of blues-based musics available to a wide audience of American readers from a black author. Lorenzo paused and looked around as he pronounced this fact. Much as my students now sometimes find it difficult to credit that segregation, at least of the de jure stripe, ended so recently that I witnessed the somewhat premature declarations of its final days, so it is hard for younger readers now to grasp what it meant that as recently as the March on Washington, any book about this foundational African American cultural form you picked up in a retail book store would likely have been by a white author. Which is not to say that any number of black music historians and critics hadn't been doing the work and doing it phenomenally well. The pathbreaking projects of Fisk University's prodigious, too often unsung, and intriguingly named Professor John Wesley Work III are well worth considering in this context. But it is to say that America's official publishing culture throughout most of the twentieth century said to black America a version of what some Abolitionists had tried to say to Frederick Douglass: you just tell your story and leave the theory to us. Baraka's *Blues People* put an end to that once and for all, and the audience in the Schomburg could hear in Lorenzo Thomas's voice what it had meant to him to read that book when it appeared in his youth, which was always just a few well-placed time steps ahead of my own.

Reading *Blues People* simply was part of the "Black Intellectual Tradition," and the book itself was a way of saying to the world what Lorenzo Thomas's title says again, "Don't deny my name." In this book, Thomas again and again checks those original sources, cites those half-remembered foretastes. From Amiri Baraka and Larry Neal's *Cricket*, Thomas elicits Albert Ayler's "To Mr. Jones—I Had a Vision." Readers are recalled to the *Black World* of 1973 for Marion Brown's "Improvisation and the Aural Tradition in Afro-American Music." In sharpest contrast to so many of those white writers prior to Baraka's *Blues People*, Thomas himself attends to the thoughts of the musicians. Whether citing the published writings of composers Ayler and Brown, reciting the lyrics of The Whispers, or talking all day with Juke Boy Bonner, Thomas gives us colloquy with the great thinkers who are his subject. For generations now, critics have written of the conversation that is the blues, but how many of them actually, acutely, listened; didn't just outline call and response, but answered the call? It is one thing, as so many presenters do at academic conferences, to argue that there is theory to be found in the cultural productions of everyday people; it is another entirely to act as if you really believe that. Thomas never doubted.

Thomas sets out upon his great migration, a man from farther south whose father took him north to New York, now transplanted himself not just into the American South, but into that particular mélange of South and West known as Texas, a land of grits and groceries where a Mance Lipscomb played guitar with a pocket knife even as Ornette Coleman was marching in the school band. It is in the endless circuits of his own intellectual travel that Thomas finds the blues a body of literature, one that, as he writes here, "explicitly confronts the situation of" the African American migrants to the urban North and the new western territories. But explicit is as explicit does, and sometimes the blues, if it is to serve, as Thomas has it, "as an ameliorative agency in the transaction from rural to urban," sometimes the explicit explodes with the implicit. "Sometimes I wonder, can a matchbox hold my clothes."

One of those in whose footsteps Thomas follows is Sterling Brown, among the first poet-critics to examine the blues explicitly *as* literary form. Brown inhabited a popular culture in which, as Thomas reminds us, *George White's Scandals* was a Broadway smash, with songs like (after all, his name was "White") "That's Why Darkies Were Born." Brown was having no truck with White, and had a few things to say in the *Opportunity* of 1932[5] about what led lyricists of the day to such dizzy excitements over the "startling rediscovery of Alabammy" as a rhyme "for their key word" (one that appears nowhere in Raymond Williams's *Keywords*) *mammy*. "It is against this kind of doggerel," observes Thomas, "that Brown built a levee of authentic African American folksong." Brown's levee, it has to be said, has held, and it was in Brown's basement that Howard University student LeRoi Jones, having adopted a poetic "I" but not yet "Amiri Baraka," listened to Muddy Waters and began to think the thoughts that led to *Blues People.*

Like some cosmic Exoduster, Lorenzo Thomas follows those thoughts from Brown to Brownsville, from the second Sonny Boy Williamson to the first Eric Dolphy, from Langston to LeRoi and back to Lorenzo. He pauses to talk along the way, and in this his book is closer in spirit to Baraka's *Black Music* than to *Blues People,* close cousin to A. B. Spellman's *Four Lives in the BeBop*

Business. There is a day spent with Juke Boy Bonner and Peppermint Harris. And, not content simply to look at photos of Sonny Boy Williamson from his days on the King Biscuit Time radio broadcast (there is something oddly satisfying about photographs of radio programs, but it's not enough), Thomas interviews Sam Anderson, the school superintendent who decided to open the legendry station KFFA in Helena, Arkansas, and then he talks with the Moore brothers, whose King Biscuit flour became the sponsoring vehicle by which Sonny Boy Williamson reached out to the whole delta and beyond. These conversations come from fieldwork, from a trip Lorenzo Thomas made to Arkansas in the early eighties in the company of filmmaker Louis Guida, who later published the volume *Blues Music in Arkansas*.

And always, Thomas is thinking through the manifold implications of poets' responses to the music. By the time his itinerary brings us to the Black Arts era, Thomas is no longer an engaged interviewer but is a participant observer. In much the way that he follows the evolution of the music from the blues, through the work of the territory bands and onto the terrain of bop, Thomas pursues the poetics of the blues and the blues of poets from the thoughts of Hughes and Brown through to the musical engagements of Baraka, Larry Neal, Henry Dumas, and into the studio trackings of the grandchildren of the blues, tracking their treatment of what all of them see as the redemptive powers of jazz.

NOTES

1. Lorenzo Thomas, *The Bathers* (New York: I. Reed Books, 1981), 59.
2. Lorenzo Thomas, *Time Step* (East Bay, Calif.: Kenning Editions, 2004), n.p.
3. Lorenzo Thomas, *There Are Witnesses/Es Gibt Zeugen* (Osnabrück, Germany: OBEMA, 1996), 32.
4. Lorenzo Thomas, *Dancing on Main Street* (Minneapolis: Coffee House Press, 2004), 14.
5. Sterling A. Brown, "Weep Some More My Ladie," *Opportunity* 10 (March 1932): 87.

ONE　All Blues: Roots and Extensions

A Sense of Community

Blues Music as Primer for Urbanization

Mobility as Blues Motif

"The popular song," wrote Sigmund Spaeth in his delightful book *The Facts of Life in Popular Song*, "has become a most revealing index to American life in general. It sums up the ethics, the habits, the slang, the intimate character of every generation, and it will tell as much to future students of current civilization as any histories, biographies, or newspapers of the time" (v–vi).

Spaeth's perception is easily and most appropriately applicable to African American music in both its contemporary popular incarnation and its folk origins. "The chief concern of African music," writes Miles Mark Fisher, "was to recite the history of the people," and it is clear that that concern survived the Middle Passage (1). As Lawrence W. Levine points out,

> In their songs, as in their tales, aphorisms, proverbs, anecdotes, and jokes, African-American slaves, following the practices of the African cultures they had been forced to leave behind them, assigned a central role to the spoken arts, encouraged and rewarded verbal improvisation, maintained the participatory nature of their expressive culture, and utilized the spoken arts to voice criticism as well as to *uphold traditional values and group cohesion.* (6)

While we generally understand folk song as an anonymous and communal product, Fisher insists that the songs of slavery "are best understood when they are considered as expressions of individual Negroes which can be dated and assigned to a geographical locale. They are, in brief, historical documents" (xi).

Similarly, Abbe Niles wrote in 1926: "The blues sprang up, probably within the last quarter-century, among illiterate and more or less despised classes of Southern Negroes. . . . A spiritual is matter for choral treatment; a blues was a one-man affair, originating typically as the expression of the singer's feeling" (9). Other writers also pointed out that the historicity of blues lyrics was not merely accidental. "The blues singer," wrote John W. Work in *American Negro Songs* (1940), "translated every happening into his own intimate inconvenience. To the spiritual creators, the great Mississippi flood of a few years ago [1927] would have been considered a visitation of a wrathful God upon a sinful community. To a blues singer it simply raised the question, 'Where can a po' girl go?'" (28).

"Where to go" is a good question that is often pondered by the blues singer. Mobility is a major motif of the blues—but it is often the picaresque mobility of escape, of the driven, of the optimistic and sometimes fruitless quest. The success and longevity of the motif in blues poetry has, of course, to do with a certain glamour. "During the days a long time ago," says singer Peppermint Harris, "cat's living out in the country, he wants to get to some urban center, you understand. He'd want to get on down to Memphis or Cairo, Illinois. Somewhere where it was jumping."

On the other hand, much of the mobility recounted in the blues has a more sinister genesis—as Richard Wright testifies in his story "Big Boy Leaves Home" or as Sonny Boy Williamson affirms as he sings, "I got to leave this town." Sometimes the journey is made necessary by some deep disappointment in life. It is a soured domestic situation that prompts Elmore James to sing,

> I'm goin' get up in the mornin'
> I believe I'll dust my broom

What is immediately apparent in examining these "songs of mobility," these "traveling songs," is that they are normally addressed to an audience that shares the singer's experience and worldview—sometimes to the extent that, like the casual vernacular of African American people in the United States, the lyrics are not easily comprehended by listeners outside of the singer's circle.

It should be stressed, however, that the theme of mobility is not merely a lyrical convention such as the Romantic poets' *la belle dame sans merci*; the blues metaphors have a certain (i.e., exact) empirical interpretation. The songs are historical documentation of the central drama of Afro-American life in the twentieth century.

War, Displacement, Separation, and Blues

As we fret beneath the Damoclean sword of possible nuclear destruction, it is not too much to say that war—ever more frightening and efficiently lethal—has determined the character of our century. War has one inevitable product: change. The most obvious change, of course, is seen in the physical geography of the fire zone but, curiously, the five major wars fought by the United States since 1898 have not produced physical destruction of our landscape. The changes have been social and economic, thus more difficult to see.

Mythology protects our sensibility. When we think of the last days of the Civil War, for example, we envision the emancipated slaves shouting and dancing in jubilation. We do not see hundreds of thousands of desperate, wretched refugees fleeing the plantations in an attempt to seek safety behind Union army lines.

Poetically speaking, it is that picture that is the motif of twentieth-century African American reality. Details and specifics may change, but that image is indelible and emblematic. And it might be said that the art form needed to record and express this drama almost miraculously arrives in the blues—clever dramatic monologues that run a scale from sentimentality to mocking satire to a genre of cautionary tales.

The power of a blues performance and the tension it creates has been discussed by Paul Carter Harrison, who considers such performances "modal style theatre." In *The Drama of Nommo*, Harrison meticulously describes the drama created by Bobby Bland and his backup singers in a performance transcribed by Charles Keil. "With the song *Yield Not To Temptation*," Harrison writes, Bland "designated the church modality, appointing himself as preacher and the girls as choir—the spiritual representatives of the community/audience which has become the congregation anticipating the revelation of an event. Though Bobby addresses the congregation as if the story reflects his personal problem, the song reveals the moral predicament of infidelity that is the concern of the entire community" (64).

Lest anyone be misled by Harrison's extended church metaphor, be aware that the burden of the song is "Yield not / to temptation . . . while I'm away." It is a song about mature carnal love.

Through ironic understatement, satirical overdramatization, and careful instigative reporting, the blues singer reinforces deeply held community ideals and protests the depredations of an urban status quo geared to bring out the worst in people. Diagnostic in design, the blues is often remedial in effect.

The cautionary blues are guidelines for behavior in love and on the job, and—most importantly—caveats about accepting other people at face value or by their own advertisements for themselves.

Blues as Cautionary Tales

It is the blues as cautionary tale that I'd like to discuss; the songs that express the historical reality of the great African American population migrations of the twentieth century that amounted to a domestic diaspora. I choose this genre specifically because too often blues is defined as depression or hedonism. We need to understand its third dimension as the normative force described by Lawrence W. Levine.

In *Black Men, White Cities*, Ira Katznelson noted that much urban ethnography is based on the premise that the culture shared by black migrants to the cities is dysfunctional and an impediment to social and economic mobility. I suggest that the blues, an integral element of this culture, includes an important body of literature that explicitly confronts the situation of the migrants and—in fact—functions as an ameliorative agency in the transition from rural to urban lifestyles. As might be expected, many of these lyrics compare the two lifestyles and, borrowing from the store of biblical allusions preserved in the "sorrow songs," insist that we learn (as Guitar Slim sings) that "the things that I used to do / I just won't do no more" and that (as Wilson Pickett sang) "99 and a half just won't do."

It is useful to examine the historical impact of the great migration to understand the importance of this genre of blues lyric.

A full generation after slavery's end, almost 90 percent of all African Americans lived in the rural South. The migratory rush from that region to the industrial cities at the dawn of the twentieth century was as great and as disruptive a phenomenon as the slave trade itself had been.

The plague of boll weevils in the cotton fields and the Great War in Europe were the catalysts of the migration, which was also encouraged by an energetic "antiracism" campaign launched by the *Chicago Defender* and fueled by the availability of industrial jobs in northern cities. According to Robert B. Grant,

Northern employers, prior to 1915, had come to depend for much of their labor supply upon the great numbers of European immigrants arriving in the United States. Except during strikes, employers had generally drawn the color line. The war changed this situation. Immigration fell from an all-time high in 1914, of 1,218,480 to . . . 110, 618 in 1918. At the same time production demands leaped ahead. (14)

The result was that between 1910 and 1920, the black population of Los Angeles increased 105 percent; Chicago, 148 percent; Cleveland, 307 percent; Detroit, 611 percent; and Gary, Indiana, 1,283 percent. New York City's 66 percent increase effectively made Harlem the "Negro metropolis of the United States" (Walrond 942).

What African American artists—painters, blues singers, poets—recorded of the era was not statistical data, but the social, psychological, and spiritual impact of the period. "The migrant masses," wrote Alain Locke in 1925,

shifting from countryside to city, hurdle several generations of experience at a leap, but more important, the same thing happens spiritually in the life-attitudes and self-expression of the young Negro, in his poetry, his education and his new outlook, with the additional advantage, of course, of the poise and greater certainty of knowing what it is all about. (*New Negro* 4–5)

If he didn't know, the New Negro certainly found out very quickly. Grant writes:

The reaction of northern whites to the arrival of southern blacks was heavily dependent on racist preconceptions. The preconceptions . . . were amply supported by the behavior of the undereducated, unhealthy black masses flocking to the cities, for the migrants generally lacked both industrial skills and preparation for urban life. Whereas these deficiencies were often characteristic of white immigrant groups and of city in-migrants generally, Negroes felt the disapproval of Caucasians with special force. At its worst, race prejudice led to violence and even murder. (10–11)

While the cruel reception many migrants received is well documented and sometimes discussed in the poetry of the Harlem Renaissance, that was not the subject of the blues.

The blues, after all, remained essentially a dramatic conversation confined to, and carefully encoded for, those who intimately shared the same experience. While sophisticated white people in the 1920s were avid for African American music, the blues and jazz were not primarily designed for their amusement. The songs were more likely intended as a crash course in urban survival—cautionary tales designed to get the new arrival "hep" as quickly as possible.

The truth of the matter is, perhaps, hidden and revealed in that word *hep* and its current version *hip*. The word is certainly not derived, as a sociolinguist once suggested, from a "kinetic cryptosememe from the role the hip plays in dancing, where it can be viewed as a synecdoche for the body and the locus of movement" (Kochman 168). Our word *hip* is, rather, a rendering of southern black refugees' dialect pronunciation of the word *help*. Nineteenth-century writers recording black or white southern speech might have spelled it *he'p*. The true significance of the expression can be guessed by reconstructing the circumstances of its usage in the early part of this century. The first thing the migrant to the big city needs is help. His homefolks will help him find a room, tell him where they're hiring workers, tell him what's what and what's happening. Of course, the city also harbors those who would help the newcomer to hand over his traveling cash, the belongings in his bag, and anything else they might get away with. As Louis Armstrong wrote of his experiences in the years before the first World War: "As the days rolled on, I commenced getting hep to the jive. I learned a great deal about life and people" (192).

There are any number of blues songs that carefully detail the dangers of city life for the newcomer's benefit. The lineage of this genre might also include Paul Laurence Dunbar's novel *Sport of the Gods* (1902), which describes the moral destruction of a black family forced to flee the South only to end in the decadent clutches of New York City. It should be noted that Dunbar sees white racism as a malignant force that works hand in hand with ordinary urban vice.

An intense ambiguity was experienced by the African American migrants. What was at stake was a traumatic estrangement from lifestyles and values developed over the space of two centuries in the rural South. Certainly the blues was appropriate as a medium for expressing the situation's urgency; the blues, after all, might be seen as analogous to the European immigrants' language brought from "the old country." It would be *understood* and the blues would maintain its rural imagery until such time as it became feasible and necessary to adopt an urban vocabulary.

In its earliest manifestations, the songs of the migration are straightforward in their references—expressions of disillusionment bordering on anomie. The feeling of estrangement comes from both ends of the Illinois Central line.

> He left me standin' on the railroad track
> Wavin' my hands and tryin' to call him back

say those left behind, while those in the North say,

> Down in the delta
> Down in the delta
> away from ice and snows
> Down in the delta
> away from ice and snows
> I wanna be where
> the weather suit my clothes

These lines from Spencer Williams's "Mississippi Delta Blues" (1926) express the homesickness of the migrants in an emblematic manner that is characteristic of the blues. Another verse alludes to what has been lost

> These Northern women
> They sure do worry me
> They're always hungry
> they live on toast and tea

(Handy, *Blues: An Anthology* 123–25)

In other words, the down-to-earth vitality of southern life has been replaced with a veneer of urbane sophistication that is ultimately unsatisfying and, perhaps, as fraudulent as the standard photograph sent home of the traveler leaning against somebody else's brand-new luxury automobile. W. C. Handy gave us a similar picture of

> High-falutin' lowbrows under gobs of paint
> Pretendin' like they is, when they know darn well they ain't

There are other songs that describe the experience of those who actually managed to grasp some of the city's glitter and fast fortune, only to lose it as quickly. The story is told by Washboard Sam's "Life Is Just A Book" (1941):

> Now once I had money: could go most anywhere
> Wouldn't wear a shirt: after it tear
> Now my money's gone: done pawned all my clothes
> And if I don't make some changes: I'll be sleeping outdoors

and wailed by Cab Calloway:

> I'm a striver from up on Striver's Row
> And I'm jiving the very best I know,
> But hard times got me topsy-turvy.
> Once I used to have so much money
> and then I used to dress up debonair
> But now I'm on my uppers
> And old Lady Luck she won't let me go nowhere

Other migrants settled for somewhat more stable situations as urban workers, but this lifestyle also had its frustrations. The same frustrations endured by the European immigrants were felt by relocated blacks. "He was a fool to have married," thinks Jurgis Rudkus in Sinclair's The Jungle (1906), "he had tied himself down, had made himself a slave. It was all because he was a married man that he was compelled to stay in the yards; if it had not been for that he might have gone off like Jonas, and to hell with the packers" (139). The very same sentiment appears in Howlin' Wolf's "Killing Floor":

I should have left you a long time ago
I should have left you a long time ago
Then I wouldn't be here now, down on the killing floor

Naturally, the blues also suggested better ways to deal with the situation, as in Memphis Slim's "You Got To Help Me Some" (1941):

Now if I'm the Pullman porter
Girl, you got to be the maid
So when every Sunday comes
We both can get paid

I'm not suggesting that frustration and poverty is unknown in the South, only that these songs specifically confront urban situations.

The seriousness and depth of the disjunction from a comfortably remembered rural life to a difficult urban existence appears in Weldon "Juke Boy" Bonner's lines:

Here I am in the big city
And I'm about to starve to death
And my sister that lives in the country
Got cows and hogs and chickens laying in the nest

Dunbar's theme of the vicious city is also cleverly recorded in a story from North Carolina that folklorist J. Mason Brewer classified among "migrant tales":

The Mother's Last Words to Her Son in the Country

One time there was an old Negro lady who had a son that she tried to rear to be a respectable young man.

When the son became twenty-one years old he left her and went to live in town. While there, he got in trouble and had to go to court. The judge sentenced him to death in the electric chair.

The son was carried home to see his mother for the last time. When they got there, the guards asked her to say her final words to him.

She looked at her son and said, "Now, John, you know I tried to raise you like good people. So you just go on down there and get 'lectro-cuted, and then come back home and act like you got some sense. (150)

A similar theme is explored, with a much more pleasant denouement, in Rudolph Fisher's wonderful story "Miss Cynthie," and there are many folk-tales that turn on the pretensions of migrants returning home from the city for visits.

I have not attempted to present a linear history for these songs for two rea-sons: (1) they are best appreciated as examples of a genre, such as the pas-toral in English-language poetry, that can be flexible in use; and (2) because the massive black migration of the World War I era is, in fact, repeated a gen-eration later with the advent of World War II. Nor does it end there—World War II slides almost imperceptibly into the Korean War, which produces sim-ilar social changes and similar songs.

There are, of course, important differences between 1919 and 1949. One is the advance of desegregation policies in the military and on the home front; another is the replacement of the early migrants' disillusionment with a new dream of success quite as energetic as Alain Locke's 1925 prescription for the "New Negro" of the 1920s.

By the late 1940s, the blues cautionary tale has progressed to the point that it is the matter of popular black movies such as *Souls of Sin* (1949), and *Reet, Petite and Gone* (1947). Both films are entertainingly didactic, cautionary tales depicting the dangers lurking in Harlem for innocent newcomers. The stars of these films—Savannah Churchill, June Richmond, and Louis Jordan—have impeccable blues credentials and, in a sense, extend the genre to a new medium. The films of the 1940s also signal a final and irrevocable adaptation to urban life. In 1928, Big Bill Broonzy could sing:

> Down to the depot mama, Lord
>   I looked up on the board
> Lord, I asked the ticket agent
>   how long the southbound train been gone
> Lord, if the train don't come
>   there's going to be some walking done

Two decades later the mood is quite different. In *Reet, Petite and Gone*, two southern girls arriving in New York to collect an inheritance are met at the airport by a crooked Harlem lawyer who gives them five hundred dollars to turn around and go home. They are tempted, but then Big June Richmond says, "Look, we've got five hundred dollars. We can get an apartment!" Of course, the girls discover that things aren't so easy, but the film gives the 1940s filmgoers the happy ending they want in the big city.

The imagery of rhythm-and-blues songs of later decades exemplifies the decision to stay in the urban environment and survive. Even the early phase of "rap" songs demonstrates this fact. "It's a jungle out there," raps Melle Mel with Grandmaster Flash and the Furious Five on a 1983 hit record:

> sometimes it makes me wonder
> how I keep from going under

and he warns,

> Don't push me, cause I'm close to the edge
> I'm trying not to lose my head

The language is new, tough, and entirely urban; but the message is not new.

We still have our cautionary tales, and there are still artists who expand African American expressive art forms to carry the message that somehow, we survive.

Authenticity and Elevation

Sterling Brown's Theory of the Blues

Every poet must confront a serious problem: how to reconcile one's private preoccupations with the need to make poetry that is both accessible and useful to others. A failure in this area does not, of course, prevent the production of poems. Indeed, some poems—like many of T. S. Eliot's—may be records of this struggle, while others have the disturbingly eloquent beauty of church testifying or twelve-step program witness. One manner of reconciliation is an embrace of what may be called *tradition*, but even this is problematic.

The idea of tradition made Eliot uneasy; at best he saw it as a living artist's colloquy and competition with the dead (48–50). In his essay "Tradition and the Individual Talent," Eliot points out that acquiring the "consciousness of the past" is both necessary and perilous for a poet (52–53).

As a poet somewhat younger than Eliot, Sterling A. Brown delighted in experimentation yet also valued his role as a contributor to a tradition. In the poems he composed in the 1920s, Brown "sought to combine the musical forms of the blues, work songs, ballads, and spirituals with poetic expression in such a way as to preserve the originality of the former and achieve the complexity of the latter" (Gabbin 42). Brown's relationship to tradition was, in other words, something like a mirror image of Eliot's. Where Eliot cringed before a weighty past, Brown—focusing on the African American vernacular tradition—perceived an originality and creativity to be mastered and then practiced in an even more original manner. In fact, Brown's poetics document an attitude toward tradition that is not very different from the one held by the blues singers themselves.

An intriguing discussion of how the New Negro movement attempted to resite the idea of tradition is offered by Charles H. Rowell's view of the poet as a sort of adept: "In a word, when Brown taught and traveled in the South,

he became an insider to the multifarious traditions and verbal art forms indigenous to black folk, and through his adaptations of their verbal art forms
and spirit he, as poet, became an instrument for their myriad voices. Hence,
Southern Road" (134). How this approach to reclaiming tradition in the service
of literary innovation also served Alain Locke's program for the arts as an instrument of race "redemption" via political and social progress is indicated
by a comment from Langston Hughes and Arna Bontemps in their introduction to The Book of Negro Folklore (1959): "The blues provided a tap-root of
tremendous vitality for season after season, vogue after vogue of popular
music, and became an American idiom in a broad sense" (vii).

It is worth noting, also, that Brown did not necessarily see his valorization
of African American folk tradition as inconsistent with his practice of contemporary poetic experiment. Just as Hart Crane and others fled the stultifying worldview of their parents, Brown could warn against "an arising snob-
bishness; a delayed Victorianism" among educated African Americans ("Our
Literary Audience" 42). And when he analyzed the blues, Brown discerned a
poetic approach that paralleled the imagists and other modernists "in sub-
stituting the thing seen for the bookish dressing up and sentimentalizing"
that characterized nineteenth-century literary verse ("Blues as Folk Poetry"
378).

In addition to addressing the dilemma of privacy and access, of the proper
value of tradition, Sterling Brown's work also shows how one writer negoti-
ated the relationship of the creative arts—both "highbrow" and "folk"—to
the political agenda of the African American struggle for self-determination
as it developed in the period between the two world wars. In choosing to
study the blues, Brown found himself engaged with a genre of poetry that offers its own clever solutions to these problems. The blues, Brown discovered,
"has a bitter honesty. This is the way the blues singers and their poets have
found life to be. And their audiences agree" ("The Blues" 288). Indeed, it is
this agreement between poet and audience that is the reality and the purpose
of the blues.

Houston A. Baker, Jr., has rightly noted the unusual circumstance of the
awesomely intellectual young Sterling Brown embracing a form devised by
the unlettered (Modernism 92–95), and perhaps an important clue is found in
Brown's poem "Ma Rainey." Rainey's art and its powerful effect on her audience, her ability to "jes catch hold of us, somekindaway" (Collected Poems 63)
through song, is precisely the ambition of every poet, and may explain one

source of Brown's attraction to the blues. There are some other possibilities as well. Whether or not one sees Brown's poetry as part of the modernist direction—or of the regionalism that seemed to make a number of largely regional "splashes" during the 1930s—Brown's poems also clearly embody and represent two decidedly premodern projects. One of these is the "corrective" gesture of African American scholarship, and the other is the desire of both poets and critics to create a "national literature" for black Americans.

In 1930, Brown declared "a deep concern with the development of a literature worthy of our past, and of our destiny; without which literature we can never come to much." He added, "I have deep concern with the development of an audience worthy of such literature" ("Our Literary Audience" 42). In a sense this aim balances Brown's modernist tendencies and leads him toward the compilation of "antiquities" found in the folk tradition. As Charles H. Rowell has noted, Brown belonged to a group of writers who "realized that to express the souls of black folk, the artist has to divest himself of preconceived and false notions about black people, and create an art whose foundation is the ethos from which spring black life, history, culture, and traditions" (131). This effort is also consistent with the "correctionist" mission first assumed by David Walker in his 1829 rebuttal of Thomas Jefferson's racial slurs in *Notes on the State of Virginia* and continued by Carter G. Woodson, J. A. Rogers, Lerone Bennett, Jr., Ivan van Sertima, and others.

Sterling Brown's contribution to this effort was to identify and analyze the stereotypes—derogatory in varying degrees but *never* "just clean fun"—that proliferate in literature and the media. This he did in both scholarly and popular arenas—as both critic and poet. The urgency of Brown's efforts derives from his understanding, as stated in *The Negro Caravan*, that "white authors dealing with the American Negro have interpreted him in a way to justify his exploitation. Creative literature has often been a handmaiden to social policy" (Brown et al. 3). As critic Brown exposed these vicious and persistent stereotypes; as a creative artist, he sought to counter them with a social realist portraiture based on forms indigenous to the African American community.

The need for this type of work should not be underestimated. Although blackface minstrelsy began in the 1830s, it was—incredibly—still going strong a century later. In 1922, for example, George Gershwin and Buddy DeSylva wrote *Blue Monday Blues*, a one-act "jazz opera," for a Broadway musical production. As a run-up to Gershwin's classic *Porgy and Bess* (1935) this was more like a stumble. The review in the *New York World* called it "the most dismal, stupid and incredible blackface sketch that has probably ever been perpetrated. In it a dusky soprano finally killed her gambling man. She should have shot all her associates the moment they appeared and then turned the pistol on herself" (qtd. in Goldberg 122). As late as 1932, *George White's Scandals* filled seats on Broadway with songs such as "That's Why Darkies Were Born." Writing in *Opportunity*, Brown acknowledged the popular and degradingly inaccurate depictions of the Negro from Stephen Foster to Al Jolson as an "epidemic" that spread its contagion anywhere money was to be made: "Tin Pan Alley, most of whose dwellers had been no further south than Perth Amboy, frantically sought rhymes for the southern states, cheered over the startling rediscovery of Alabammy and Miami for their key word Mammy" ("Weep" 87). It is against this tide of doggerel that Brown built a levee of authentic African American folksong.

As poet also, notes Stephen E. Henderson, Brown's subtle and insightful understanding of the folk forms "extends the literary range of the blues without losing their authenticity." In fact, Brown approaches the African American folk forms of spiritual, shout, work song, and blues exactly as he had used "the formal measures of the English poets" in his earliest attempts at writing poetry (S. Henderson, "Heavy Blues" 32). It is clear that, for Brown, these stanzas had achieved an equal dignity and utility as literary models.

Among the formal qualities of the blues, Brown's study also focused on language and dialect. Brown's important essay "The Blues as Folk Poetry" (1930) is not so theoretically elaborate or ambitious as the archetype of "Ebonics" offered in Zora Neale Hurston's "Characteristics of Negro Expression" (1934). While the dialect recorded in folklore is integral for Brown, it is not of mystical import:

> There is nothing "degraded" about dialect. Dialectical peculiarities are universal. There is something about Negro dialect, in the idiom, the turn of phrase, the music of the vowels and consonants that is worth treasuring. ("Our Literary Audience" 45)

In "The Blues as Folk Poetry," Brown finds that the images presented in this dialect form are "highly compressed, concrete, imaginative, original" (382). He cites beautifully conceived lines such as

My gal's got teeth lak a lighthouse on de sea.
Every time she smiles she throws a light on me.

But Brown was not primarily interested in collecting poetic, or more numerous quaint, expressions. As he noted in 1946, his interest in folk materials "was first attracted by certain qualities that I thought the speech of the people had, and I wanted to get for my own writing a flavor, a color, a pungency of speech. Then later I came to something more important—I wanted to get an understanding of people, to acquire an accuracy in the portrayal of their lives" ("Approach" 506).

Brown's work also participates in the creation of an African American "national literature" by endorsing and contributing to a project carefully outlined by Alain Locke in the 1920s. This is not a modernist program but a modernized replication of the model first articulated in Europe by those who saw a national literature as the refinement of indigenous folk expression. Locke and James Weldon Johnson applied this nineteenth-century model quite specifically to music, seeing in the spirituals the materials that—in the hands of gifted black composers—would escape "the lapsing conditions and fragile vehicle of folk art and come firmly into the context of formal music" (Locke, *The New Negro* 199). The Fisk Jubilee Singers, performing concert settings composed by R. Nathaniel Dett and others, represent the first movement of Locke's envisioned symphony.

Folklorist Arthur Huff Fauset applied the same principle to literature. Writing in Locke's *The New Negro*, Fauset decried the derogatory misrepresentations of authentic African folklore in its American survivals, called for a more professional ethnographic study of it, and predicted that "Negro writers themselves will shortly, no doubt[,] be developing [the folktales and oral traditions of the South] as arduously as [Joel] Chandler Harris, and we hope as successfully, or even more so" (243–44).

While Locke foresaw a great classical music born of the folk forms shaped by slavery, James Weldon Johnson surveyed Broadway's stages and declared a victory for Negro genius, citing the rhythmic impulse of African American music as "the genesis and foundation of our national popular medium for musical expression" (Johnson and Johnson 31). Johnson's political interpretation of this development was not hidden. In the preface to his 1926 collection of Negro spirituals, he noted that "America would not be precisely the America it is except for the silent power the Negro has exerted upon it, both positive and negative" (Johnson and Johnson 19). Johnson also asserted that authentic folk art posed a serious challenge for any academically trained artist who aspired to transcend, or even match, its distinctive qualities of honesty and emotionally overwhelming beauty.

That the type of reclamation effort Arthur Huff Fauset prescribed for African American folktales should also be required for the blues—a form that only emerged in the first decade of the century—should not surprise those who consider the carefully built and well-maintained mechanism of racism that was running full throttle before World War II.

Texas A & M College professor Will H. Thomas's *Some Current Folk-Songs of the Negro* was the very first publication of the Texas Folklore Society. While this essay provides evidence that the blues was a widespread and authentic form in Texas in 1912—two years before W. C. Handy published "The St. Louis Blues" and launched its commercial development—the paper also offers disturbing documentation of white academics sitting around enjoying their own genteel version of "darkie" jokes. Sympathetic song collectors were also somewhat tainted by the general paternalism of the region and era. Folklorist John A. Lomax, one of the earliest commentators on the blues, characterized them as "Negro songs of self-pity" in an article published in *The Nation* in 1917. Even when employed by a liberal, such terminology supported the negative social construction of the African American image that James Weldon Johnson succinctly summarized as the view that black people were, at best, "wards" of American society.

Benjamin A. Botkin, writing in 1927, accepted the Texas folklorists' idea that self-pity was "a trait of the Negro, bred in him by centuries of oppression" (231); but Botkin was perceptive enough to understand that out of this "sense of self-pity develops an inevitable conviction of social injustice and an indictment of the existing order" (233). Botkin and Sterling Brown would become allies. They were the same age and shared similar interests in folklore, the experiments of the New Poetry movement, and a high regard for proletarian self-expression as encouraged by intellectuals connected with *The New Masses* and similar journals (Hutchinson 271–73). Typically placing important but accessible essays by scholars such as Henry Nash Smith in the company of poems by John Gould Fletcher and others, Botkin's annual anthology *Folk-Say: A Regional Miscellany* was more literary anthology than academic journal (Hirsch 12–14). *Folk-Say* provided a venue for Brown's essays and the blues-influenced poems collected in *Southern Road*.

"The blues," wrote Brown in *Negro Poetry and Drama*, "tell a great deal about folk-life. The genteel turn away from them in distaste, but blues persist with their terse and tonic shrewdness about human nature" (27). It is also true that the blues differ from the spirituals because the secular form highlights vicarious and ventriloquial qualities. "Ain't nobody here can go there for you, / You got to go there by yourself" is, as Brown puts it, the "sour truth" of the ancient spiritual ("Lonesome Valley," *Poems* 98–99). The message of any blues, of course, is just the opposite. The blues singer bids his listener to learn from his or her example before, as Roosevelt Sykes put it, you "make a mistake in life." The poems Brown originally published as a sort of suite titled "Lonesome Valley" in Botkin's 1931 *Folk-Say* seem designed to explore this aspect of blues songs.

Sterling Brown actually uses the blues stanza form in three ways in his own poems. The earliest approach is found in "Ma Rainey," first published in *Folk-Say* in 1930. Here, as in Langston Hughes's poem "The Weary Blues," the actual blues verses are set within a more elaborate structure of different free-verse stanzas. The 1931 edition of *Folk-Say* contains Brown's "Tin Roof Blues" and "New St. Louis Blues," both of which are entirely composed in the standard three-line blues stanza form. In 1932 Brown published "Long Track Blues" and "Rent Day Blues"—and here the blues stanzas are disguised as quatrains.

Brown's three-part "The New St. Louis Blues" is deeply and pugnaciously political. In the first poem, even the natural disasters that are so often the topic of blues songs are politicized. After a tornado brings destruction and a flood of refugees, Brown sings:

Newcomers dodge de mansions, and knocked on de po' folks' do',
Dodged most uh de mansions, and knocked down de po' folks' do',
Never knew us po' folks so popular befo'.

("Lonesome Valley" 119)

When he turns his attention to the way things go in the man-made world, the picture is bleaker still:

Woman done quit me, my boy lies fast in jail.
Woman done quit me, pardner lies fast in jail,
Kin bum tobacco but I cain't bum de jack fo' bail.

Church don't help me, 'cause I ain't got no Sunday clothes,
Church don't help me, got no show-off Sunday clothes,
Preachers and deacons, don't look to get no help from those.

Dice are loaded an' de deck's all marked to hell,
Dice are loaded an' de deck's all marked to hell,
Whoever runs dis gamble sholy runs it well.

("Lonesome Valley" 121)

Another poem, "Convicts"—not written in the blues stanza form—comments on the southern penal system. Jim, serving ninety days on the chain gang, passes his own home each day as he shuttles between "handcuffs / And a dingy cell, / Daytime on the highways, / Nights in hell" (115).

The system of local prison farms and the practice of leasing convict labor were major concerns to African Americans in the South in the early years of the century. As Lawrence Gellert noted regarding his travels in South Carolina and Georgia in the 1920s, "These roads are kept in repair by chain-gangs. Work on them, of course, is in proportion to the number of convicts available. Hence no crime goes long unpunished. Not if there can be found a stray Negro within a hundred-mile radius" (229). This system was in place as early as 1906, as Ray Stannard Baker reported in *Following the Color Line* (95–99). John L. Spivak's contribution to Nancy Cunard's *Negro: An Anthology* includes photographs of prisoners in Georgia being tortured by fastening in stocks or being stretched between posts, situations even more brutally repressive than those recorded by Baker a quarter-century earlier. "No pretext had been necessary to kidnap Africans and bring them to America as slaves. But pretexts would be necessary to kidnap Black Americans and reenslave them," observes H. Bruce Franklin. The answer was, of course, that "the victims would have to be perceived as criminals" (102).

In the poems grouped as "Lonesome Valley," Brown is quite deliberately revising both the folklorists' and the Broadway song-pluggers' misinterpretations of the blues. In his prose writings on the blues from the late 1930s to the early 1950s, Brown would explicitly restate the principles that informed his blues poems. "As well as self-pity there is stoicism in the blues," Brown wrote in 1937. He also directed attention to the collector Lawrence Gellert's discovery of songs that contained searing evidence of "otherwise inarticulate resentment against injustice." The arch language used here is, of course, intended to mock the southern (and, perhaps also, academic) etiquette of oppression. Brown characterizes the songs Gellert collected as ironic, coded, but defiant protest, representing not self-pity but "a very adept self-portraiture" (*Negro Poetry and Drama* 27–29). The kinds of songs Gellert collected can be judged by the following verses, recorded in Southern Pines, North Carolina:

> Ah wants no ruckus, but ah ain't dat kin'
> What lets you all shoe-shine on mah behin'.
>
> ("Negro Songs" 233)

Gellert, a contributor to *The New Masses*, met Brown in Boston while traveling with Nancy Cunard in 1932. The three impressed each other greatly (Gellert, "Remembering" 142–43). For his part, Brown cites Gellert's work in almost every article on the blues he subsequently published.

The development of the blues simultaneously as a folk music, vulnerable to scholarly misinterpretation, and as an offering of the commercial music industry, on phonograph records and on the vaudeville stage, is intriguing. For those interested in the study of "pure forms" this dual development offered problems from the start. Nevertheless, unlike Alain Locke, Sterling Brown seemed unworried about the possible fading away of authentic folk expression or its commercial exploitation. What remained important to him was that "the vigor of the creative impulse has not been snapped, even in the slums" of big cities, as far from the source of southern tradition as anyone might imagine ("Negro Folk Expression" 61). Brown also clearly articulated his understanding of what the living blues form represented, and what the true purpose of the "creative impulse" embodied in the blues really is. "Socially considered," Brown wrote in 1952,

> the blues tell a great deal about one segment of Negro life. It is inaccurate, however, to consider them completely revelatory of the Negro folk, or of the folk transplanted in the cities, or of the lower class in general. The blues represent the secular, the profane, where the spirituals and gospel songs represent the religious. ("The Blues" 291)

As he had pointed out in 1930,

> There are so many Blues that any preconception might be proved about Negro folk life, as well as its opposite. As documentary proof of dogma

about the Negro peasant, then, the Blues are satisfactory and unsatis-
factory. As documents about humanity they are invaluable. ("Blues as
Folk Poetry" 372)

What becomes apparent to anyone who dips into the considerable musico-
logical and sociological literature about African American music published
in recent years is that Sterling Brown's early efforts to properly complicate
our interpretations have, indeed, achieved a great measure of success.

The same cannot be said of Brown's interest in building a literary edifice
on the unique blues form. Though Langston Hughes created masterpieces
with that form, and though W. H. Auden, Raymond Patterson, James
Emanuel, and Sterling Plumpp have—like Brown himself—also created notable blues works, the attempt to elevate the blues stanza to literary rank has
not been so successful as the campaign for the sonnet. It may be fair to consider, however, that the partisans of the sonnet began to promote it three
hundred years before Sterling Brown discovered the blues.

What Brown certainly did accomplish, however, was to identify the authentic poetic voice of black America, making it heard above the din of racist parody and well-intentioned, sympathetic misinterpretation. In 1953, during the
height of McCarthyism's assault on creative expression, Brown saw fit to foreground the political power inherent in the blues songs composed by his friend
Waring Cuney and by the popular Josh White. These songs "on poverty, hard-
ship, poor housing and jim crow military service, come from conscious pro-
pagandists, not truly folk," Brown wrote. "They make use of the folk idiom in
both text and music, however, and the folk listen and applaud. They know very
well what Josh White is talking about" ("Negro Folk Expression" 60).

Testifying before the House Committee on Un-American Activities, White
explained his performing for Communist-organized benefits and rallies in
the following statement: "Dozens of artists of all races and colors . . . have
also given their names and talent and time under the innocent impression
that they were on the side of charity and equality. Let me make it clear, if I can,
that I am still on that side. The fact that Communists are exploiting grievances
for their own purpose does not make those grievances any less real" (33).

It is interesting—and a subtle index of Sterling A. Brown's character—to
note that, while in "Ma Rainey," written in 1930, he was content to quote an
audience member's appreciation that "she jes catch hold of us, somekindaway," in the 1950s—at a time when it mattered—he was brave enough to explain exactly why.

TWO   Learning the Changes

"Pass the Biscuits, Please"

Lunchtime with Sonny Boy Williamson

Imagine this:

Live! from Elaine . . . Marianna . . . Marvell . . . Mellwood . . . Forrest
City . . . Clarksdale . . . Helena . . . it's . . .

No, not *Saturday Night*, not *Monty Python*, but . . . "*King Biscuit Time!*" The per-
former was the late Sonny Boy Williamson, and his music was the blues.

In 1979 John Belushi and Dan Akroyd made magazine covers and Top 10
album listings all over the country as "The Blues Brothers." In a society
where the truth often sounds less plausible than the spoof, it may be that the
spoof is the true signature of our times. We have all been trained to worship
the power of the media without even understanding what it is. It's a shame,
really. But, as Walter Cronkite used to say on a daily basis, that's the way it is.

Somebody's always definitely taking it to the bank, but it's disappointing
that our younger generations were getting their knowledge of the beautiful
blues music that originated right here at home from British musical clones
and lampoon comedians and have little inkling of the real story behind it.

The blues, originating in the delta environs of Arkansas, Mississippi, and
Louisiana and in the farmlands of East Texas, on black minstrel tours of the
Deep South and in the fast cities of Memphis, Houston, and St. Louis, has become the basis of popular music all over the world. Elvis Presley and other
performers built multi-million-dollar careers on these roots, but a regional
daily broadcast from Helena, Arkansas, radio station KFFA in the early 1940s
may have been the most historically important and influential outlet of this
hundred-year-old American musical style.

Cotton, or as it was called, "white gold," made 1937 a boom year in

Arkansas. That year, while the nation was busily licking the depression, Arkansas's delta counties produced a record 1,975,000 bales. In those days, cotton was produced by the labor of mules and men, and its cultivation dictated much of the region's lifestyle. Rural schools arranged their class schedules so that students could assist in the cotton harvest. Less than half the state had electricity, and the plantation system was not much changed from the previous century. It was hard work and determination that produced the cotton that pulled Arkansas out of the depression years.

During that time, Sam W. Anderson, a country school superintendent in eastern Arkansas, had a hopeful and expansive vision of Arkansas's future. By 1939, he decided to leave his position at Dyess in Mississippi County to found a corporation that would build a radio station at Helena. His station, KFFA, went on the air November 19, 1941. The station's most successful program, *King Biscuit Time*, hit the airwaves a few days later. Back then, the medium of radio was barely twenty years old, but KFFA was born for good luck; and *King Biscuit Time* was part of its good fortune.

"Sonny Boy Williamson came in one day," Anderson told me, "and said he wanted to be on the air. He played French harp. So I said, 'Let's go down to the studio and hear how it sounds.' I was new in the radio business, and I didn't know what kind of program you could do with just a French harp. But I was born and reared around here and I understood something about the black people's music. Sonny Boy had a little suitcase and opened it up . . . had all kinds of harps. And he played.

"I said, 'Well, Sonny Boy, the station is new and we can't afford to pay you a salary; but if I can sell the program to a sponsor, then we'll get the sponsor to pay you.' But Sonny Boy wasn't really interested in a salary, he wanted to be on the air to publicize his personal appearances. He played somewhere virtually every night."

Anderson got to work right away to find a sponsor for his new talent, and he was fortunate in his search. A couple of blocks from his new radio station was the Interstate Grocer Company building. A wholesale distributor serving stores in both Arkansas and Mississippi, Interstate had been organized in 1913 by Earl P. Moore and Watt W. Moore, two brothers from Batesville. Anderson found an attentive ear in executive Max S. Moore, who later became the company's president. Interstate had begun marketing King Biscuit brand flour in 1938, and Moore found Anderson's sales pitch interesting.

"We were interested in establishing our own private brand of flour,"

Moore recalled in the spring of 1979, "and Anderson called us up to audition these two guys, Robert Junior Lockwood and Sonny Boy Williamson, because we wanted to hit the colored trade. The biggest population in the area was black; they were farming people with large families and used flour. Many of the white people then would just go out and buy bread."

"It's changed now," Moore told me, "it's all tractors and wages. But, then, it was large families that worked the farms themselves."

"I knew," said Anderson, "that any advertiser needed to reach the black population to be successful in the delta." Blacks, after all, constituted 75 percent of the total population then and now, even though property ownership and other socioeconomic black representation in the delta was and is almost the reverse statistically.

Lockwood and Williamson seemed right for Moore's advertising purposes, and Interstate agreed to sponsor a program that Moore proudly claimed as "the oldest radio show in the country." Sonny Payne, however, producer of *King Biscuit Time* for more than twenty-three years, seemed a bit uneasy about that claim. The *Grand Ole Opry*, broadcast on Nashville's WSM since 1926, is usually considered the world's oldest continuously broadcast radio program. But there is support for the grocery company executive's boast. *Grand Ole Opry* is a weekly program, and by the end of the 1970s the daily *King Biscuit Time* had logged more than nine thousand continuous broadcasts since its 1941 premiere.

Sponsored by Interstate, Sonny Boy Williamson's program went on the air in December 1941, and his initial salary, was, according to Max Moore, "approximately nothing." The show was aired on KFFA each afternoon from 12:15 to 12:30. Williamson performed alone with his French harp or with Lockwood on guitar until June 1942, when he added drummer James F. (Peck) Curtis and pianist Robert (Dudlow) Taylor to the broadcast. In later years he would employ bluesmen such as Joe Willie Wilkens, Willie Love, and Joe (Pinetop) Perkins. People like B. B. King and Memphis Slim would also be guests on the KFFA program.

Williamson—born Willie Rice Miller in Glendora, Mississippi—was an interesting, difficult, and talented man. He had a considerable poetic and musical gift and could be both generous and bullying toward other musicians. He was also ambitious and dedicated to making a living from his music. "Sonny Boy," said Anderson, "was the kind of man who could have made a living at anything. He was an individual; nobody could handle him. He was a real big man . . . about six foot six, weighed 250 when he was fat and around 230 when he was skinny. Wore a size 14 shoe . . . a big man."

Williamson's poetic gift was even more impressive than his physical presence. Everyone who has written about him recognizes Williamson as a unique talent, and his popularity in the delta during the 1940s and 1950s suggests that he was also capable of communicating to his audiences on their own terms. The poetry in Williamson's songs—and in Robert Junior Lockwood's—came right out of the delta style of storytelling and everyday speech. The embellishment and humorous exaggeration that are prized and cultivated in the region also shape the words of Williamson's songs, which are characterized by their lyrical originality. Songs like "One Way Out," "Unseen Eye," and "Eyesight To The Blind" are good examples of his artistry. It is also a refreshing escape from the nagging whine of saccharine easy-listening ballads like "You Don't Send Me Flowers (Anymore)" to again hear Williamson's starkly funny lines:

> Don't send me no flowers
> When I'm in the graveyard
> 'Cause then I can't smell 'em.

All of Williamson's songs have a strange, unique tone to them. They do not boast like Muddy Waters's famous "I'm Ready" or threaten with mocking bitterness like B. B. King's "Outskirts Of Town," but they do speak of troubles and disappointments in a way that we have come to expect from the blues. One of Williamson's songs says,

> I've got to leave this town
> Nobody seems to want me around

but there is no sense of self-pity or martyrdom in the tone of his utterance. Even when he feels like bragging, it's not bragging on himself but on his good fortune in meeting a woman so beautiful that she could "bring eyesight to the blind." But much of the information conveyed in Sonny Boy Williamson songs can't really be called good news. Several of Williamson's songs—including the delightfully titled "Don't Start Me To Talking or I'll Tell Everything I Know"—examine the dynamics of gossip. Such concerns seem appropriate to a bard whose persona complains about romantic involvements with two women who "live so close together / I can't see one for seeing the other." Just as generations of college philosophy students may have pondered the true import of such lyrics far into the night, well-known music critics such as Charles Keil and Michael Haralambos have tried to define the essence of Sonny Boy's music, but it still remains effectively elusive. Even if we decide that blues is merely an individual's self-expression, Williamson, as he revealed himself in his songs, comes across as a mysteriously ambiguous character, as, perhaps, he was.

Though it is difficult to define, the image Williamson projected in his songs and style seems to have been the key to his early popularity in the delta and his spreading fame. "We got the show going so good," recalled Interstate's Max Moore, "because Sonny Boy was so well known." Why he was so well known in a region as full of blues singers as a trailer full of cotton in December is another question.

"When he was on live and the show was successful," said Anderson, "we averaged a thousand pieces of mail a week. The area and the nature of Sonny Boy's music was what made the radio program successful. It was music that the black people enjoyed; and it fit their patterns of life. The wording of his songs always dealt with the feelings and emotions of black people. Radio had to be closer to the people . . . to the audience . . . than television has ever been. Radio was live and happened right next door to them. It still operates that way."

In the broadcasting of King Biscuit Time, KFFA was definitely next door—in many more ways than one. It is hard to say how natural or calculated was the image projected by Williamson, on the air or otherwise; as it is even today in the media, when television networks employ huge staffs of motivational psychologists, pollsters, and researchers, and switchboards light up if a news anchorman appears wearing his reading glasses instead of the usual contact lenses. For his part, Williamson was by all accounts ingratiating, gentlemanly, and quite outrageous. Sometimes his behavior fit both the racist stereotypes and racist realities of the Arkansas delta. Though blacks might have been denied educational opportunities in those days, there was no control on intelligence and no such thing as either separate or equal aspirations. Only a fool would attempt to determine the true motives of any human being who was aware of being defined as less than a man by the social—and, in those days, legal—craziness of racial segregation.

For all his talent and graciousness, Williamson's charisma was not entirely without fault. He did not always get along with his fellow blues musicians and, at times, he drank a bit. "I used to tell him," said Anderson, employing the characteristic delta-style exaggeration, "that he drank enough to float a battleship. One time, I had to bail him out on Saturday night four times in a month! I told him:

"Sonny Boy, you're going to spend half your salary on paying fines."
And he said: "Mr. Sam, if you were a black man one Saturday night, you'd never want to be white again!"

"Everybody seems to have a story about Sonny Boy," writes veteran delta journalist George De Man in *Helena: The Bridge, the River, the Romance.* De Man relates the tale of Williamson and a fellow bluesman arrested for vagrancy. As in all those old late-night chain gang movies, they are naturally singing the blues in their cell: you know, "Mmmmmm hmm hmm . . . I have had my fun . . . hmmm . . . hmmm mmmmmm." This time—as the oral tradition would have it—a tornado touches down just then, demolishes the jailhouse, and the two freed men walk away, singing, into the whirlwind.

Apochryphal or not, after hearing a story like that, who could resist the next opportunity to hear Sonny Boy Williamson sing?

KFFA and the Interstate Grocer Company didn't miss a beat in making sure that their star was not only on the radio but "right next door." And the ambitious Williamson wouldn't have let them, either. The sponsor had a bus, and two or three days a week, but mostly on Saturdays, Williamson and his group would make personal appearances at grocery stores in Clarksdale, Marvell, Elaine, Forrest City, as well as the rural areas. "The tours were the company's idea," said John Rogers, a tall, lean man who was the Interstate Grocer Company boss in Max Moore's absence.

"We'd go somewhere every week or, at least, not less than every other week," Rogers said. "I made some tours with them in 1951 and 1952 and I know there were more than a thousand people who'd come out in Mississippi and Marvell. That was the time they had those old cars and wagons. There were more than a thousand people out there one day in Sherard, Mississippi."

The tours were documented after a fashion by a billboard full of dusty photographs in the Interstate office lobby. Some of the pictures show concerts in towns like Haynes, Forrest City, Mellwood, and Clarendon. Photos from a tour to Marianna on June 27, 1942, show several hundred people sur-rounding a bandstand in a park setting. The date and size of the crowd attest to the almost immediate popularity of Sonny Boy Williamson's music and of the *King Biscuit Time* show. The radio program became so popular, in fact, that the company introduced a new product in 1947, Sonny Boy Corn Meal. "That's his picture on the package," noted Rogers.

Besides the company's tours, Williamson also had a heavy schedule of dances and clubs where he and his band performed. "He always announced on the program the places he'd be playing," said Rogers, "whether it was on the tour or his own dances. He would also advertise the products at those dances. That was part of the contract. Between the tours and his own shows it kept the band busy all the time. And it kept the company's name before the public."

It is doubtful that Williamson thought of himself as a potential trademark when he first approached Anderson at KFFA in 1941 and was asked about the idea for the *King Biscuit Time* program. There was apparently no long-range strategic plan in anyone's briefcase. John Rogers said simply: "Sonny Boy was looking for a job, and the radio station convinced us to sponsor the show; it was convenient for everybody."

Of course, that may really be *too* simple.

What is not simple is trying to imagine what impulse makes a man who everyone expects to be usefully satisfied picking delta cotton decide to be-come an artist—a radio and recording artist—a bluesman. Certainly it is not the constraints of city life, for Helena long suffered from its rural and planta-tion heritage; for several years, despite its choice location on the Mississippi River, the city was not able to develop its economic potential. Williamson may have been frustrated in his ambitions, and that could have sparked his energy.

Williamson's ambition sometimes created problems for his Arkansas friends. "He'd be here about six months and everything would be fine," An-derson recalled, "and then I'd miss him. Peck Curtis and his pianist Dudlow wouldn't travel with him when he left town, and I'd ask Peck Curtis where Sonny Boy was and he wouldn't know. In about three days I might get a call from Detroit or Chicago and he'd ask me to wire him some money so that he could get back. He'd be up there on some recording deal and they'd beat him out of the money they promised. He was always with a lot of small companies that would give him big promises, you know."

Sonny Boy Williamson also spent a lot of time going to Jackson, Mississippi, to record for Lillian McMurray's Trumpet Records. When Trumpet finally scored a hit with Elmore James's "Dust My Broom" (with Williamson playing harp on the record) in the early 1950s, McMurray was able to sell Sonny Boy's recording contract to the Chess label in Chicago, and Williamson began to acquire an audience beyond the delta and the big-city blues clubs he played in whenever he was away from Helena and *King Biscuit Time*. Eventually, following friends such as Memphis Slim, Williamson wound up in Europe, where he was greeted by blues fans who had heard of him but never heard him. "He played at the Palladium in London for six weeks," Anderson exaggerated. "That was their biggest hall then, and they couldn't get all the people in. The Beatles, you know, they were just little fellows then, but they made it big imitating what Sonny Boy did."

That statement may sound strange at first, until you remember the almost surrealistic tone of Williamson's beautiful spontaneous lyrics on KFFA's *King Biscuit Time* (like Houston's Lightnin' Hopkins, he often made up songs on the spot) and compare them to Lennon and McCartney's hits. Interestingly enough, the Beatles were also introduced to the United States, on rock-and-roller Little Richard's recommendation, by the small black-owned VeeJay label in Chicago, the same company that made a star of Mississippi delta bluesman Jimmy Reed.

Partly because of Sonny Boy Williamson's presence in Europe in the early 1960s, groups like the Beatles, Animals, Moody Blues, Herman's Hermits, and Rolling Stones made their earliest hits with direct copies or lovingly imitated re-creations of the electrified blues that were not usually (except at KFFA, Memphis's WDIA, and a few other stations) considered worthy of airplay in the land where the music originated.

Besides influencing young European rock musicians such as Led Zeppelin's Jimmy Page, Williamson also inspired a very beautiful composition by avant-garde jazzman Archie Shepp. In the liner notes to Shepp's 1968 recording *On This Night* (Impulse Records), jazz critic Nat Hentoff quotes Shepp's remarks concerning the younger musician's meeting in Denmark with Williamson in 1963:

He came into the club in which we were playing one night. We talked, and he sent me out for his brief case. I got it and when he opened it up, it was full of harmonicas. Then he began to tell stories of his wanderings across America, and from that night I wanted to do a portrait of the man and what he represents.

One of the most intriguing tunes on Shepp's record is his musical portrait of Sonny Boy Williamson.

After a couple years in Europe, Williamson returned to Arkansas and again walked into the KFFA offices to see Anderson. He did the *King Biscuit Time* program live again until his death in 1965. With the young British rock and rollers he had inspired filling up the Top 10 radio charts, it was almost as if his contribution had come full circle, and the lifestyle of the black people that he had entertained and had advertised to had changed considerably—even though the realities of such broadcasting in the early 1940s are not really appreciated in the present day and time.

It is a little hard to understand these days. "Radio," writes Ray Poindexter in *Arkansas Airwaves*, "has not left its own recorded history. Because of the intangible nature of its product, its past has for the most part, disappeared into thin air" (vi). Television, which feeds on everything recorded throughout the twentieth century, is, in its own way, even less real. It is important, though, to understand what the combined artistry of Sonny Boy Williamson and the producers and sponsor of *King Biscuit Time* was really about.

Certainly, the existence of the station, the program, the sponsoring company, and the talented black musicians who performed and have since received critical attention from all over the world is something that the civic groups in all the towns involved should be concerned about. More than that, these people in the 1940s provided a real Arkansas heritage of which we should be proud.

When *King Biscuit Time* hit the air just after Pearl Harbor, music by black artists was still relegated to the "race record" category. Even for artists with a major commercial contract, black music was virtually banned from the airwaves. Anderson and younger radio people have vivid memories of those times. Tom Usslemann, a Houston independent record producer and former Philadelphia disc jockey, recalled almost being fired from an eastern radio station in the early 1950s for playing records by black singers. "The only reason I didn't lose the job," he says, "is that three companies called up wanting to sponsor the show!" He had found the records in a box labeled "Race Records—Do Not Play." And that was pretty much the way it was in those days.

Anderson, interested in building his station at Helena, was not much concerned with such trends; instead, he wanted to provide the delta with programming that was meaningful. "Gospel quartet singing was very popular
then," he says of the 1940s, "and we still play a lot of that live on Sunday
mornings." Regional stations in Jackson and Vicksburg did also, as did
KCAT in Pine Bluff. If heard at all—since many stations, including KFFA, are
currently programmed directly from communications satellite "mass market" feeds uploaded in New York or Los Angeles—such programming (including the blues) seems nostalgic and wholesomely innocuous enough
now, but it was daring a half century ago.

"I gave a talk at the Kiwanis Club in December 1941," Anderson recalls.
"Some of them were upset with me because I had Sonny Boy and about four
quartets on the air. They wanted to know why I put blacks on the radio station. Of course, that's not the word they used . . . they said 'niggers.' Well, I
told them, you're the retail businessmen of Helena and I operate the radio
station. If you want to advertise to the black people, they have to have some
representation. I said, 'If you will put up signs in your places "No Niggers Allowed," I'll be happy to take 'em off the air.'"

He smiled and added, "I haven't had any trouble with them since."

Anderson's understanding of his territory resulted in the creation of a
program whose longevity is phenomenal in the broadcast media, made a
valuable contribution to the shaping of American culture, and offered an in-
structively tangible boost to local business. The program that he, Sonny Boy
Williamson, and Max Moore dreamed up in 1941 received a backhanded
compliment from the so-called counterculture when a syndicated FM hard
rock series chose the name "King Biscuit Flower Hour"—the wording and
spelling changed to honor the cosmic consciousness of Love as well as pay
homage to the delta originators and avoid copyright infringements. On the
other hand, the rock program may be less a tribute than a rip-off—something like Akroyd and Belushi with their ersatz *Briefcase Full of Blues*. Max
Moore says that the rock show producers never asked permission to use the
name, but he didn't seem much concerned. KFFA producer Payne bluntly
says that such programs were "just trying to capitalize on Sonny Boy's
name."

In the 1980s, the Interstate Grocer Company cut back its commercial
commitment. *King Biscuit Time* retained its original time slot but was only
heard on KFFA three days a week with no print media promotion of the show.

After Williamson's death in Helena in 1965, there were no more country Saturday afternoon tours. But the program stayed on the air with recordings by Sonny Boy Williamson and Robert Junior Lockwood, and kept the cards and letters coming in.

"Things have changed," Anderson told me. "All the supermarket chains around here—Safeway, Kroger, Big Star—have their own company brand of flour now, but they have to stock the King Biscuit brand if they're gonna sell flour. They may not want to, but they have to. The people ask for it."

Then, he leaned forward, looking serious, and said, "It's a general purpose flour, you know."

Bayou City Blues

Lightnin' Hopkins, Juke Boy Bonner, and Peppermint Harris

Gimme Shelter from the Danger Zone

There's just something about the blues. John Lee Hooker said that whether you call today's musical forms rock, jazz, "heavy metal," soul, or disco, it all goes back to the blues.

And that original American art form has been very difficult to pin down. For every intellectual urban sociologist who hears a strong racial protest, you can also find a pious "saved" parson who sincerely hears in the blues anthems of defeat and disgrace.

Perhaps the music's range is just that wide. Good-time, living-for-the-weekend music, yeah . . . pain and heartache, yeah . . . so damn mad I'm fit to act the fool and die, oh new!

A few years back, the hip musical question was "play that funky music till you die . . . till you die?!!?!" No, that's not the attitude aimed at by the blues. Rather, the blues is more in line with the thoughts of a wise street poet who once told me, plainly, "Hey, little brother, dying just ain't my bag."

Likewise, the blues will never die. It's about life and living. Singing, dancing, just being in the blues is soulful affirmative action toward the goal of survival with all of your senses intact.

In fact, to move from paradigms to paradiddles, the blues burst into its vibrant life at Liberty Hall when two of its greatest sons beamed down on Houston. Clifton Chenier and Lightnin' Hopkins promised to piece the space city into ever more thrilling orbits that weekend.

A bluesman whose biggest hits are sung in French, Clifton Chenier always has the pots on. *Living Blues* magazine tailed Chenier's group America's number one R & B band, but that's not news. "In terms of modern zydeco bands," wrote music critic Joseph F. Lomax, "there is Clifton Chenier's band and there are the others" (216). Clifton really is in a class by himself. Poet Tom Dent took one listen to Chenier at the 1974 New Orleans Jazz and Heritage Festival and declared, simply, "He's a genius."

Chenier's music has its roots in the traditional zydeco style of French-speaking people in Louisiana, but it includes a lot of newfangled boogie as well. Chenier himself said that he provided the old good-time music "with new hinges . . . so she can swing." And Cliff swings harder than the Cincinnati Reds!

The band is called Red Hot and their music retains the best of the classic years of rhythm and blues (when New Orleans and the Gulf Coast ruled the pop charts with hits by Fats Domino, Lloyd Price, Ernie K. Doe, Aaron Neville, the Meters: and the list goes on and on), yet there is nothing dated about the excitement they produce. Hot? Hot Hot. And sizzling.

Lightnin' Hopkins produces excitement in another dimension. While Clifton Chenier and his partners will arouse the spirits that govern the body's electricity, Lightnin' has licks that refreshingly resurrect the mind. A poet in the living tradition of the Third World, Hopkins can be topical, quiet, witty, introspective and make you want to dance . . . all in the same song.

"My songs," Hopkins once said, "are practically all true songs. They are, something real to, my way of knowing . . . trouble up home, or when they got me on the country road gang, or had to say goodbye to some good girl, or be thinking of going to Galveston Beach—all that's liable to come up in my songs. Call 'em true songs."

For those of you under the spell of the latest "blues is protest" theory, let's point out that Lightnin' Hopkins works in the tradition of the blues singers as a kind of collective voice of the community. So did the late Papa Hop Wilson, the great steel guitar genius who played a long stand at Houston's famous Hayes Lounge. The troubles, suspicions, and joys that the blues speak of are not personally the singer's or anyone else's . . . they are possibilities that all poor black folks realize are only too dreadfully, or sweetly, possible . . . given the predictable uncertainty of our everyday lives.

In other words, even in the happy creole French of Clifton Chenier, *protest* is not a strong enough word to describe the sense of the blues. For those who have grown up to believe that Cronkite and Barbara Walters are "commentators," the truly collective voice of the blues must be somewhat shocking.

For example, Lightnin's most haunting song (recorded in the late 1950s for VeeJay Records) is "The Devil Is Watching You":

The devil finish working
And go home to his wife
He hug and kiss and tell her
"I got 'em goin' twice"
Lord it's nothin' impossible Lord
For the devil to do

The lyrics, like the folk sermons of James Weldon Johnson's *God's Trombones,* testify to the black man's inability to conceive of abstract evil. Heh heh hah. Or perhaps, it is just everyday mother wit that informs these lyrics . . . the survival wisdom (and sly sass) that made its way from Africa through slavery days and is dadgum still alive and well bespoken in the works of a great singer like Lightnin' Hopkins.

Another song from the same session is called "War Is Starting Again" and was recorded in Houston. It's about the Korean War and is cold-bloodedly direct. "You know," Hopkins begins, "the world is a shame. I hear they fixin' to start a war again." Later, he admits:

My girlfriend got a boyfriend in the Army
That fool gotta go overseas
Now you know I don't hate it so much now
It's just a better break for me

Protest song? You tell me. More like Jody's national anthem? Maybe that's the ticket. For my money, the only later song so excruciatingly subtle and plain is Johnny "Guitar" Watson's "Sometimes You Don't Treat Me Like Your Man" (on Fantasy Records). If you understand these songs, you will know more about America and the peculiar demands this country makes on those who want to live life.

The ups and downs. The chugholes in life's highway. Or farm-to-market road, as the mood strikes you. The black man, as we all know, is an expert in the sudden diminishing of self-image, and it is no accident that the blues, in those sad days after bombings, assassinations kidnappings of blonde resignations just before the Impeachment lynchers find enough rope Four DEAD IN

OHIO Harlem riots Lockheed scandals etc. etc. etc. . . . the blues seems appropriate to America's Badness. And it is going to be the generator of new joy.

Ray Charles sang Percy Mayfield's "Danger Zone" (a song inspired by the Eisenhower years of "cold war" and pre-Kissinger chip-on-shoulder diplomacy) with ghastly whoops, shrieks, and diminuendos:

Sometimes I sit here
In this chair
and I wonder . . .

The danger zone is everywhere!

And you better believe, even now, it still is. We live in the day that the prophets spoke of, the day when there is no rock under which to hide. The only shelter is the truth. Truth, disguised as music, is what people like Lightnin' Hopkins and Clifton Chenier deal in. Find shelter *there.*

Juke Boy Bonner Sang the Blues

African cultures had a role for the griot, a combination entertainer, minstrel, and tribal historian who served as the keeper of tradition by virtue of knowing the tunes and time of every necessary celebration, and some of the impromptu ones, too. In slavery days, the griot's place was taken by the plantation fiddler. After slavery, as the lifestyles and music of black people changed, the blues singer held that office.

A man who understood that role and, indeed, lived it, was Houston singer Weldon "Juke Boy" Bonner. He got his nickname as a young man when, in the days before the fancy discotheques on Old Spanish Trail, he sang in all those little beer and set-up places, so-called juke joints. Bonner sang the blues in the old, traditional way: one man with a guitar and a mouth harp, and his own words about what he and his neighbors knew of life. Juke Boy Bonner died In June 1978, singing the blues almost until the end.

Bonner was born on a farm near Bellville, Texas, in 1932. Life there wasn't easy. His family worked cotton for a share. When he was two years old his father died, and his mother passed away six years later. Young Weldon lived with relatives, chopped cotton, and learned to play the guitar well enough to be paid for performing at church socials and parties in nearby towns. At fifteen he left the country and settled in Houston's Fifth Ward.

It's doubtful that the young people who frequent the clubs on Old Spanish

Trail today would even have recognized the Houston that Juke Boy Bonner discovered. Sixty years ago, before surround sound and air conditioning, most of the music was blues, and the hot strip was the Fifth Ward's Lyons Avenue, which was lined with cafés and clubs catering to hip fun-seekers of the day. The Roxy Theater (like New York's Apollo, Chicago's Regal, and Washington, D.C.'s Howard) featured motion pictures as well as live music by touring stars such as the young B. B. King.

The Lincoln, downtown on Prairie, was the other major black theater. The house opened in the 1920s with vaudeville and Oscar Michaux's pioneering black movies and, until its demolition, survived as the Majestic Theater (finally featuring the new wave of so-called blaxploitation films and Bruce Lee movies) drawing young black folks in as it had always done. In the late 1940s, the Lincoln was the site of disc jockey Trummy Cain's weekly talent show, where Bonner, brand new in the city, began his professional music career. After winning the contest, Juke Boy made several radio appearances sponsored by Lyons Avenue impresario Henry Atlas.

Bonner soon began playing clubs in Houston and managed an ambitious trip to California. In Oakland, he recorded for Bob Geddin's small but active Irma label with a group that included Lafayette Thomas, an inventive guitarist from Shreveport, Louisiana, who was just a couple of years older than Juke Boy and already traveling with Jimmy McCracklin's popular band. The recordings are collector's items now, but they went nowhere when they were released. Bonner eventually returned to Houston but was to make many trips back to the Bay Area, where he performed and recorded over the years.

Some of Juke Boy's California experiences were not so successful. His stay in Los Angeles was dismal, and his brilliant song "Over Ten Years Ago" recalled one incident:

You know I walked all the way
    From 5th Street out to Watts
I walked all the way
    From 5th Street out to Watts

Played my harmonica on the sidewalk
For whatever little coins I got

> It was at the Jack-in-the-Box on Central
>   That I met poor Mercy Dee
> At the Jack-in-the-Box on Central
>   That's where I met poor Mercy Dee
> He was nice enough just to lay a meal on me

Back in Houston, Bonner struggled to make a living with his music. But he was caught in the midst of a major change in the music business and in the city itself. The major recording companies were busily buying out or bankrupting the smaller rhythm-and-blues labels, creating new stars, and slowly putting an end to the black touring circuit. Lyons Avenue, through a combination of overcrowding, absentee landlords, and bank redlining, was becoming a less glittering street, while the Fifth Ward itself became more and more a depressed area.

Before it became known as the wonder city of the Sunbelt, Houston was very much a typical southern city, rigidly segregated in social and economic terms. During the 1950s, for example, with the "boom" underway and the black population almost doubling, black male unemployment in Houston increased from 5.4 percent to 7.3 percent, as compared with a 2.4 percent for whites. Because of widespread job discrimination, half of those blacks who did work made less than four thousand dollars.

Some of Juke Boy's lyrics faithfully, and movingly, recorded the situation just the way it was:

> It don't take too much
> Make you feel the world is doing you wrong
> It don't take too much
> To think the world is doing you wrong
> Especially when you can't find no job
>
> You can't take care of your wife and your home
>
> Don't take too much
>   When you gave all that you could give
> Don't take too much
>   After you gave all that you can give

Look like upper class people
Don't care how the lower class of people live

Another song spoke of the disappointment that many blacks, like Bonner himself, found after leaving the rural areas with hopes of a better life in Houston.

Here I am in the big city
     And I'm just about to starve to death
I'm in the big city
     And I'm just about to starve to death
And my sister that lives in the country
Got cattle, hogs, and chickens laying in the nest

Other songs were just as graphic and direct in their description of the everyday situation in those times. While there may not be overt protest in these songs, there is certainly no note of passivity or nostalgia that some people expect from the blues.

In *The Legacy of the Blues*, bluesologist Samuel Charters pointed out the importance of what Bonner's songs accomplished: "It's difficult," he wrote, "to be very poetic about the world that most of the people have to live in, in the cities of the United States or Europe. Even if there's money, clothes, a house—it still is difficult to find a poetic language to deal with it" (68). He added that Bonner's approach was "his own expression of the kind of personal news that never gets on the pages of a newspaper, but still makes up the sum of a life" (68).

Bonner's own poetic blossoming began after 1963, when major surgery almost put an end to his career. Too ill to perform, he began writing poems that became a regular feature in Houston's *Forward Times*, and when he was able to take the stage again his voice was definitely his own. "I think he was primarily a poet," said Chris Strachwitz, Juke Boy's producer at Arhoolie Records. "He was very emotional; he really felt things. And he worried about who would listen to him. Maybe he felt that he had to follow in Lightnin' Hopkins' footsteps in being a musical poet . . . to get people's attention."

He did get some attention, though not as much as he deserved. Though the old blues clubs in the black neighborhoods continued to fade into memory, a new, young audience at places such as Liberty Hall began to listen. And

Juke Boy continued to present his uncompromising music his way. "Most singers lay out when they sing," said Strachwitz. "They get used to having a band behind them. Juke Boy played the harmonica and guitar all the time when he performed. That was very difficult and took a lot of concentration." His approach was also unique. One of his songs is an obvious derivative of one of Lightnin' Hopkins' favorite riffs, but no one but Bonner would sing "Life is a nightmare / . . . Full of ups and downs / With a valley of shattered dreams." Another song, "Railroad Tracks," matches the traditional blues locomotive rhythm and train-whistle harmonica with lyrics alluding to police harassment in black neighborhoods.

Bonner made his first trip to Europe in 1969 on tour with Clifton Chenier, Magic Sam, and Dallas pianist Alex Moore. His artistry was well received, and on subsequent tours his popularity increased as he played to huge, enthusiastic audiences at the Montreux Jazz Festival in Switzerland, and other festivals. Back in Houston, he collaborated with Barbara Marshall's Urban Theatre, providing the musical score for their production *Stay Strong for the Harvest*, a Bicentennial reappraisal of black history. The show received good notices when it was staged at the Southern Black Cultural Association Festival in New Orleans in November 1976.

After that Bonner was off again on another successful European tour, but his circumstances upon returning proved just as much a struggle as ever before. He had few, if any, music jobs and stayed in a rented room in the Fifth Ward writing poems and music. Again, his health began to fail.

Then, Juke Boy appeared at SUM Concerts' Juneteenth festival at Miller Theater. Though seriously ill, he performed well, expressing great dignity and pride as he sat onstage, as he always did: a man alone with guitar and harp and a strong voice singing songs about his and his neighbors' experience of life. KPFT-FM producer Lawrence Jones told me that in conversation with Bonner backstage, Juke Boy expressed a somewhat bitter satisfaction that he had just performed for the largest audience he had ever had in Houston, his hometown for thirty years.

No one knew it then—but it had been his last session. Juke Boy Bonner died on the twenty-ninth day of that month, June 1978. Though the official cause of Weldon Bonner's death was listed as cirrhosis of the liver, one may suspect some other factors. "He was a beautiful man," said Barbara Marshall, "and he was like so many other Houstonians—dead before his time— because Houston kills its artists." And there is something else, too; something LeRoi Jones wrote about long ago discussing the plight of blacks who left bad conditions in the countryside. Specifically, it's what a man once named for me "unnatural adversity." It is social, it is economic, it is cultural and historical.

Juke Boy Bonner was one of those singers, a man who personally suffered that "unnatural adversity," he was an artist who—in the African tradition handed down to us in the music—served as a voice for the people. As he said in one of his songs, "It's a struggle in Houston / Just to stay alive"; and in yet another:

> You got to keep on pushing at a mountain
>   And it never seems to move

It's here, perhaps, that one might find the real meaning of the blues that black people—with or without much thought to tradition—hold dear. The blues tell us that, though a man suffers, his life is still his own; that even when one cannot speak out directly, there is yet no need to suffer in silence. And the blues tell us, as did the life of Weldon Juke Boy Bonner, that no matter how stubborn the mountain seems, we gain our dignity when we keep on pushing. Someday, now, it's got to move.

A Conversation with Peppermint Harris: "Our landmarks cease to be . . ."

> How long must I suffer
>   For one mistake
>   I made?
> How long must I suffer
>   For one mistake
>   I made?
> If I've been mean
>   and evil,
>   Well, you know darn
>   well I paid
>   —Peppermint Harris

Harrison Nelson, professionally known as Peppermint Harris, was born in 1925 and grew up around Texarkana. A talented poet and guitarist, he began recording for Houston's Gold Star and Sittin' In With labels in 1947 and enjoyed some local success. He moved on to Los Angeles in 1950, where he joined the group of expatriate Ark-La-Tex blues musicians who produced the exciting Aladdin/Modern/Specialty brand of rhythm and blues that shaped the early rock-and-roll sound. The musicians might have been from the country, but the sound they developed was the precursor of what critic Charlie Gillette aptly termed "the sound of the city."

A key element of this sound was the blend of blues vocals and guitar with jazz orchestrations provided by saxophonists such as Maxwell Davis, a brilliant innovator who is not as well remembered as he should be. Arnold Shaw, in *Honkers and Shouters: The Golden Years of Rhythm & Blues*, places Davis in the same "incandescent" ranks as Red Prysock, Sit Austin, and King Curtis. Harris's early Houston recordings won him a job working with Davis at Aladdin Records when he arrived in California. Though mostly appreciated as a songwriter, Harris made the charts with "Raining In My Heart" in 1950 and produced a number one record with the classic "I Got Loaded" in 1951.

Resettling in Houston in 1960, Harris went to work as a songwriter and recording artist for Don Robey's Duke and Peacock labels. Peacock, of course, was the major black-owned record company of the early 1950s with a roster of stars including Clarence "Gatemouth" Brown, Johnny Ace, Big Mama Thornton, Bobby Bland, and a studio full of outstanding local musicians Shortly before Robey's death in 1975, the company's catalog was sold to ABC Records.

In 1977, Peppermint Harris was working a day gig at Houston Records, a disc pressing plant. Tom Usslemann, a former disc jockey and blues enthusiast, went there to inquire about prices, found Harris at work, and began a collaboration with him that resulted in the reissue of the early Sittin' In With recordings on Usslemann's shoestring Lunar #2 label.

For a while Peppermint Harris's music received growing appreciation both at home and abroad. Canadian musicologist Hank Davis edited several European releases, and Harris had become active with appearances at Houston's annual Juneteenth Blues Festival, club dates, and work with Howard Harris's community-oriented People's Workshop Orchestra. Perhaps his most long-lasting contribution was launching the career of his brilliant young bandleader-guitarist Sherman Robertson. Eventually, Harris settled in Sacramento, California, for several years and then moved to New Jersey, where he died at age seventy-three in 1999.

(The People's Workshop deserves an chapter all its own, because it is amazingly representative of a city with a black community that supports the Fresh Festival as well as five regular blues radio programs, and the Community Music Center of Houston, which is devoted to the works of Deft, Kay, and the great Afro-American classical music tradition, including contemporary composers such as T. J. Anderson and Earl Stewart.)

My conversations with Peppermint Harris were always fascinating, partly because of his friendly charm . . . and partly because his experiences, extending from country blues to the early days of the high-powered contemporary music industry. He also had firsthand knowledge of the black urban milieu that produced and supported the music. Pep's interest in motion pictures and other entertainment modes is also significant. Spike Lee, Mario Van Peebles, and other directors have made self-serving and exaggerated claims for their films as historical texts; yet Harris's comments point out that some black history does seem to be disseminated *only* in the movies and, consequently, in an unreliable, fictionalized, and sensationalized form.

Most of this interview was conducted in August 1978 at Harris's sister's home in Houston's Fifth Ward just around the corner from a vacant relic that had been the headquarters of Don Robey's Peacock Records.

Thomas: The big-band sound of blues records in the late 1940s and small group or solo blues sound of earlier years—how did it work?

Harris: We would arrange . . . I wouldn't write for the singer, I'd just write for the band, and the singer was more or less on his own, you understand. But as things changed, as the singer became the big person, you'd see people like . . . Billy Eckstine, June Richmond.

Thomas: Billy Eckstine had a really popular band in the late forties.

Harris: Well see, before he got his band he was singing with Fatha Hines. Here's what they used to do. For instance, I played the blues guitar, and you can notice on some records where I had Maxwell Davis arranging . . . you'll notice the big band. But, see, it's written so the band might play a riff [*sings*] like that. And the guitar and the singer would play [*sings*] against that.

Thomas: Like T-Bone Walker.

Harris: Yeah. But this type of thing . . . that's the way they were writing then.

Thomas: Pee Wee Crayton?

Harris: Yeah, and B. B. King's early records.

Thomas: Did Maxwell Davis also arrange those?

Harris: What happened is this: I was on Aladdin Records; so was Amos Milburn, Charles Brown. During that time Maxwell was with Aladdin Records; he was the arranger there. The A & R man there. And Floyd Dixon was there. They had success after success, but he left Aladdin and went to Modern—that's the parent company of Crown, RPM, all of this. I left at the same time and went over there, but I still had a writing contract with Aladdin Records.

Oh, Max and I were real good friends. As a result people like Etta James, Johnny Watson, Jesse Belvin, Richard Perry . . . a player named Lee Mays; he was on the label, too. So you can see the play. Even at Specialty, Maxwell did all those things when Percy Mayfield was on there. So, you see, if you listen to all those records you can hear that pattern, hear that big round sound of Maxwell Davis.

Thomas: That's an important era.

Harris: What I would really like to do is get a national booking firm . . . be able to play colleges, maybe with a narrator like Larry Steele did, and build a show, say, "The Early Twenties Up Till Now."

Thomas: Larry Steele?

Harris: Like Larry Steele's Smart Affairs . . . it was a dance company based at the Club Harlem in Atlantic City. Larry Steele and all those beautiful girls. We worked a show in Atlanta with him.

Thomas: Everything that has been done about black society, black culture—all of these folks seem to get left out. The reason for that I think is because black people are not usually in charge of what is said. These are all the people I remember hearing about when I was a little kid, the people my parents enjoyed.

Harris: Well, you take people like this . . . what they did was this (which I think we're in sore need of now) . . . what they did, they took their raw culture and presented it in a grand manner. It unfolds.

Actually, the show I'm talking about is a historical type of thing because of this: It starts out with the Roaring Twenties and shows one era to another era right on up to the current time. Then you can see just a whole picture, just like a flower growing. Then you see where it has gone from its roots to there. And in order to enjoy the final result, if blacks know what the beginning was, then, you understand, you can appreciate it more. By knowing the whole story.

Thomas: We do have to turn around the whole thing and put the people that we think, or have thought, were important in a prominent place . . . not people someone else thinks

Harris: Yeah! In other words, there are a lot of people who made very definite contributions . . . a lot of people are lost, forgotten. Just like if you wanted to say things and there's not enough time or something, or you don't have it prepared . . . there's a lot of things you forget. Back when we were talking about B. B. King . . . like a lot of those jazz musicians worked with B.B. in Los Angeles.

Things were like this. When Maxwell was at Aladdin there were one or two guys . . . it was like a clique, you understand. Maxwell called the people that he wanted on his sessions . . . as A & R man. So, as a result, he liked good musicians.

Now, I recorded with Red Callender . . . what's his name . . . a jazz piano player. I can't think of his name . . . Tiny Wells. They were on my very first records. These people seem heavy, but these were Maxwell's friends, you understand. Only thing they would do for this is make sessions, they didn't play gigs. I'm trying to think of that jazz piano player . . . he recorded on Blue Note and he's on my very first record for Aladdin Records. So you can see these jazz people behind a novice and country blues singer! Ha-ha! But this is the caliber of musicians that they used.

Thomas: What's the real difference actually between jazz and country blues?

Harris: I'm not qualified really to answer this. I don't know enough about it. In my opinion there is a very definite difference because the people in jazz are really superb musicians. Well-trained musicians. Sometimes they improvise, but this is already studied. They know what they're improvising . . . unless you're Erroll Garner or somebody like this. Tiny Bradshaw. But usually they're very, very fine musicians. But the bridge, to me, seems very narrow. You take Ray Charles, he's a very learned musician, you understand . . . but he can play lowdown dirty blues. But—on another level—just like spirituals, blues . . . I don't see that much difference.

Thomas: Would you say, realizing the fact of how well trained in music most jazz players are, that their concern with the blues is because of the color situation . . . that they're not able to go into the films, classical music, or Broadway?

Harris: Oh, I don't think that that is their concern at all. I believe they just like to play good music.

Thomas: And the blues is that.

Harris: Yes. Jazz came out of blues. It's just an embellishment and they do different things and use different structures. I mean, they are so far advanced musically until they can take a straight "Saints Go Marching In" but they're playing all kinds of things. I knew this guy, Ike Royal, a piano player from Los Angeles. I made a blues tune and he used nothing but three pieces—bass, guitar, he played piano. He used all Rachmaninoff chords.

Thomas: Playing blues?

Harris: That's what I was singing! So, I mean, there's different ideas.

Thomas: Where do your ideas in music come from?

Harris: I don't know. I just know what I like, what I hear. A lot of different sounds, you know. For instance, I like all kinds of music. There's that song "I'll Learn To Love Again" [on *the Penthouse in the Ghetto* CD] I wrote a couple of years ago. Junior Parker recorded it. I don't have nothing to play it on now, or I'd play it. Ha-ha-ha! The jukebox down the street . . . Ha-ha!

To show you the difference: if you listen to that or you listen to "Sweet Black Angels" or "Red River Blues" . . . it's a different person altogether. This thing goes:

> Although my heart has been
> kicked around . . .
> > and I have found
> Your lips are sin;

> Now that I'm free
> > don't pity me—
> > > I'll learn to love again . . .

It's got a nice group on the background.

Thomas: Yes. I remember the record. Do you remember the Masters of Soul?

Harris: Yeah.

Thomas: Fred Kibble of the Masters told me that he started out working for Don Robey. He was just a kid still going to school. His job was to sing songs, I guess they'd tape them.

Harris: Yes they did.

Thomas: . . . and send them out to Bobby Bland so he could choose which one he wanted. Fred's job was just to tape songs for Bobby Bland.

Harris: Joe Medwick, who wrote "I Pity The Fool," did the same thing. We all did. When I was writing down there, that's what you'd do—just put 'em on tape and send them to the artists. Like Larry Davis did this thing . . . "Angels in Houston." That's what I called it then.

Bobby did a record of "Lost Sight On The World." Junior did "Stranded In St. Louis" and he sang "I'll Learn To Love Again." We used to put them on tape for the singers—Joe Hinton, those guys.

Thomas: Joe Hinton had an R & B hit with a Willie Nelson country tune, "Funny How Time Slips Away."

Harris: Was that a Willie Nelson tune?

Thomas: Yeah.

Harris: I didn't know who did that. I heard it a long time ago, and a lot of artists have done it. And there's another song:

> So little time, and so much
>   so much to do

Joe . . . I was hoping he would do that. He did a lot of things.

You see I've written about a million tunes, I guess. Practically everybody who was anybody, all the big stars . . . . I had a hit with B. B. King "Whole Lotta Lovin." And also "Careful With The Fool" that B. B. did. He got a hit off "Whole Lotta Lovin'." Etta James's second thing she did was number one; and Junior Parker's "Stranded In St. Louis."

Thomas: Was "Stranded In St. Louis" a personal lyric?

Harris: Naw!

Thomas: You just made it up?

Harris: I write a lot of things. I don't know why, but to me there's something about Memphis, Texas . . . . I've used a lot of phrases about Texas and Tennessee. I guess because the blues to me is like Tennessee, like the Mississippi delta. That's its home, you know. Memphis, being a sporting center . . .

Did you see the movie *Leadbelly?* When I was a kid in my hometown, they had places where people tasted their homebrew, you know. Drank beer. They'd have a little corn liquor there. They'd sit back, you know. Sunday mornings, Sunday evenings, something like that. They'd be at a house . . . called it a "house." Out in the country, law didn't come around there.

They had these dudes . . . I knew these two cats. One had a violin, one had a guitar. See, they'd come there and play for drinks. Pass the hat, you understand. And get down!

Thomas: That was a show?

Harris: Yes, sir! Just like guys would play on the streets. Mostly they'd go around to those houses that I was talking about.

They'd have a little party sometimes, what they'd call "suppers." There'd be a "supper" at somebody's house. What they'd mean, see, is that they'd have fish and stuff for sale, you understand. Beer and homebrew, bootleg whiskey. They'd have somebody over in the corner with the records playing or the piano . . . somebody'd be going in the back gambling. You know, breaking on down till daylight.

Thomas: Wasn't there a time there was a lot of music on the street in Houston? On Dowling Street?

Harris: Um-hmm. Lightnin' Hopkins played on Dowling.

Thomas: Who'd they play for?

Harris: Anybody that would listen. I never actually seen it, but he was telling me about it. Man, there's so much . . . . I'd like to see somebody write a book that is *authentic*.

Thomas: You wrote "Sweet Black Angels" with . . .

Harris: Joe Hughes. I put Joe Hughes's name on it because he helped me a lot. "Red River Blues" was written with Nelson Carson. I'll tell you why. I was over at Nelson's house in Ashdown, Arkansas, one day visiting. There's a creek runs around by his house and he said, "Listen at this: 'Red River, Red River / Red River runs right by my door.'" But that's all I remembered. But I liked the phrase, I liked the idea, so I just wrote a song about Red River. Since I got the idea from him, I put his name on it. But I wrote the lyrics.

Thomas: Was that the Red River in Texas?

Harris: Oh, I don't know what river it is! Ha-ha! I just pictured "Red River" and I see where it's coming from. What I'm saying, you can see it, just living down in the country. Just like "One Room Country Shack." What it says is this, you can understand. Like I wrote about Tennessee.

During the days a long time ago when folks was around and up and down Red River, well . . . Cat's living out in the country, he wants to get to some urban center, you understand. He'd want to get on down to Memphis or Cairo, Illinois. Somewhere where it was jumping. During them times they were like nice hustling towns for "sweetbacks," they called 'em. Pimps, gamblers. Blues singers. They'd sing "Drop me off in Memphis . . ." or anywhere down the line.

Just like the *Leadbelly* movie: You see how they rode all those freight trains and things until they found one of those good towns, some of them broads, you understand. He's home free, he's sharp.

I'll tell you what I like . . . there's a song B. B. did. I like the mention of towns, especially historical towns as far as the Negro or black culture is concerned. We have a lot of songs like that. I mean, songs about Harlem, songs about Forty-seventh Street in Chicago, songs about Eighteenth and Vine in Kansas City, Beale Street in Memphis. You see, these were landmarks. We lost a lot of this with the advent of integration. Our landmarks cease to be, now.

If you really covered historical . . . like you say—uh, as Big Joe says:

> Well, I been to Kansas City
> > Boy, everything was really all right
> Well, the lads jump and sing
> > Until the broad daylight

He say,

> Well, I dreamed last night
> > I was standing on Eighteenth and Vine

You know he's into where it is!

> Yes, I dreamed last night
> > I was standing on Eighteenth and Vine
> I shook hands with Piney Brown
> > And I could hardly keep from crying.

Well, see, anybody from around Kansas City would know he's talking about the hustling kind of people . . . they'd always be on Eighteenth and Vine. Then he said, and guess what:

> I took a stroll on Forty-seventh Street . . .

Hey Jack! That was Big June Richmond or somebody . . . [She] did that song about Forty-seventh Street in Chicago.

Thomas: Do you know anything about Oklahoma City? Ever been there?

Harris: Yeah, I've played Oklahoma City but I didn't know much about it.

Thomas: Well, I guess Sixth Street would have been the scene in Oklahoma City. But it hasn't worn well at all . . . . Well, like everything else, I guess.

Harris: Um-hmm. You take our landmarks . . . Dowling Street and Lyons Avenue in Houston are known all over the world. If you wanted to see somebody from your hometown in Houston, man, they would show up there.

Thomas: As you said, the whole business of integration has really changed our life a great deal.

Harris: Yeah, for instance; you take the Theresa Hotel in Harlem. Everybody used to be at the Theresa.

Thomas: Fidel Castro stayed there, I think.

Harris: Yeah, man. Whoever's who! When you're in New York . . .

Thomas: Fidel Castro, when he came from Cuba in the early sixties to speak at the United Nations. Kennedy didn't like that, but Castro says: This is the scene where the *people* are. Ha-ha-ha!

Harris: Hey, man! Ha-ha!

When I first went to New York, I was working for a promoter out of West Virginia called "the beautiful Red" . . . Apple Red Taylor. So I went on to New York when I finished his tour. I'd never been to New York before. My manager was Ben Da Costa and I stayed downtown with Ben a day or two. I didn't know Red was coming to town. So Red came on and came on downtown. He told us, "Well, come on, Slim. I'm gonna take you up to Harlem; you don't want to be down here with no paddy folks."

So we went to the Theresa Hotel, so I wanted to get a room and they said they didn't have no room. But, see, Red's a gangster out of West Virginia . . . all his friends are like Bumpy Johnson, (Casper) Holstein. They were called "partners," they were just like *that!* All gangsters. So they said they didn't have a room; we said, "Well, that's all right."

So we went in the bar, you know. Arthur Finley was in there with Johnson. . . . She sees who I'm with. Hey! The bitch came a-runnin' and got me a *suite!* Ha ha! But they didn't have no room! Heh heh heh!

Thomas: Yeah, right . . .

Thomas: The numbers?

Harris: In Harlem. But, see, Bumpy'd rob all their runners. He'd just *take* the money!

See, the mob was trying to run the niggers out of business in Harlem . . .

They were going to take over Harlem. But Bumpy'd just take the money away from 'em. Like Red said, "Bumpy just walked up and down 125th Street. He'd just go up and talk to 'em and tell 'em how much money he wanted."

Thomas: And then take it?

Harris: They gonna *give* it to him! They was paying off. They'd just pay him off, you know, at certain times. They'd rather do that than have him blow them up. Oh, and he looked like a little doctor! Bald-head dude.

That *Shaft* picture had a cat portraying Bumpy . . . in that first *Shaft* picture. But I met Bumpy. Boy, he was a hell of a gangster.

But the Theresa, just like I said, had the original thing honoring Joe Louis. And, you know, Sugar Ray Robinson's joint was right almost next door. All the players hung out there. Willie Bryant.

Thomas: Palm Cafe?

Harris: Well, the Palm Cafe was . . . like the Theresa's here and you go down this way . . .

Thomas: Yeah, about half a block.

Harris: Yeah, across 125th Street there, the same side the Apollo Theatre is on. The Palm and the Shalimar. Ralph Cooper was broadcasting there.

Thomas: I was just about to ask you about Ralph Cooper. He was another one, like Larry Steele, who needs to be talked about.

Harris: Yeah, Willie Bryant, too. Ralph Cooper was a real light-skinned dude; he played in a lot of black movies that were produced out of New York.

Thomas: Ralph Cooper was interesting. When I was a kid he was producing a lot of shows. At that time, they were rock-and-roll shows. He wasn't making it as big as Alan Freed because he didn't have the same kind of connections. But he was producing a show at the Valencia Theatre in Jamaica . . . a talent show and rock-and-roll show. Like I say, Alan Freed had people like Fats Domino and Buddy Holly . . . Cooper had acts with lesser names, but they were still stars as far as us kids were concerned—I remember Ralph Cooper very well; that was toward the very end of his career when I first saw him.

Harris: Well, you know, when I was a kid . . . Ralph Cooper, Mantan Moreland, Willie Bryant . . . a host of 'em . . . did a lot of good things. But it was to a limited audience.

Thomas: An all-black audience?

Harris: Yes. And you take people like Nipsey Russell and Jackie "Moms" Mabley, Bill Bailey, Slappy White, Redd Foxx, and those guys . . . they were never seen down here. Because there were no theaters down here for them to work in. Until television.

Thomas: What about downtown Houston and the old Lincoln Theatre?

Harris: Acts like that didn't come there. Pigmeat Markham might have come there, every once in a blue moon.

Thomas: Was there not enough money down here?

Harris: I don't think it was a matter of money so much as it was the matter of a place to play. The theaters didn't do the kind of thing down here, I mean, like they did on the East Coast.

Thomas: Houston was still pretty much "country South"?

Harris: Like it is now. But it's just a funny thing . . . you didn't find that on the West Coast, either. It was strictly like Virginia . . .

Thomas: . . . out to Chicago and Ohio?

Harris: Yeah.

Thomas: What about Birmingham and thereabouts?

Harris: I don't know. I played Birmingham . . . but it was just one-nighters, so I don't know.

Thomas: How about Kentucky? Louisville?

Harris: I don't know. I doubt it, but that influence may have reached down there, too.

Thomas: It's interesting that they had one tradition on the East Coast that didn't get out to the rest of the country.

Harris: The Lincoln is a good example. They had shows, but they didn't have the big acts. They had some dancers there . . . they were all local talent. They played at the Peacock Club, that you passed there on the corner. That was a big nightclub; and the El Dorado Ballroom on Dowling Street. But Moms and that, that was an East Coast thing.

Goin' to Kansas City

Milt Larkin and the Best of the Territory Bands

"Little of beauty has America given the world," wrote W. E. B. DuBois in *The Souls of Black Folk*: "The Negro folk-song—the rhythmic cry of the slave—stands today not simply as the sole American music, but as the most beautiful expression of human existence born this side [of] the seas." For DuBois, this music was "the singular spiritual heritage of the nation and the greatest gift of the Negro people" (732).

The ambiguity of DuBois's phrasing is purposeful and suggestive. Yes, DuBois means that this music is what is properly called a *talent*, a gift to the Negro from God; and yes, he also means that it is the Negro's gift to the American nation. The givers of gifts—as DuBois, a genteel and impeccably Victorian gentleman would have known—never admit to desiring anything in return. Two decades after DuBois wrote on the spirituals, however, African American scholars such as James Weldon Johnson and Alain Locke upped the ante. Locke, a professor of philosophy at Howard University and the first African American to study at Oxford University as a Rhodes scholar, was the most ambitious in his hopes for African American art, particularly music. In the arena of culture, wrote Locke in his essay "The New Negro," the serious African American artist

> becomes a conscious contributor and lays aside the status of a beneficiary and ward for that of a collaborator and participant in American civilization. The great social gain in this is the releasing of our talented group from the arid fields of controversy and debate to the productive fields of creative expression. The especially cultural recognition they win should in turn prove the key to that revaluation of the Negro which

must precede or accompany any considerable further betterment of race relationships. (15)

This view was, to an extraordinary degree, shared by the artists themselves and—indeed—accepted as a personal responsibility to the race that coincided with their own individual aspirations.

Whether or not he was an avid reader of Professor Locke's widely published essays, Houston jazz bandleader Milton Larkin epitomizes the type of artist Locke envisioned in 1925.The fact that Larkin was a masterful practitioner of what we call the *popular arts*, and that Locke really was proposing that African American composers should elevate the spirituals into an American *classical* music, raises a number of questions that must occupy some of our attention.

The serious critique of American popular culture and the role of the mass media does not begin with Theodor Adorno, Max Horkheimer, and the Frankfort School—though we are indebted to them for coining the perfect phrase *the culture industry* to describe it. As early as 1927, Southern Methodist University professor Henry Nash Smith had identified the problem that Adorno and others analyzed so cogently. In an article entitled " 'Culture,' " published in the *Southwest Review*, Smith noted:

the masses of our city people are living, not in Texas, but in a queer milieu patched together from shreds of the musical ideas of New York song-writers, the artistic and ethical conceptions of California moving-picture producers, the mechanical triumphs of Detroit automotive engineers, the journalism of national syndicate writers, and the skill of professional athletes. Of course, this unreal world has been necessary. . . . Unable to find culture, we have tried desperately to content ourselves with . . . amusements of escape. (253–54)

As a description of a nation without "high art" traditions, lacking appreciation of local expressions, in a curious way Smith's statement echoes that of DuBois; further, though he is not concerned with race, Smith also reinforces Locke's call for the development of an indigenous and authentic culture. When applied to black folks, what is characteristic of the United States in general can become a bit complicated. The study of African American cultural expression actually presents two very complex problems, and both of them involve the proper evaluation of the *local* in what we celebrate as *culture*.

First, for political reasons, African American cultural leaders such as Alain Locke have attempted since the 1920s to depict African American culture as a *national* culture. This effort, particularly in the case of black music, was also promoted by the commercial distribution systems for popular culture that were developing at the same time. African American entrepreneurs such as Harry Pace and W. C. Handy were involved in this aspect of "the show business," but they did not have the economic power to compete at the level that Berry Gordy, Jr. achieved with Motown Records in the 1960s.

Alain Locke and James Weldon Johnson proudly—and accurately—declared that African American music was *American* music (and vice versa), the only genuine cultural expression created in the United States. In time, the poet Langston Hughes understood the "downside" of this reality and expressed it poignantly in his poem "Note on Commercial Theatre" (1940):

> You've taken my blues and gone
> You sing 'em on Broadway
> And you sing 'em in Hollywood Bowl,
> And you mixed 'em up with symphonies
> And you fixed 'em
> So they don't sound like me.
> Yep, you done taken my blues and gone.
>
> *(Collected Poems* 215–16)

From an artist's point of view, Hughes raises the question of authenticity and—perhaps more importantly—copyright. But the larger issue of accurate representation, and cultural self-representation, was central to the participants of the Harlem Renaissance. For the artists who participated in the Black Arts Movement of the 1960s and 1970s—for whom this Hughes poem could almost be a precursive manifesto—this question very easily became a metaphor for *political* "self-determination."

The historical development of popular African American music offers an especially useful vantage on these issues. In the late 1930s and 1940s big-band jazz became enormously popular through live broadcasts on the CBS and NBC radio networks or independent stations with powerful nighttime transmitters, such as Chicago's WGN. But while the nation could listen to bands such as Benny Goodman's or Tommy Dorsey's on the radio, most of the innovation in jazz came from black "territory bands" that worked grueling itineraries of one-night stands through the South and Midwest playing a regular circuit of nightclubs and dance halls. As Gunther Schuller wrote in *The Swing Era* the territory bands developed a musical vocabulary that "was eventually exported to New York and there established itself in what would become in turn a national style" (772). These bands also were the proving grounds of the best black jazz musicians in the country.

It could easily be said that the territory bands reveal what both the art and the *business* of jazz is really about. In a still very segregated America, these artists reworked the folk roots of African American music and created exciting new forms. As blues singer Peppermint Harris put it, "They took their raw culture and presented it in a grand manner." Scholars, of course, may want to know a little more about how that was done than blues singers are usually willing to tell; and focusing on a particular band may answer some questions or, at least, help frame some areas for further investigation.

Although never recorded, the Milton Larkin Orchestra based in Houston, Texas, is reputed to have been among the most accomplished and innovative of the territory bands. The group is perhaps best known as the launching pad for artists such as pianist-arrangers Cedric Haywood and William "Wild Bill" Davis, Gil Askey (later conductor for the Temptations), George Rhodes (arranger-conductor for Sammy Davis, Jr.), and the extraordinary saxophonists Arnett Cobb, Eddie "Cleanhead" Vinson, Jimmy Ford, and Illinois Jacquet.

It was Illinois Jacquet who, as a nineteen-year-old Larkin alumnus, found instant and undying fame with Lionel Hampton's band. According to pianist Hank Jones, Jacquet's astonishing rave-up tenor sax solo on "Flying Home" (1942) was "the most influential solo in the entire history of music" (Evans A17).

Perhaps Jones was being expansive; but his comment illuminates a major issue that jazz critics must confront.

David W. Stowe's excellent commentary on the territory bands in "Jazz in the West" raises some important questions regarding what he calls "images of the mythic West" in much of the available critical writing and oral histories (58). There is often a question of whether we are dealing with jazz legends or jazz history; and if we are honest we will all admit that the grand mythologies of jazz—constructed with the equal efforts of critics, fans, and the musicians themselves—were initially (and perhaps remain) as exciting and attractive to us as the music is. That being the case, it is not always easy to look behind the myths or to feel pleased by what we sometimes find when we do. In the very first place, we are talking about an art form that developed in a social atmosphere dominated by race and an economic system skewed by racism. At the same time that the radio was making swing music recognizable as "mainstream American music," it was clear that the originators of the musical style were less generously rewarded than the white bands. In March 1945 when Benny Carter's band, the King Cole Trio, and Savannah Churchill were booked for a month at the Trocadero on Hollywood's Sunset Strip, the booking was hailed as a breakthrough for black performers. For Carter's show as a package, the club paid fifty-six hundred dollars per week; yet Frank Sinatra, as a single, was offered seventy-five hundred dollars per week by the club. Similar disparities in pay scales are found throughout jazz literature (Berger et al., vol. 1, 224). To add insult to the inequities of the status quo, a *Down Beat* writer of the period claimed that black bands were "doomed" as far as economics was concerned "because the white bands had learned to play their style and could get the choice bookings" (Berger et al., vol. 1, 241). In other words, no one was kept in the dark about what was going on or the rationale behind it.

You will say, "That was then, this is now," but this bad history continues to create a problem for jazz scholarship. Aside from the fact that much of the earlier writing about jazz is mythmaking or press-agentry, those who would strive for some accuracy and sensible interpretation are immediately confronted with an Archimedean dilemma. As Amiri Baraka eloquently noted, the view from the top of the hill is different from the view from the bottom. Perhaps a single example will suffice: How and why did the territory bands develop a distinctive style?

According to most critics this style is explained as the result of the relative isolation of the region from the "mainstream" of the culture industry (Stowe 64). If that is true, what we are talking about is style as a type of response to deprivation; or, at best, a happy result of geographical accident similar to the discovery of a surviving specimen of something long thought to be extinct—in this case, artistic originality. For Baraka in *Blues People* and William Barlow in "*Looking Up at Down": The Emergence of Blues Culture* there is a different answer drawn from a positive understanding of the alchemy of the dance hall, evidence of what Baraka calls "the Blues continuum." The sound of the territory bands developed because, Baraka writes, "Negroes in the Southwest still wanted a great part of their music to be blues-oriented, even if it was played by a large dance band" (167). And those bands, adds Barlow, responded to the wishes of "the new black urban proletariat" that bought the tickets (249). At this point, however, we are faced with yet another problem (see Beeth and Wintz 99). Do we know even as much about this urban proletariat—its origins and aspirations, its character—as we do about obscure musicians? As Ted Vincent notes in *Keep Cool: The Black Activists Who Built the Jazz Age* (1995):

Accurate chronicling of music history demands not only a close look at how Black society dealt with its own music . . . but also a look at how music fitted within the larger context of life, a context with a political side. (187)

The Milt Larkin Orchestra

A close look at the Milton Larkin Orchestra will perhaps illuminate several of the concerns we have been discussing, especially in terms of providing a way toward understanding the development of professionalism among these musicians.

Milton Larkin was born in 1910 in Navasota, Texas. His family soon moved about seventy-five miles to Houston, but by the age of thirteen he had lost both parents, and after graduating from Houston's Booker T. Washington High School in 1927 he was on his own. A mostly self-taught trumpeter, trombonist, and excellent vocalist, Larkin formed his first band in 1936. But getting to that point took some effort, and to understand the social context of Larkin's early years it may be worth a moment's digression to look at exactly what came with the territory.

Navasota, in Grimes County, is a farming town of about seven thousand located about twenty miles from Texas A & M University. It is not a tourist destination. On the Greyhound bus run between Houston and Dallas there are never more than one or two passengers getting off or on at Navasota except at Thanksgiving or Christmas, when perhaps half of each busload will be relatives going to visit relatives at the prison farm just outside of town.

On the wall at McDonald's, just down the road from Navasota High School, in recent years—after Spike Lee's *Do the Right Thing* shook everybody awake—you could find a framed photograph of folk singer Mance Lipscomb, who lived in this county all his life. But Lipscomb recalled Navasota in the late 1920s and 1930s as "the dirtiest place there in the world," an area ruled by the Ku Klux Klan. "They kilt niggas for the fun of it," said Lipscomb. "Specially if a man try to hold up fur his rights, they gonna kill him" (Lipscomb and Alyn 142). The period Lipscomb recalled was the tail-end of an ugly half-century in Texas history. In the early years of Reconstruction, Navasota and towns in nearby counties elected black candidates to various offices. Following the election of Governor Richard Coke in 1873, however, a reign of unbridled violence and terrorism drove hundreds of black and sympathetic white residents out of the region (Smallwood 155–57). Even though the city council of Houston had recently enacted segregation ordinances, one needs very little imagination to understand why the Larkin family moved there from Navasota a few years after Milton was born. The great African American migration of this period swelled the populations not only of New York and Chicago, but also cities such as St. Louis (which many migrants considered "the North") and Houston. The allure of such places included the possibility of economic and political advancement; even if Houston government continued to tighten segregation laws between 1903 and 1922, the city also offered sixteen elementary and three high schools for blacks. As Howard Beeth and Cary D. Wintz point out in *Black Dixie: Afro-Texan History and Culture in Houston*, by 1930 "the percentage of Houston's black youth attending school was greater than that of either Atlanta or New Orleans, although it was not quite as high as that of New York or Detroit" (96–97).

This situation was particularly important to a youth like Milt Larkin. His interest in music first led him to purchase a used trumpet and an Otto Langley instruction book and then drew him to the kids who were in Percy McDavid's band program at the city's Phillis Wheatley High School. He developed a close friendship at after-school practice sessions with Illinois and Russell Jacquet and their pal Arnett Cobb. The Jacquet brothers' father maintained a family band, and Larkin was soon an honorary member, learning songs such as "Dinah" and "Tiger Rag," and memorizing papa Gilbert Jacquet's favorite Louis Armstrong records (Thomas, "Jazz Angel" 54).

Larkin eventually landed a spot in the Giles Mitchell band, which rehearsed on Mondays. "They'd let you come to rehearsals," he recalled. "The first man in the section would listen to you and tell the leader whether you could make it or not . . . and every Monday I was wondering if I'd be with them for the next week. Rehearsals were mainly 'cutting time.' If you saw another two or three trumpets come around, you knew they were looking to take your seat." Larkin lasted, but soon moved up to a job with Chester Boone's band, and by 1936 had formed his own aggregation (L. Thomas, "Jazz Angel" 55). The early days with his own band were tough indeed; band members shared the driving between gigs, and Larkin's wife Cathryn worked as hard as anyone—cooking two meals a day for the band and ironing the musicians' dress shirts. As Lionel Hampton and others have noted, the matter of band uniforms was not just a minor detail. For Milt Larkin, who saw a musical career as a step toward upward mobility, it was a matter of great importance. As a teenager, in fact, his interest in music was first attracted by reading about Noble Sissle in a magazine and being impressed by the photographic evidence of the bandleader's urbane stylishness. Photos of the Larkin Orchestra underscore the point (see W. Hampton 76; Fernett 144).

By the late 1930s Larkin's reputation allowed him to draw upon the most talented players in Houston and to attract men who had been trained in Bernard Adams's bands at Wiley College in Marshall, Texas. Wiley, founded in 1873 and perhaps best known for poet Melvin B. Tolson's award-winning debate teams of the 1930s and 1940s, was the oldest black college west of the Mississippi. Professor Tolson's men compiled a phenomenally triumphal record, traveling across the country and trouncing teams from the University of Southern California and Yale, among others. Professor Adams was a demanding coach, too, and the band included talented students such as trumpeter Volley Bastine and Kenney Dorham, and William "Wild Bill" Davis. Pioneer bebop drummer Roy Porter left Wiley to join Larkin in 1943 (Porter 40–41, 46). Others who played with the Larkin band in the period included Willy "Blip" Thompkins and guitarist Sonny Boy Franklin (Howard 15).

The color line as it was drawn in Houston did, however, affect the band's fortunes. "When I did broadcasts from the Aragon Ballroom," said Larkin, "I hoped that it might become a regular job, but that didn't work out. The white kids got too familiar with us. The owner called me at my break and told me how wonderful the band was—but he was afraid to try it" (L. Thomas, "Jazz Angel" 106). Nevertheless, aspiring young white musicians such as Jimmy Ford—who later earned the national spotlight with Maynard Ferguson's band—and Ed Gerlach devotedly followed the Larkin band around to gigs at black venues such as the El Dorado Ballroom. The other territory bands also heard Larkin there. In *Blues People*, Baraka notes that the local musicians were always "impressed most by [the touring name band players'] musicianship and elegance, but they did not want to sound as 'thin' as that" (158). Quite as important, perhaps, was the reciprocal influence. At the Harlem Grill in Houston, Larkin's band played against these touring stars and the sidemen in those bands were not ashamed to be caught literally "taking notes" from the local jazzmen. Illinois Jacquet remembers that visiting members of the Ellington, Basie, and Lunceford bands made it a point to catch the Larkin Orchestra's midnight set and—as in the legendary late shows in Kansas City—the visitors often sat in with the guys onstage, sometimes with exciting results. Says Jacquet:

> I remember when the Cab Calloway Band came through and Chu Berry their top sax player thought he was going to show us up. Well, Arnett lit into him and then I did. Oh. did he get a lesson! (Howard 15)

Knowing what was at stake for the young Texas musicians suggests that Jacquet's reminiscence is not merely self-serving exaggeration. It was their reputation among other musicians, after all, that got first Jacquet and then Cobb calls to go with Lionel Hampton's band in the mid-1940s.

Despite the fact that all musical organizations needed to make tours—even with today's instant international marketing and around-the-clock-videos beamed from space satellites, they still do—the goal of every territory band was to hit the big jackpot, which meant a long and lucrative stand at a prestigious venue. Following well-received performances at Eddie Spitz's College Inn in Kansas City, and national notices in Down Beat, Larkin was invited to do two weeks at Joe Louis's Rhumboogie Club in Chicago in 1940. The club's musical director, Marl Young (later music director for Desilu Productions) created a spectacular show featuring Aaron "T-Bone" Walker and the Milt Larkin Orchestra that, in fact, ran for almost a year. The crowds didn't stop coming, but one by one and then seemingly two by two Larkin's musicians were—to quote Nat "King" Cole's hit song of the period—gone with the draft. Eventually, Larkin himself was drafted and spent his hitch in an army band that included the brilliant arranger Sy Oliver (Dance 63–64; L. Thomas, "Jazz Angel" 55, 105). After the war, Larkin settled in New York, where he was director of the Apollo Theatre band, among many other accomplishments. He returned to Houston in the 1970s, created the Get Involved Now Foundation to bring music to hospital patients, and continued to be involved with music until his death, at age eighty-five, in August 1996.

We can perhaps fix the Milt Larkin Orchestra in a proper historical and artistic context by comparing it with another legendary southwestern band— Alphonso Trent and His Orchestra (see Fernett 40–42). Trent found the end of his rainbow quite early; by 1927, sponsored by a group of white businessmen, Trent became the headliner at Dallas's Adolphus Hotel and did nightly broadcasts on WFAA. Trent's sidemen supposedly earned salaries on a par with big-name New York orchestras, and legend has it that they all drove Cadillacs (Russell 61–63). After 1934, however, Trent was merely a legend. "His sections could swing," wrote Ross Russell, "but Trent did not know how to develop or present his potentially great solo talents" (64). That, of course, is precisely where Milton Larkin excelled.

Some bands are literally schools where young musicians learn from a consummate maestro. Art Blakey's Jazz Messengers, for example, enjoyed a success in this regard unsurpassed by any academic conservatory. Other bands are more like workshops, where talented players improve each other by virtue of close association and shared artistic interests. Such, perhaps, was Larkin's. As a leader he had both the perceptiveness and reputation to attract the most promising young musicians in southeast Texas; and he had the organizational acumen and personal self-assuredness to allow them to shine.

It is impossible, of course, to know how a band that never recorded really sounded; but Milt Larkin's All Stars (often featuring Arnett Cobb, Eddie Vinson, and Jimmy Ford) performed frequently in Houston in the 1970s, and Cedric Haywood's original charts were kept from gathering dust by Sonny Franklin at the Sportsman's Lounge and the Continental Ballroom on Monday nights for many years into the 1980s. The workingman's "blue Monday" is, of course, also traditionally the player's day off; and because it was a one-night-a-week commitment and a labor of love, Franklin's big band included most of the best jazz players in Houston.

On any of those nights it was clear as a bell that school was still in session.

Outward Bound

Eric Dolphy's Migrant Muse

Much of the wonderfulness of Eric Dolphy's music is found in the audible evidence of his far-ranging inspirations. Equally adventurous and at home on flute, alto sax, and bass clarinet, Dolphy was also master of many musical styles and traditions. Nowadays collectors talk about "world music"—a category that includes vernacular forms from many nations and cultures. In a way, following the dictates of his muse, Dolphy was a prescient embodiment of that idea. His thrillingly raucous "Music Matador," for example, goes beyond a Latin tinge to reveal the true fire of central American and Caribbean salsa; while "245" expresses authentic blues, his reading of Ellington's heartbreakingly lovely "Come Sunday" (in duet with Richard Davis) uniquely combines the classical étude with gospel tent testifying. The range is indeed impressive, and also illustrates Dolphy's aesthetic grounding.

"There is no doubt," write biographers Vladimir Simosko and Barry Tepperman, "that Eric Dolphy was an important figure in jazz at a time of transition . . . as well as an enormously vital creative musician with one of the most exciting and rewarding musical personalities ever recorded" (4).

"Music," Eric Dolphy told *Down Beat's* Don DeMichael, "is a reflection of everything. And it's universal" (22). His brilliant but tragically short career was a demonstration of his sincere belief in that principle, yet it also brings into high relief the cultural contradictions that continue to affect African American artists.

In 1960, writer Martin Williams introduced Dolphy to a national audience as a veteran of the "Los Angeles jazz underground . . . of talented musicians, only a few of whom make the recording studios or are able to earn their livings by playing their horns." Dolphy had just completed an acclaimed tenure with Chico Hamilton's quintet and settled in New York, where his collaborations with Charles Mingus, John Coltrane, and Ornette Coleman would change the direction of jazz.

"It is really wonderful to feel I can make my living as a musician now," Dolphy said, "because I never wanted to do anything else" (Williams 16).

"You can have Los Angeles," he told former schoolmate and fellow saxophonist Vi Redd. "I've fallen in love with New York because there's so much happening here and it's so much better for me" (Robertson 6B).

While his reputation soared, making a living as a creative musician in New York was exceedingly difficult. After a number of successful European tours with Coltrane and Mingus, Dolphy decided to settle there for a while in 1964 and became, perhaps unintentionally, another in the remarkable list of African American expatriate artists.

One usually expects to find experiences of American racism as the spur to expatriation. In Dolphy's case there isn't anything quite as blatant as the testimony of Richard Wright's *Black Boy*, yet there is a sense in which the cultural issues that attach to race in America shaped both his life and career. Dolphy's death in a West Berlin hospital may have been the result of a triage error (tantamount to malpractice) after he collapsed on the stage of the Tangent Club on June 27, 1964.

What is perhaps most fascinating about Dolphy is how carefully his talent was nurtured. Almost obsessively devoted to the art of music, from early childhood Dolphy was a brilliantly adept beneficiary of all the methods of music education available to him: traditional individual instruction, formal academic training; the jazz and rhythm-and-blues popular music bandstand; and the African American church. But while Dolphy's avidity and ambition urged him to take advantage of every opportunity to learn his craft, he did not enjoy similarly abundant opportunities for expression once he had mastered his instruments. In the 1920s, writes Berndt Ostendorf in *Black Literature in White America*, "Benny Goodman debated in his youth whether he should stay in the classics or go into jazz. He chose jazz because there was more money in it. . . . Many black musicians have no such choice. Whites could *choose* jazz, but blacks were typecast" (104).

Eric Allan Dolphy, Jr. (1928–64) is, perhaps, the most remarkable example of the truth of Ostendorf's statement. As a mature artist he was also the epitome of the classic definition of the jazz musician as not merely a player but a creative and spontaneous composer. Russell J. Linnemann reminds us that this role was established rather early in the history of jazz, that Louis Armstrong pointed out in the 1930s that the jazz player "must learn to read expertly and be just as able to play the score as any regular musician. Then he must never forget for one moment of his life that the true spirit of swing music lies in free playing" (115). That's one thing Eric Dolphy never had to worry about.

"No jazz musician," noted Dolphy's obituary in *Overture*, the Los Angeles musicians' union journal, "ever had a better musical education or foundation" ("Jazz Loses" 3). He, in fact, profited from music instruction in several parallel or interconnected institutions. His enormous talent and tireless dedication brought recognition in ever-widening circles. At thirteen, Eric received a "Superior" award on clarinet in the California School Band and Orchestra festival. The African American church has also been central to the training of the community's musicians, and this was true in Dolphy's case as well. His mother was a gifted choir singer, and she encouraged his participation in church music early. By 1946, Eric was codirector of the Youth Choir at Reverend Hampton B. Hawes's Westminster Presbyterian Church. The pastor's son, of course, became an estimable bebop pianist.

At Dorsey High School, Eric was among seven black students in the 1947 graduating class of more than a hundred. During his years there he studied oboe with orchestra director Phil Martin. He had begun studying that instrument in junior high school and was good enough to aspire to a professional symphonic chair. Dolphy had actually begun music lessons at age six and worked with private teachers Lloyd Reese and Mrs. Ola Ebinger on clarinet and saxophone. Later he studied and mastered the flute and the bass clarinet. There is unanimous agreement that as a multi-instrumentalist Dolphy was extraordinarily accomplished.

The years 1948–50 found Dolphy at Los Angeles City College, a reluctant student except when in the rehearsal hall. Afternoons he practiced Stravinsky's *L'Histoire du Soldat* with trombonist Jimmy Knepper. At night, both collegians—along with Joe Howard, brothers Addison and Art Farmer, Anthony Ortega, and vocalist Damita Jo—were members of Roy Porter's 17 Beboppers. For Eric, the nights provided an even better music school than the college did. In his autobiography *There and Back*, Roy Porter recalls:

I'll never forget one incident at the Hole in the Wall. It was just a small beer joint with sawdust on the floor and no bandstand, down from the Lincoln Theater on Central Avenue. The piano and the whole band were on the floor right there with the people. There were no mikes or anything, but one night [Leroy] Sweetpea Robinson and Eric Dolphy got to blowing and battling for chorus after chorus on *Sippin' with Cisco.* . . . This battle of the alto saxes must have lasted damn near an hour. . . . The Hole in the Wall was on fire that night! Those kind of things made it all worth while even when the money wasn't happening. (82)

Bebop, Amiri Baraka has written, was an artistic rebellion that "had to do with reversing the stereotypes or escaping them. Black people began breaking out of the ghetto and the music did too" (*The Music* 184).

"Our rebellion," wrote pianist Hampton Hawes in his book *Raise Up Off Me,* "was a form of survival. If we didn't do that what could we do? Get your hair gassed, brothers, put on your bow ties and a funny smile and play pretty for the rich white folks" (9). A similar reluctance to be denied appropriate respect for his creative expression led Dolphy, during a rather lean period in Los Angeles, to pass up a job with Eddie Beal playing Dixieland in segregated Las Vegas.

The existence of racism in the United States was more pervasive six decades ago than anyone can reasonably imagine today. Willis Conover, longtime director of jazz programming for the Voice of America, has talked candidly about the nation's capital as "a segregated southern town" during World War II: "When Sarah Vaughan and I can dance at the White House [Festival of the Arts in June 1965] and she observes that the last time we danced in D. C. we had to go to an illegal uptown after-hours club, there has been change" (7). But such change had not yet arrived during the Korean War in 1952 when Dolphy, assigned to the prestigious U.S. Naval School of Music, stopped at a restaurant with his fellow GI bandsmen. "You fellows can order what you like," the soldiers were told, "but that colored boy can't come in here. You could take a sandwich out to him, though." Eric's anger was somewhat assuaged when all of the men left the place in disgust.

After he came home from the army, Dolphy's combo Men of Modern Jazz held down a yearlong gig at the Club Oasis, and he made a few recording sessions, some with Gerald Wilson's orchestra backing the Platters (Simosko and Tepperman 36; Keller 14). Writing in *Jazz Times,* David Keller provided valuable details on Dolphy's activities and associations on the LA jazz scene. "Eric," remembered his trombonist Lester Robinson, "had a tremendous collection of classical lps: Mozart, Stravinsky, Debussy, Webern, Ravel and Bartók along with many others. Bebop and modern composers, that was our number one hookup" (Keller 14). Gunther Schuller, who included Dolphy as a soloist in his early "Third Stream" concerts, noted that "Eric was one of those rare musicians who loved and wanted to understand all music. His musical appetite was voracious" and extended from older jazz styles to the classical avant-garde ("In Tribute" 12).

Not everyone was as appreciative of Dolphy's talent as Schuller was. According to his mother, Sadie Dolphy, Eric "was very talented as a classical musician [and] was qualified to play with the Burbank Symphony, but in those days blacks could not perform with the symphony orchestra. Just when he was about to go on the road with Chico Hamilton [in 1958], he got a call asking him to perform with the Burbank Symphony, but then it was too late" ("Remembering Eric" 11–12). "When he told me that one of his ambitions was to be among the first black musicians to play in the LA Philharmonic Orchestra," wrote drummer Roy Porter, "I had to respect him" (85–86). The fact that those who do the hiring for American symphony orchestras did not respect Dolphy is a cultural scandal of the first magnitude.

According to Howard Shanet, the first full-time black musician hired by the century-old New York Philharmonic was violinist Stanford Allen in 1962 (Shanet 347). A decade later there were only a handful of players in symphony orchestras across the country and only one musical director. As far as wielding the baton is concerned, Philip Hart noted in the 1970s that "resident conductors of Japanese origin among our orchestras outnumber native blacks" (394). At the beginning of the 1990s the Houston Symphony Orchestra launched an internship program with two local universities in an attempt to rectify the absence of minority performers (Cunningham D2).

The cultural politics involved here, of course, are more complex than insults at roadside restaurants or auditions for local orchestras. Yet such cases demonstrate the prevalence of the problem of race in the United States—in the arts as in all other areas of society. In the United States, writes John Gennari, there persists "a cultural pecking order in which the Philharmonic always and forever stands higher than the World Saxophone Quartet, in which the Julliard String Quartet is assumed to operate at a higher level of musical expression than the Modern Jazz Quartet" (25). The result of this cultural prejudice is that orchestras devoted to preserving and showcasing the European classical music tradition are highly esteemed and economically subsidized by government and corporations.

But one should not imagine unbounded largesse. "In a primitive society," writes Philip Hart in *Orpheus in the New World: The Symphony Orchestra as an*

American Cultural Institution, "the arts were an essential part of ritual or of group experience, supported as part of the religious and social life of the community. In Western civilization, as the arts became increasingly specialized, the church or state maintained them as a matter of course. But in the capitalist economy of the 19th century, centered on the profitable production and distribution of goods and services, the arts became an economic anachronism" (296). It is fair to say that, in the United States, even those who fund it consider culture a "frill."

Responding to Gennari, Herb Snitzer reminds us that "Mozart died a pauper," observing that racial prejudice combines with the politics of cultural prestige to the extent that "the white world in general has ignored black jazz, except where it has been economically beneficial not to do so—as in the case of the many white promoters who have made vast sums of money exploiting black artists" (34).

During the early 1960s a major symphony orchestra player, though guaranteed a full season of work, would not have made more money than Eric Dolphy managed to eke out of his hectic schedule of recording sessions and club dates (Hart 307). But money is not usually the primary motivation for musicians. Philip Hart found, while teaching at Julliard, that many excellent players in smaller cities "were happier supplementing their modest symphony income with a varied career of teaching and free-lance work than they would be in subjecting themselves to the full-time routine of a year-round symphony contract" (467). Such reluctance to accept the rigorous performance schedule would certainly not have been Dolphy's position. He was, says Roy Porter, "a practiceaholic" (85). Eric himself admitted that playing his instruments was his greatest enjoyment.

"He never had an agent," said Dolphy's father. "I can read and write, and I can handle my own business, he'd say." This may have been a serious mistake. John Coltrane, for example, enjoyed the relative security of a fifty-thousand-dollar recording contract with Impulse Records and was represented by the Shaw Agency, which booked his band—with Dolphy on reeds—for twenty-five hundred dollars a week in 1961–62 (J. C. Thomas 143–44). During the same period, Dolphy was never able to book his own group consistently or at such a pay scale, and in early 1963 much of his income was derived from one or two recording sessions a month working as a sideman (Simosko and Tepperman 74).

Comparing long-playing records to artist's work sheets and contracts might offer us a way to calculate the precise cost of American racism. In order to pretend that the African American was inferior, American society had to *prevent him* from excelling—hence the prohibitions created by segregation. Furthermore, it became impossible to accord jazz its rightful place because the notion of "white supremacy" could not be defended once it was admitted that black people had created (and continue to create) the most vital and distinctive of American art forms.

Amiri Baraka (LeRoi Jones) identified the cultural dilemma of the African American jazz artist in an important 1961 *Metronome* essay titled "The Jazz Avant Garde." "Ornette Coleman," he wrote, "has had to live with the atti- tudes responsible for Anton Webern's music whether he knows that music or not." Baraka recognized the potential in this for cultural oppression, but he also noted that "the formal music of Europe can be used by modern jazz musicians to solve technical problems" (*Black Music* 70). Baraka took his lead in this discussion from the musicians themselves. Eric Dolphy, for one, knew Webern's music well and regularly practiced pages from Alban Berg's *Wozzeck* on his electric piano during 1961 and 1962. This was a period when Dolphy also routinely and daily talked on the telephone with John Coltrane— not about gossip or politics—about *business;* specifically, musical problems of tone and saxophone fingering. When these two men were on the phone with each other they were working. They might talk for an hour at a time, literally fine-tuning their compositional and improvisation ideas by playing passages for each other on their horns. For Coltrane and Dolphy, playing music was serious business—the business of creative musicianship.

In 1962, critics like Kenneth Tynan—whose own creative efforts gave the world the nude Broadway musical *Oh Calcutta!*—denounced the musical explorations of Coltrane and Dolphy as "anti-jazz." The term was widely explicated in the music press. "It's kind of alarming to the musician," Eric told *Down Beat's* Don DeMichael, "when someone has written something bad about what the musician plays but never asks the musician anything about it. Sometimes it really hurts, because a musician not only loves his work but depends on it for a living" (23).

Dolphy was not suffering an existential or emotional crisis. In a letter to Reverend John Doherty, he managed a tone of characteristic optimism:

This year has been . . . an interesting and busy year for me, although not profitable. I gave a concert in November with a poet and since then I have had a few club dates. I am hoping that this year [1963] I will be able to do more.

This attitude was not new. His mother Sadie wrote to Simosko about Eric's struggles in the mid-1950s:

> During that early era jobs were scarce and work was rare indeed. Employment for musicians was more the now and then type rather than the rule of full employment. Often he and his colleagues played in the parks on Sunday afternoons (band concerts). As my memory goes way back to those lean years, Eric received very little pay for work then—but was always happy to take advantage of an opportunity to play.

Whenever Eric Dolphy did find an opportunity to play he usually also found applause.

"Everywhere he would go in Europe," said Dolphy's father, "he would get a nice hand from the people; he made a lot of records and did a lot of concerts. They wanted him, and they understood and appreciated his music. It was much harder over here. It took *me* a long time to get used to his music" ("Remembering Eric" 12).

"People over there have more respect for the music and musicians," says trumpeter Calvin Owens, who spent a decade based in Brussels beginning in 1984. He believes that the economic outlook was also better for him in Europe than in the United States.

"European audiences listen more carefully," agrees Joyce Mordecai, a dancer who had been engaged to marry Eric Dolphy. "They place jazz artists on the same parallel as classical music, even if they're playing in a nightclub. They have more respect for the musicians. And, for the musicians, it's not necessarily a matter of more money but more consistency of work and respect."

The receptive climate for jazz in Europe was nurtured by the pioneering French critics Hugues Panassie and Charles Delaunay. And pioneers are really what they were. "Being a jazz lover in Paris in the twenties," Delaunay told Whitney Balliett, "was like being an early Christian in Rome" (Balliett 9). Panassie, however, had "the gift to communicate his enthusiasm for the music," and, as Berndt Ostendorf has pointed out, European listeners were often able to relate to jazz as art without questioning "the seriousness or legitimacy of this American contribution to modernist culture" (Balliett 15; Ostendorf vii).

Charles Delaunay, the son of painters Robert and Sonia, grew up in a household frequented by visitors such as poet Guillaume Apollinaire, composer Igor Stravinsky, and other modernist artists who shared an avid enthusiasm for "primitive art" (Balliett 13). It is not surprising, then, that Delaunay's comments on jazz sometimes parallel contemporary responses to African sculpture. That fact also suggests that care be taken when reading such critics. In the early years of the twentieth century, the "mainstream" response of aesthetically adventurous Europeans and some advanced Americans to what was called "Negro art" often saw it, according to critic Matthew Pratt Guterl, as a type of vital modernist primitivism that could serve as "a panacea for a neurasthenic, overcivilized Western culture" (163).

Ted Gioia, in *The Imperfect Art: Reflections on Jazz and Modern Culture* (1988), points out that while treating the music as worthy of scholarly attention, some European critics "saw the jazz artist as a creature of inspiration who, in his own rough and unskilled way, would forge a musical statement that was of the heart and not necessarily of the mind" (29). It is worth noting that Gioia, himself a teacher of jazz studies at Stanford University, admits that he "could not imagine a Charles Mingus or a Thelonious Monk thriving in an environment in which artistic success depended on access to fellowships, government grants, academic appointments, and the like" (83–84). At first such a statement seems flattering to the black artist. Looking a bit closer, though, consider how its logic might apply to an artist such as Eric Dolphy— who actually managed to work for Mingus. Could any foundation functionary or academic administrator be more stupidly abusive than Mingus was to Dolphy on their last European tour?

If jazz was initially viewed by the white American community (and is sometimes seen even today) as somewhat lacking in cultural value, it was not always given a higher place among African Americans. "Except for the poet Langston Hughes," writes Paul Burgett in Samuel A. Floyd's *Black Music in the Harlem Renaissance*, "none of the Harlem intellectuals took jazz seriously. While people like James Weldon Johnson and Alain Locke respected jazz as an example of folk music, their greatest expectations lay in its transformation into serious music of high culture by some race genius in the tradition of a Dvořák or a Smetana" (29–30). In his popular book *The Negro and His Music*, Alain Locke became a booster of what he called "classical jazz" as epitomized by Ellington and was optimistic about its potential to produce an African American maestro equal to Dvořák.

Locke's idea was not resented by black musicians, even those he would have considered folk artists. Bandleader Clarence "Gatemouth" Brown has stated that predecessors such as Ellington, Basie, and the beboppers demonstrated to him in the 1940s that he did not have to be an "Uncle Tom" or minstrel clown but could play jazz, blues, and R & B while maintaining his dignity as a serious artist.

There can be little doubt that jazz musicians of Eric Dolphy's generation, and social background, coming of age in the 1940s, were greatly influenced by Locke's ideas. Musicians trained in the bebop style took Louis Armstrong's statement that the jazz musician was a "spontaneous composer" quite literally and certainly considered their music to be a higher level of musical expression than the popular Tin Pan Alley songs they transformed every night into smoldering mysteries or blazing jewels.

Putting yourself in someone else's shoes is often a good thing—so says everyone from religious leaders to corporate consultants. So, I think, it might be a very useful exercise (even for the most unshakably self-secure jazz devotee) to try to experience the astonishment of the nightclub owners who heard this music for the first time. Hell, they hire somebody they hoped could play a somewhat recognizable facsimile of current hit songs . . . and here these guys get on the bandstand and spin out suites and little syncopated symphonies!

Eric Dolphy's influence on an entire generation of reed players has been enormous and can be heard in much music of the 1980s and 1990s. But Dolphy's composing and arranging talents, write his biographers, "never found an outlet, at least beyond his closest circle of friends." Some indications of what he might have achieved can be found in Dolphy's orchestral arrangements for Coltrane's "Africa" and in his own Love Suite (1964), which is similarly scored for an unconventional ensemble (Simosko and Tepperman 17). "Africa," in Bill Cole's opinion, is a significant work (126). While Gunther Schuller's reconstruction of Love Suite has not been widely heard, four compositions created in 1962 for a concert with metaphysical poet Ree Dragonette have also never been fully assessed. Dolphy's approach to the project, the poet told Down Beat's Bill Coss, "is original, perhaps radical, but it is so structured, and it goes back into so much jazz that went before. I feel that we are much alike and his response to my work has been greater and better than I would normally find from some other poet" (Coss 42). Dolphy spent several months reading and analyzing Dragonette's poems, and the fact that he later recorded only one of these compositions—"Mandrake" on Iron Man, Douglas SD875 (1963) and, as it was originally titled, "The Madrig Speaks, The

Panther Walks" on *Last Date*, Limelight LM82013 (1964)—raises the question of whether or not he thought of these pieces, which are not traditional "settings" of the poems but rather musical commentaries on them, as an extended work or suite.

Eric Dolphy's headstone bears the inscription *He Lives In His Music*. He also lived *for* music. As Simosko and Tepperman wrote: "He was a totally dedicated artist, one for whom music was more important than considerations of economics, race, culture, or even ego" (23–24). Dolphy's geographical journeyings—from West Coast to East, across oceans—were merely steps in a quest for a place to support his material existence while he continued his much more important intellectual, artistic, and spiritual journey. For a brief moment he found that place, and the respect—indeed love—of interested audiences and fellow musicians, in Europe. The tragedy is that his last date was played so soon.

THREE America's Classical Music

Evolution of the Bop Aesthetic

If you have to ask, you'll never know.
—Louis Armstrong

The music of the late 1940s called bebop is usually seen, like most avant-garde movements, as an "artistic rebellion." That view, however, often neglects any investigation into the predominant intellectual traditions of the African American community from which bebop musicians emerged. The aesthetic concerns implicit in the bebop style may be traced to the ideological roots of the "New Negro movement" beginning at the turn of the century that found its grandest expression in the Harlem Renaissance of the 1920s. Howard University philosopher Alain Locke (1886–1954) and other leaders of the Harlem Renaissance saw in African American folk music and jazz the raw material awaiting "transformation into serious music of high culture by some race genius in the tradition of a Dvořák or a Smetana" (Burgett 29–30). Black musicians who developed the bebop style in the 1940s and 1950s were greatly influenced by such ideas. They also took quite literally Louis Armstrong's statement that the jazz player was a "spontaneous composer" but understood their own relation to musical tradition in a way that Locke was unable to fully anticipate.

In an excellent PBS documentary on her career, diva Marian Anderson succinctly stated the ethos of African American musicians and their relation to their audiences and to tradition. "I had a special feeling for some of the spirituals," she says, "because they pictured what was going on even as we were singing them." Miss Anderson, in her regal way, was referring to the fact that the sorrow songs, to the shame of our country, have remained eerily contemporary for more than a hundred years. Inasmuch as all African American musical genres reflect an African musical origin shaped by the historical experience of the West, her statement might easily be applied to any genre and—in fact—has been by the musicians themselves.

"Africa is the creative source," states pianist and composer Randy Weston. "Wherever African people have settled, they have created a new music which is based on African rhythms." And Dizzy Gillespie reported that "when somebody asked [Cuban percussionist Chano Pozo], 'How do you and Dizzy converse?' he would say. 'Dizzy no peaky pani I no peaky engly, but boff peak African' " (A. Taylor 19, 132).

Examining the musicians' testimony makes it clear that this sense of shared identity is understood in terms beyond the mere technical requirement of producing sounds in concert. Orchestra leader James Reese Europe made the issue clear in 1914 when he told a newspaper interviewer:

We colored people have our own music that is part of us. It's the product of our souls; it's been created by the sufferings and miseries of our race. Some of the old melodies we played Wednesday night [at Carnegie Hall] were made up by slaves of the old days, and others were handed down from the days before we left Africa. (Hare 137n)

And one can trust Duke Ellington to sum up the matter with his characteristic elegance. "The music of my race is something more than the American idiom. What we could not say openly we expressed in music" (Walton 79).

It is necessary to establish these artists' idea of a tradition because the place historically accorded African people in this country makes any discussion of African American aesthetics problematic. What we find is that we must usually filter our discussion through a sociological lens precisely because black people have been so long and so often excluded from the spectrum of discourses assumed to be operational when we examine European culture. Parallel is not the same as parity. It is no secret, for example, that Fernando Ortiz's brilliant turn-of-the-century fieldwork on African traditions in Cuba—publications including Los Negros Brujos (1906)—was undertaken and funded to provide data for an exercise in criminology. Eventually, however, Ortiz's research led to a more positive evaluation of the African contribution to Cuban culture (Boggs).

In our own country, H. Bruce Franklin has shown that this was a period when black Americans—as a race—were being defined as criminals. Between 1890 and 1910, a rigorous combination of peonage, disenfranchisement, and segregation ordinances effectively reduced African Americans in the South to conditions not far removed from antebellum slavery (Franklin 101–4). Our recent critical adoption of the French term translated as the Other does not really change the implications of such views.

The African American intellectuals who launched the "New Negro movement" at the turn of the century were acutely aware of the pariah status being imposed upon their people. In 1874 William Wells Brown had written of the freedmen, "Slavery had bequeathed them nothing but poverty, ignorance, and dependence upon their former owners" (413–14). Brown had the credentials to back up this assessment. Himself a fugitive slave, Brown became a prominent abolitionist and prolific author of articles and books. Brown's works—including *Clotel; or, the President's Daughter* (1853), thought to be the first novel published by a black American—were widely read and highly esteemed by African American intellectuals. The black struggle for recognition as citizens during the last quarter of the nineteenth century was met with increasing hostility and, finally, legalized racial segregation. The black leadership tried to counter these developments, in part, by demonstrating yet again the humanity and aptitude of black people. Often this meant drawing attention to the former slaves' mastery of Western cultural standards.

W. E. B. DuBois, editor of the NAACP's *Crisis* magazine beginning in 1910, penned numerous accolades for African American performers of European classical music or skilled interpreters of the spirituals; but nowhere, notes Richard A. Long, "do we find Du Bois mentioning Armstrong, or Ellington, or . . . Fletcher Henderson" (130). Other intellectual leaders of the period such as James Weldon Johnson and Alain Locke were somewhat more approving of black popular music, and, of course, such younger members of the Harlem Renaissance as poet Langston Hughes were enthusiasts (Long 131–33; Ogren 117–18). In the campaign to gain racial respect, however, many African American intellectuals adopted a decidedly Eurocentric cultural outlook.

Because my own students all take it as a matter of fact that American popular music both owes its origins to African American creative expression and stands as the unique cultural achievement of the United States—a claim first advanced specifically for the spirituals by DuBois and James Weldon Johnson—they are aghast when they encounter Maud Cuney Hare's comments on jazz in her *Negro Musicians and Their Music*. Ever the social and intellectual aristocrat; Cuney Hare writes: "So far did the Rag craze and Jazz spread, that in traveling to many institutions of learning, the author found that the musical taste of the youth was being poisoned." Jazz, for her, was most usually the term used to describe "acrobatics and monkey-ish antics on the part of the performers, and the grotesque use of instruments" (133). Hare's discussion plainly reveals the burden shouldered by the New Negro:

> It has been claimed that Jazz will divide itself and follow two strains—"the Negro and the Intellectual." This aptly describes the situation. Many regard Negro music as synonymous with comedy and buffoonery, rhythmic oddities and random lines. But thoughtful musicians differentiate between music as expressed by trained and cultivated Negro Americans and Negro music of the above named style. (131)

Hare's tone reveals the sort of race consciousness that W. O. Brown, a contemporary sociologist, defined as "oppression psychosis" accompanied by "excessive sensitivity" to insult (90–91). Alain Locke was also sensitive to the possibilities of defamatory images and lingering minstrel stereotypes, but, as Kathy J. Ogren points out, Locke "located the controversial qualities of jazz in the white-dominated commercial music industry—not in black performance traditions" (125).

Locke was, indeed, a perceptive critic and effective advocate. Like Maud Cuney Hare, Locke was properly appreciative of the European. classical tradition, but he was less interested in adopting it wholesale than in tracing the parallel evolution of an African American culture from folklore to high art. He was able clearly to distinguish authentic black folk culture from commercialized caricature, even if the terms he used seem quaintly romanticized today. In *The Negro and His Music*, Locke wrote:

> Today's jazz is a cosmopolitan affair, an amalgam of modern tempo and mood. But original jazz is more than syncopation and close eccentric harmony. With it goes, like Gipsy music, a distinctive racial intensity of mood and a peculiar style of technical performance, that can be imitated, it is true, but of which the original pattern was Negro. Moreover it is inborn in the typical or folky type of Negro. It can be detected even in a stevedore's swing, preacher's sway, or a bootblack's flick; and heard equally in an amen-corner quaver, a blue cadence or a chromatic cascade of Negro laughter. (72)

Locke was not, however, content to leave his analysis at a level that could easily be misconstrued as a poetic embellishment of the notion of "natural rhythm." Locke was quite specific in defining what he called the African American musician's "instinctive gift" for jazz improvisation. "There is a modern delusion," noted Locke's colleague Horace M. Kallen, "cultivated by the lazy and the arty, that originality is the prerogative of ignorance. Nothing could be farther than the facts of record" (146). As an amateur musician himself, Locke understood precisely what made jazz music possible:

> For the process of composing by group improvisation, the jazz musician must have a whole chain of musical expertness, a sure musical ear, an instinctive feeling for harmony, the courage and gift to improvise and interpolate, and a canny sense for the total effect. This free style that Negro musicians introduced . . . really has generations of experience back of it; it is derived from the vocal tricks and vocal habits characteristic of Negro choral singing. (Negro and His Music 79)

Nevertheless, the Eurocentric element of Locke's thought led him to the scenario that would produce symphonies from jazz in much the way that eighteenth- and nineteenth-century European composers "elevated" and refined simple folk airs into chamber music and symphonic motifs. Locke was also unabashedly academic, and these concerns led him to a statement that must have rankled the jazz musicians who read The Negro and His Music: "The white musicians, proceeding oftener with a guiding thread of theory, have often been able to go farther by logic in the development of the more serious aspects of jazz than the Negro musicians have, moving too much under the mere guidance of instinct." Thus, Locke concluded with the disappointed tone of a professor prodding his favorite underachiever, "It has been white musicians and critics, who for the most part have capitalized on jazz, both commercially and artistically" (86).

II

It is not at all difficult to imagine the black musicians' response to Locke's statement.

Jazz, said Charles Mingus in 1971, is "the American Negro's tradition; it's his music. White people don't have a right to play it, it's colored folk music. You had your Shakespeare and Marx and Einstein and Jesus Christ and Guy Lombardo but we came up with Jazz" (qtd. in Walton 156). There's no doubt one might have heard similar sentiments expressed in the 1930s when top African American bandsmen in Philadelphia were making ten dollars a night—about a week's wage for an ordinary civilian lucky enough to have a job (W. O. Smith 33–34). Youngsters like Dizzy Gillespie made two dollars a gig, but the white commercial jazzmen that Alain Locke alluded to were paid like movie stars.

Nor was it merely a matter of locale or reputation. It was as simple as black and white. In a 1938 letter to Abbe Niles, W. C. Handy, composer of "St. Louis Blues," world-renowned at age sixty-five and owner of a highly successful music publishing company he established in 1912, reported:

I had my first aeroplane flight Friday morning to Charleston, S.C. The Carolina Air Line will not carry a Negro, so I could only buy a round trip on the Eastern Air Lines. I drove by automobile from Charleston to Columbia, arriving there in a little more than two hours (120 miles), and witnessed a performance of a play "Cavalcade of the Blues," written by a 17-year-old colored girl around my life and work. (Handy, Father viii)

Handy, who had read William Wells Brown's The Rising Son in his youth, had achieved both commercial and artistic success in the music business yet felt as confined by the system of racial segregation as he had been at the beginning of his extraordinary career. The story of his airplane flight can be set next to a much earlier experience recorded in his autobiography, Father of the Blues:

As a side line in Clarksdale [in 1903] I did a kind of bootleg business in Northern Negro newspapers and magazines. Not only did I supply the colored folks of the town, but also got the trade of the farmers, the croppers and the hands from the outlying country. They would come to my house on their weekly visits to the city, give me the high sign, and I would slip them their copies of the Chicago Defender, the Indianapolis Freeman or the Voice of the Negro.

This may sound like a tame enough enterprise to those whose memories are short. . . . But because I was favorably known to most of the white folks as the leader of the band that gave the weekly concerts on the main street, they never suspected me of such dark business as distributing Northern literature to Negroes of the community. (79–80)

The "New Negro movement" was, of course, inaugurated by those very publications with the paired objectives of elevating black race consciousness and winning respect and equal treatment from the white community. The Harlem Renaissance merely focused this campaign in the cultural arena, using the arts as both medium and message.

The intellectual leaders of the Harlem Renaissance could not overlook the more practical aspects of the musical profession. The art form soon to be inherited by Charles Parker, John Birks Gillespie, Charles Mingus, Bud Powell, and Max Roach operated within the cruel inequities of segregated America. Though he acknowledged the music's African origins, Paul Whiteman probably did not have any African American musicians in mind when, in 1926, he envisioned "chairs of jazz in universities (Whiteman and McBride 279). Even in the far less rarified atmosphere of the popular dance music business, the disparity of economic reward and critical approval along racial lines was glaringly evident.

In his 1926 book *Jazz*, Whiteman expressed a vision of the music's future that paralleled Alain Locke's; he had, after all, been the conductor of Gershwin's *Rhapsody in Blue* at its 1924 Carnegie Hall premiere. Echoing Emerson's 1844 essay on poetry, Whiteman wrote, "I am ambitious for jazz to develop always in [an] American way. I want to see compositions written around the great natural and geographical features of American life—written in the jazz idiom. I believe this would help Americans to appreciate their own country" (Whiteman and McBride 287). In case this noble patriotism was not enough, Whiteman also tried a little Denver-style "boosterism" to sell jazz to middle America:

Jazz has affected America . . . in a musical way, and in many more material senses. It is bulking increasingly large in economics. There are today more than 200,000 men playing it. The number of jazz arrangers is around 30,000. Thus two entirely new industries have grown up in less than ten years. They are lucrative industries, too. Players in the best of the modern jazz orchestras have come straight from the symphonies where they were paid $30, $40, or at the most $50 and $60 a week. Now they get $150 up. Jazz has made *fortunes* and bought automobiles, country houses and fur coats for many a player, composer and publisher. Indirectly it has filled the pockets of the musicians who are identified with opera and symphony, for it has interested a greater part of the population in music. (Whiteman and McBride 155–56)

The only pockets that were not being filled were the pockets of black musicians; but this annual report from the King of Jazz did not include them anyway.

African American music historian Maud Cuney Hare complained that "just as the white minstrels blackened their faces and made use of the Negro idiom, so have white orchestral players today usurped the Negro in his jazz entertainment" (148). A somewhat surrealistic historical note (sort of a preview of the *Mississippi Burning* motion picture revision of the Civil Rights era) will perhaps give an indication of exactly how bad things were for the black jazz musician: by the late 1930s *Down Beat* was running a series of articles by Marshall Stearns arguing that African American musicians were the actual originators of jazz!

Stearns, a college professor and true music devotee, published "The History of Swing Music" as a monthly feature in *Down Beat* in 1936 and 1937, often focusing on the influence of African American musicians. In response, the magazine's pages crackled with charges and countercharges in articles such as Paul Eduard Miller's "Roots of Hot White Jazz Are Negroid" and Original Dixieland Jazz Band leader Nick La Rocca's angry tirade complaining that French critic Hugues Panassie "gave entire credit for swing to early Negro bands" rather than the true inventors of the music ("White Man's Music" 1).

Alain Locke tried to find a positive way to describe the situation. Jazz, he wrote, "in spite of its racial origin, became one great interracial collaboration in which the important matter is the artistic quality of the product and neither the quantity of the distribution nor the color of the artist. The common enemy is the ever-present danger of commercialization" (*Negro and His Music* 82). It was in this atmosphere of jazz as an "interracial collaboration"—with segregated dressing rooms—that the first notes of bebop were heard.

Though it developed out of 1930s big-band swing music, bebop was a radical departure in a number of ways. The players, often with more formal training than their predecessors, thought of themselves as artists rather than entertainers. They sought both respect for their dignity and recognition for their creative genius.

The new music was worked out by young African American musicians in

Harlem after-hours joints, nightclubs along Central Avenue in Los Angeles, and in a dozen other black neighborhoods. But it leaped into the spotlight on New York's Fifty-second Street, remembered by drummer Roy Porter as "the street that never slept."

> There were places like the Three Deuces and the Famous Door on one side of the street. Across the way was the Onyx, Jimmy Ryan's, Leon & Eddie's, the Spotlight Club, and many others. All these spots were featuring name jazz musicians like Papa Jo [Jones], Shadow Wilson, Kenny Clarke, Art Blakey, Big Sid Catlett, Max Roach, Monk, Diz, Bud Powell, Fats Navarro, and one of the greatest trumpet players, Freddie Webster. (Porter 49)

The irony was that black customers were unwelcome (W. O. Smith 76, 151–52). America was still very segregated, and the unsmiling beboppers were still playing for white folks. What they were playing, however, is something else again.

Louis Armstrong, in his book *Swing That Music*, had confirmed Alain Locke's definition of the jazz musician's "instinctive gift." "To be a real swing artist," said Satchmo, "he must be a composer as well as a player" (Locke, *Negro and His Music* 79). The younger musicians took this as gospel, and many of them had the technical proficiency to make meaningful use of Armstrong's advice. Charles Mingus, for example, "trained his own ear on Beethoven, Bartók, Stravinsky, Richard Strauss. But his earliest and deepest musical influences were 'Duke Ellington records on radio' and his step-mother's Holiness Church, where they sang and swooned and carried on" (Coleman and Young 12). As for the Ellington band, it included men such as clarinetist Jimmy Hamilton, who enjoyed practicing Mozart trios in his spare time (W. O. Smith 198). "It's frightening to think of what he could have accomplished," said W. O. Smith, "had he had the college or conservatory experience" (42).

The 1930s big band, however, was a conservatory in its own right. W. O. Smith, the first band director at Texas Southern University, began his career in Philadelphia in 1935 with the Frankie Fairfax band. Members included Jimmy Hamilton, Shadow Wilson, Charlie Shavers, and Dizzy Gillespie (W. O. Smith 47). "Rehearsals." Smith recalled, "were a joy."

We learned to play hard tunes with difficult chord changes. We played these challenging tunes starting in the original key and proceeding a half step up each chorus until we returned to the original key. Imagine playing tunes like "Body and Soul," "Sweet and Lovely," and "Smoke Gets in Your Eyes" in this fashion. If nothing else, a few weeks of this would give you control of your ax. . . . A year of this with frequent rehearsals and gigs would put anybody at the top of his game. (38)

The brass and woodwind sections would improvise riffs to these tunes in the call-and-response pattern of African American church singing.

Sociologist Ortiz M. Walton—who is also a bass player who has performed with symphony orchestras and in the jazz idiom—has explained the practical matters of bebop playing with a clarity that has eluded most critics. Because the beboppers were veterans of swing bands, they were all familiar with the rehearsal style Smith describes and with the "shorthand code" or "head arrangements" such bands used. "Inasmuch as 'standards' (those compositions having greatest popularity during a particular era) were required knowledge of the professional jazz musician," Walton notes; "it was an easy step to their modified usage in the bop aggregation" (101). The bebop quintet, while reducing the number of instruments, retained the swing big band's organizational approach.

Similarly, the boppers could not entirely escape the exigencies of the nightclub. "Green Dolphin Street" became a jazz standard not only because it is a beautiful tune, but also because it was the theme song of the greatest tearjerker movie of 1947. When the big spenders (or even just the regulars) requested it in order to please their ladies, the cats had to play it. Even though "Green Dolphin Street" hails from the lost era when movie scores were conceived of almost like classical suites, what the jazz players did with it enormously overshadows and transcends its programmatic Hollywood origin.

Walton perhaps overstates the case when he writes, "Bop was a major challenge to European standards of musical excellence and the beginning of a conscious black aesthetic in music" (104). In fact, the aesthetic made explicit by the bebop pioneers was not entirely new. It was the fruit of four decades of African American intellectual debate. To offer a musical analogy, we might point out that while you can't really hear the drums on many early recordings, jazz fans know that the drums were there. Alain Locke and others were able to hear the polyrhythms of African drumming in the voices of the singers of spirituals, just as the drums of West Africa are able to replicate the voicings of tonal languages such as Yoruba.

There are two major considerations that need attention in order to understand bebop as more clearly part of an African American cultural continuum than as an unexpectedly avant-garde "artistic rebellion." On one hand, bebop challenges Eurocentric standards by aggressively interrogating their hegemonic status. While the musicians themselves accepted Locke's idea of an "evolution" from simple folk forms to sophisticated art, they also moved dance music toward self-conscious artistry without necessarily channeling it through the symphony orchestra as George Gershwin, Pines P. Johnson, and other earlier musicians had attempted to do. Nonetheless, the relationship of bebop to the "classical" tradition is complex. If one credits Charlie Parker as an intellectually curious musician capable, even though lacking formal conservatory training, of remarkably advanced composition and improvisation, then Parker's interest in Igor Stravinsky should not be more surprising than Stravinsky's own interest in Woody Herman as expressed in his *Ebony Concerto* (1945). Nor is it logical to dismiss Parker's interest in modern composers of the European tradition as mere pretentiousness or an obsession nurtured by a racial inferiority complex. Indeed, the legacy of racial bias makes this entire area of scrutiny dangerous. As jazz saxophonist and avant-garde composer Anthony Braxton reminds us—setting issues of income, social status, or perceived aesthetic hierarchy aside—our inability to understand the beboppers' primarily *musical* interest in modernist music is a powerful reflection of our society's "real interest in suppressing African intellectual dynamics" (Lock 92–94).

On the other hand, bebop does represent a development of African American cultural nationalism that identifies the evolution of a popular performance style toward a more sophisticated or "serious" art form as well as a social and political statement. As performed by Gillespie, Blakey, Randy Weston, Max Roach, and others, the style is a creative and explicit expression of racial pride that is logically and inextricably linked to the musicians' desire for artistic recognition and economic self-determination. But it is very clear that the terms of this expression can be found outlined in the aesthetic questions posed by Harlem Renaissance writers such as Alain Locke and Maud Cuney Hare.

Bebop highlights the mixture of resentment and ambition, racial pride and justified anger that Alain Locke so meticulously endeavored to simultaneously mask and reveal. The beboppers both fulfilled and rejected the ideals of Harlem Renaissance intellectuals. They pushed jazz further toward the "serious music" that Alain Locke envisioned; they revived a militant race consciousness that had, perhaps, been tactically muted by the accommodatingly genteel pose of the Renaissance aestheticians; yet, accomplished as they were in the European musical tradition, the new jazz created in the 1940s was an astonishingly appropriate and logically instinctive extension of the African way of making music that is the enduring gift of our ancestors.

Classical Jazz and the Black Arts Movement

The period between 1960 and 1970 represents an era of important and extraordinary cultural change in the United States. Long-standing issues of the relationship of ethnic vernacular art to the "mainstream," and that of the American "mainstream" to European "high art," came into focus in these years in a particularly contentious yet artistically fruitful manner.

If one recalls artists such as John Coltrane, Charles Mingus, and Eric Dolphy, it is clear that jazz musicians were never before so technically proficient on their instruments or in their mastery of European "classical" traditions. On the other hand, these artists consciously intended to foreground non-European musical influences as well as the Afrocentric and folkloristic elements of jazz. At the same time, the poets and theorists of the Black Arts Movement (including Amiri Baraka, Larry Neal, and Askia Muhammad Touré) were making a very popular case for an aesthetic conceived as openly oppositional to both European and white American culture.

The roots of the Black Arts Movement are easily traced to the Harlem Renaissance of the 1920s. That earlier movement was the first attempt by African American artists to produce work consciously grounded in their folk heritage and to utilize that work for the social advancement of the race. For Larry Neal, the Harlem Renaissance "was essentially a failure. It did not address itself to the mythology and the lifestyles of the black community" (*Visions* 78). This statement seems puzzling today, but its meaning was crystal clear in 1968 and pointed to a political philosophy underlying aesthetic discriminations.

Whereas the leaders of the Harlem Renaissance hoped to prove the cultural worthiness of African Americans by demonstrating their aptitude for cultivation, development, and progress in terms understood by white American society, the leaders of the Black Arts Movement hoped to celebrate a kind of proletarian and vaguely "African" culture. Like Zora Neale Hurston's appreciation of the folk, the Black Arts Movement sought to identify a certain intrinsic beauty and vitality in African American authenticity.

This view particularly affected the way that Black Arts Movement writers dealt with jazz. In an important essay titled "Jazz and the White Critic" (1963), Amiri Baraka declared:

In jazz criticism, no reliance on European tradition or theory will help at all. Negro music, like the Negro himself, is strictly an American phenomenon, and we have got to set up standards of judgment and aesthetic excellence that depend on our native knowledge and understanding of the underlying philosophies and local cultural references that produced blues and jazz in order to produce valid critical writing or commentary about it. (186)

By 1966, Baraka had framed the message much more concisely: "The music you hear (?) is an invention of Black lives" (Black Music 176). What was at stake, of course, was a cultural hierarchy explicit in American society. As a visiting African student once expressed it, "They love your music—but they don't love you." The Black Arts Movement asked, basically, what's love got to do with it?

In the area of music, the prevailing cultural hierarchy assigns value to the European symphonic tradition at the expense of indigenous American musical conventions. Compared to jazz, classical music has been assigned a higher cultural value, which—of course—has very little to do with music per se.

In 1948, Sidney Finkelstein noted that "the man who listens to jazz, whether 'New Orleans' or bebop, is hearing as unstandardized a set of musical scales and combinations of scales as is he who listens to Copeland or Ives." Finkelstein logically concluded that "the artificial distinction between 'classical' and 'popular' has been forced upon our times by the circumstance that the production of both . . . has become a matter for financial investment instead of art" (9).

There is, however, a definite political rationale involved that touches on aesthetic questions. The Black Arts Movement tried simply to dismiss the problem along with the European tradition. The critics of an earlier generation, however, attempted to elevate jazz by developing it as a "classical" music. A close examination of the reasoning behind each position suggests that the dynamics of assimilation and resistance in African American culture involve a dialectical movement that reflects a general tendency in American society's unresolved search for a national cultural identity.

Just as the African American is on a continuing quest to learn what is African about him, so America seems persistently clueless about what makes it American.

Many early African American critics and commentators took great pride in the notion that jazz was innovative and influential. Maud Cuney Hare was not of that opinion. Daughter of the most powerful figure in the Republican Party in Texas, as a child in Galveston she joined her brother and cousins in memorizing scenes from Shakespeare to entertain their elders after family dinners. The beautiful and talented Maud Cuney attended the New England Conservatory of Music, where she angrily resisted an attempt to deny her accommodations in the school's dormitory (Hare, Norris Wright Cuney 81; Lewis 105–6, 116). She was engaged to W. E. B. DuBois, a relationship that did not survive his relocation to Germany for graduate studies in 1892. Eventually married to a lawyer with a comfortable income, she was both "highly cultivated" and outspoken. With a column in the Crisis and wide-ranging associations, she became a powerful force in music education.

As early as 1917, Maud Cuney Hare extolled the refinement of what she called Afro-American folk music by serious musicians such as Anton Dvořák and Walter Damrosch, but she also spiritedly attacked "the ordinary songs of today . . . written in ragtime set in execrable rhymes" (Ferris 299–300). She was also prepared to diss the more pretentious adapters. Of Rhapsody in Blue (1924) Hare sniffed that "Gershwin wrote [it] within a month's time" and suffered the piece to be "orchestrated by a trained musician, Ferde Grofé" (149).

Damrosch, despite Hare's praise and his own interest in adapting Negro folk themes to symphonic forms, complained in 1928 that jazz "stifles the true musical instinct by turning away many of our talented young people from the persistent and continued study and execution of good music" (qtd. in Ogren 157–58).

Jazz, then, was appreciated by such commentators as a type of raw material. This view was surprisingly widespread, held by genteel integrationists as well as by black nationalists. "At a time when the Negro's possibilities and capabilities are discussed," wrote William H. Ferris in Garvey's *Negro World* in 1922, "it is of interest to know that the Negro has evolved a form of music which when pruned of its corruptions and developed contains wonderful possibilities" (300). Three years later, J. A. Rogers exhibited a similar cheerfulness. "Musically," he wrote, "jazz has a great future. It is rapidly being sublimated" (221).

Alain Locke, professor of philosophy at Howard University, was the most prominent spokesman of the Harlem Renaissance and the most eloquent propagator of the view that jazz should be refined into an indigenous American "classical music." Locke recognized the beauty of the spirituals and the energetic invention and originality in jazz, but he believed that his critical task was to foster their development. "In spite of the vitality and importance of folk music," he wrote, "the climax of any musical development is in the art forms and on the formal art level." Throughout his long career, Locke was also concerned with devising strategies "to raise the status of the jazz musician" in both economic and aesthetic terms ("Negro Music" 119–20).

Always on the lookout for "the vindication of the higher possibilities of jazz," Locke hoped that it would come from the works of black musicians, and he was not at all happy with the state of things in 1934: "Vital musical idioms have not been taken up sufficiently by our trained musicians; most of them have been intimidated by their academic training." Those who were most closely in touch with the folk traditions were, Locke lamented, "the very ones who are in commercial slavery to Tin Pan Alley." The few reluctant and halfhearted efforts he saw (in the attempt to place what he called Negro music on a par with the serious music of the European symphonic tradition) "resulted in an actual watering-down of these idioms by the classical tradition" ("Toward a Critique" 110–11).

The musician who most clearly embodied the direction Locke wanted to encourage was Duke Ellington, "the person most likely to create the classical jazz towards which so many are striving" ("Toward a Critique" 113). As Michael J. Budds notes in *Jazz in the Sixties*, "Ellington has exhibited an interest in these so-called 'extended forms' for several decades and continued to champion such methods until his death. By 1960 his works already included 'concerto-substitutes' for various members of his band, multi-movement and multi-section 'tone poems,' and suites" (78).

Ellington's late works for the Alvin Ailey Ballet and the Dance Theatre of Harlem might be seen as the culmination of Locke's design. Nevertheless, though orchestrated for symphony orchestra by Luther Henderson under Mercer Ellington's supervision, these works are recognizably Duke Ellington music—just played by a different band. When I say "recognizably Duke," I mean *beautiful*—luxuriant with the melodies of the spirituals and the intensity of the jazz shout.

The musician that Black Arts Movement theorist Amiri Baraka championed was Sun Ra, and it is here that two seemingly contradictory aesthetic philosophies meet in the kind of gyroscopically delightful resolution that virtuoso jazz soloists nightly pluck from the air. During the 1960s when he was based in New York and frequently performed at Baraka's Black Arts Repertory Theatre/School in Harlem and at Slug's nightclub on the Lower East Side, Sun Ra's Arkestra typically began rehearsals with Jelly Roll Morton's "King Porter's Stomp" and proceeded through jazz history decade by decade. Like the members of Charles Mingus's band—or Ellington's—they knew and were able to play any style of jazz that had ever existed. Or not play it.

In his erudite and sometimes polemical *Jazz: America's Classical Music*, Grover Sales begins where Alain Locke left off, noting that "the music of black America began as a primitive folk entertainment and grew with amazing speed into a complex and varied art form that interacted with classical music; the ethnic musics of Latin America, the Middle East, Europe, Africa, and the Orient; and with jazz's offshoots, rhythm 'n' blues and rock, and became an international language" (3). After three-quarters of a century of such development, Sales can state with assurance: "Monk, Mingus, Dolphy and the Miles Davis Sextet with Coltrane and Evans will fuel musicians of the future, just as Bach and Haydn prepare conservatory graduates" (219). What is understood here—as the musicians themselves know—is that African American music (which many of the artists, taking a cue from Mr. Ellington, do not like to call "jazz") is, in fact, a music with its own highly developed and carefully curated traditions. It is not classical music because it resembles seventeenth-, eighteenth-, or nineteenth-century European styles but because it is, partly, the result of a similar historical process. A group like the talented Uptown String Quartet might epitomize this development. These four women—employing traditional European classical instruments—perform arrangements of spirituals, bebop standards such as Parker's "Moose the Mooche," transcriptions of Max Roach drum solos—and they improvise in the genuine jazz tradition on all of these pieces.

What is especially notable about the Uptown String Quartet is that their performance embraces the entire history of jazz styles—from the collective improvisation of early jazz in New Orleans to the "free" style of collective improvisation that was the hallmark of the 1960s Black Arts Movement avant-garde. They are, as well, proficient in the European traditions associated with their instruments and the quartet ensemble.

Alain Locke was right; and even if we cannot presume to know whether he would have been pleased or displeased by today's music, I do not think he would have been surprised that it did not turn out precisely as he envisioned. Speaking for his own generation in 1925, Locke wrote: "When the racial leaders of twenty years ago spoke of developing race-pride and stimulating race-consciousness, and of the desirability of race solidarity, they could not in any accurate degree have anticipated the abrupt feeling that has surged up and now pervades the awakened centers" (New Negro 7–8). Neither would Alain Locke know the distant impact of his own exhortations. Unlike W. E. B. DuBois, Locke himself did not live to see the later 1960s, when a significant portion of the energy that was the Black Arts Movement emanated from centers he had indeed awakened.

"Communicating by Horns"

Jazz and Redemption in the Poetry of the Beats and the Black Arts Movement

For Langston Hughes and Rudolph Fisher, jazz is the backdrop for the desperate yet urbane comedy of the Harlem Renaissance. The poets of the 1950s "Beat Generation" and the militant Black Arts Movement of the 1960s and 1970s perceived jazz as a significant social critique of an oppressive social structure. Some of the works of Amiri Baraka (LeRoi Jones), Bob Kaufman, Larry Neal, and Henry Dumas explore a spiritual dimension of jazz that can be compared to an almost religious fervor, with all of the many implications of that term. For these writers, the jazz musician is not merely the custodian of an authentic folk culture or even the conscious avant-garde artist; he is the leader of rebellion against postwar conformity and the spiritual agent of the politically powerless.

Jazz, like African sculpture, fitted well with the taste for exotic primitive art that marked the modernist movement's aesthetic replication of Western economic imperialism in the early decades of the twentieth century. For many in the metropoles of Europe and America, primitive art-forms promised both a revitalization of and a protest against what they conceived as a stultifying and "tired" civilization.

In the 1920s, as Berndt Ostendorf has noted, jazz found an enthusiastic audience among young whites, because "if the Ladies Home Journal was against it, it had to be good." Even though the music could be seen as a central part of African American cultures, "For these flappers jazz was counterculture, a criticism of middleclass lifestyles and accepted values" (107). But for Theodor Adorno, who disliked jazz—and, apparently, black people as well—this idea of jazz as rebellion was an illusion.

Among Adorno's many critiques of "the culture industry" are two essays on jazz that betray a Eurocentrism that verges upon racism. Adorno contends that jazz, controlled by commercial interests, presents a false nonconformity precisely because it is no longer the expression of uncivilized blacks. "However little doubt there can be regarding the African elements in jazz," Adorno writes, "it is no less certain that everything unruly in it was from the very beginning integrated into a strict scheme, that its rebellious gestures are accompanied by the tendency to blind obeisance" ("Perennial Fashion" 122). Adorno was not only disappointed with the hepcat's behavior but was suspicious of the music's very structure. In a 1936 essay, Adorno wrote quite explicitly about the absence of a potential for liberation in jazz music:

> To the extent that we can speak of black elements in the beginnings of jazz, in Ragtime perhaps, it is still less archaic-primitive self-expression than the music of slaves; even in the autochthonal music of the African interior, syncopation within the example of a maintained measured time seems only to belong to the lower [social] level. Psychologically, the primal structure of jazz (Ur-jazz) may most closely suggest the spontaneous singing of servant girls. ("On Jazz" 53)

Unlike Alain Locke and others in the Harlem Renaissance who saw jazz and other African American musical forms as the foundations of a classical music that might rival anything produced in the European symphonic tradition, Adorno reveals a total inability to recognize blacks—even in an imagined dawn of folk expression—as people capable of creating a self-conscious and original art. Sadly, Adorno—looking to Negroes for "unruliness"—was unable to admit that an accomplished musician such as Duke Ellington, like the European composers both of them admired, was creating an artistic scheme.

While Adorno might be credited with predicting some of the excesses of music marketing through image manipulation, it is also true that the rebellious image attached to jazz has been powerful and durable. The jazz styles of the 1950s, exemplified by Charles Parker and small-band "bebop" improvisation, were—in comparison to the "swing" orchestras of the 1930s—self-consciously subversive and accurately "read" as such by both black and white aficionados. By 1960, an independent film by Ed Bland, titled The Cry of Jazz, highlighted the rebellious spirit of black musicians and black audiences in both bop and emerging "free jazz" styles. "I think what The Cry of Jazz did," Amiri Baraka recalled in a 1984 interview, "was plant the seeds in some of our minds of what the aesthetic of our music was." That is, The Cry of Jazz stimulated a more self-conscious sense of racial identity in Baraka's own work.

According to William J. Harris, Baraka's early 1960s critical essays on music allowed him "an opportunity to meditate on a profound and sophisticated art form created by blacks and to do so during a time when he was trying to find a model for his own art that was not white avant-garde" (xxiii). But it was the "Beat Generation," which started in the late 1940s, that first elevated jazz as an index of social protest to mystical proportions. As W. T. Lhamon, Jr. suggests in his book *Deliberate Speed*, novelist Jack Kerouac, poet Allen Ginsberg, and others perceived bebop's musical energy as oppositional to the fictive political stability being advertised by the establishment. Yet compared to the civil rights movement and subsequent protests against the war in Vietnam, the Beat Generation was a tame affair, as even its members acknowledge. "It is an indication," wrote Beat poet Pete Winslow, "of how innocuous pre-beat protest movements were in the fifties that the act of dropping out, assuming a new idiom, growing a beard and proceeding to live with something like intensity seemed truly revolutionary" (23).

The Beats found fuel for their intensity in jazz music, experimentation with drugs, and an imitation of what they thought was a black lifestyle. The young white poets were also inspired and given stylistic direction by black poet Bob Kaufman. The Beats were perfectly capable of intellectualizing their search for primal vitality. "Certainly," says Winslow,

> modern jazz came from the mainstream, the perfectly logical and perhaps inevitable result of men learning more about their instruments and themselves under conditions of repression and world-wide turmoil. It made more sense than any other music of the post-war era, and the beats recognized this. With jazz came the speech of the hipster. White people socially accepting blacks for the first time reacted with something like awe upon discovering the meaning of being cool. Kaufman, writing mainly for whites, utilized this feeling to the fullest, but always as the beat rather than the Negro. (23)

Bob Kaufman's strongest poetry, like that of fellow Beat soul brothers Ted Joans and Amiri Baraka, speaks in an unmistakably black accent that is deeper than the hipster idiom so easily accessible to white beatniks. In fact, Kaufman in the late 1950s had a more mature vision than either Joans or Baraka; and, unlike his white peers, his references to jazz do not invoke the questionable convention of ecstatic abandon.

Though many of the Beats may not have known it, the literary apprecia-

tion of the noble savagery of jazz was born in the same years they were.
Maxwell Bodenheim, the Greenwich Village bohemian poet of the 1920s and
1930s, was among the most colorful precursors of the Beats. His portrait, in
fact, hung over the bar in McDougal Street's Kettle of Fish. Bodenheim, in a
poem celebrating jazz and exhorting working-class consciousness, was nevertheless unable to avoid racist stereotypes:

> It takes a good, old-fashioned midnight hell
> To make a dark man twist his hips.
> He'll make your heart-beats swell until they yell
> And burn a jazz-song on your lips! . . .
> You need a dark brown sister stepping wild,
> You need a dark brown stack of joy.
> She'll put a moony, loony, baboon-child
> Right in your blood and marrow, boy!
>
> (35–36)

Much of the jazz-inspired Beat writing of the 1950s was hardly any better.
Poet Hugh Romney later moved on to try his hand at a stand-up comedy career and a few lines of his work explain why:

> And my god is tree and sky naked of final mushroom madness
> And my god is jazzbeat sun and naked teat of earth
> And my god is poet
> Self complete with torn and tear and hold as this poem is holy
>
> (53–54)

Jazz, for Bob Kaufman, suggests instead an intense and eerie sadness, a
despair for the sanity and survival of all persons. In Kaufman's poem
"Countess Erica Blaise: Chorus," jazz is "Africa's other face, stranded—in
America, yet to be saved" (*Ancient Rain* 12). An early poem like "Walking
Parker Home," prefiguring the prosody of Ntozake Shange, connects jazz
with images of heroin addiction reminiscent of the later work of William
Burroughs:

> New York altar city/ black tears/ secret disciples
> Hammer horn pounding soul marks on unswinging gates

Culture gods/ mob sounds/ visions of spikes
Panic excursions to tribal Jazz wombs and transfusions
Heroin nights of birth/ and soaring/ over boppy new ground.
Smothered rage covering pyramids of notes spontaneously exploding
Cool revelations/ shrill hopes/ beauty speared into greedy ears
Birdland nights in bop mountains, windy saxophone revolutions

(*Solitudes* 5)

All of this is "Beat," but it's more directly a black indictment of society. Kaufman's poem speaks of Charlie Parker's legacy, "our Jazz-tinted dawn," in the same tone of black outrage that Askia Muhammad Touré would later employ to eulogize John Coltrane. In his eloquent 1970 poem "JuJu," Touré suggests that the saxophonist's "Africanic song" was wasted on audiences characterized by "green beast-eyes and the carnal leer of lust and hate." Touré pointedly accuses white jazz fans of devaluing the pain expressed in Coltrane's music, the very same charge Kaufman levels in his description of Parker's extraordinary performances as "beauty speared into greedy ears."

Kaufman's line, however, contains a crucial ambiguity. He is not content to paint the jazz musician merely as a martyr sacrificed to jargon-spouting philistines in shades. Along with "black tears," the music also encodes a more aggressive response to the racially motivated humiliations that frame the jazz artist's life—and the lives of all black people. Kaufman's musicians squeeze out notes as if they are hurling spears. In "Battle Report," terse and beautiful, Kaufman devises an image of jazz instruments as weapons in a war against oppressive "square" society:

> One thousand saxophones infiltrate the city,
> Each with a man inside,
> Hidden in ordinary cases,
> Labeled FRAGILE.
> A fleet of trumpets drops their hooks,
> Inside at the outside.

Like a syncopated Homer, Kaufman continues the census of his imaginary orchestral forces and, at the end of the poem, remembers the Charles Parker bebop theme that became a popular dance tune known as "The Hucklebuck":

At last, the secret code is flashed:
Now is the time, now is the time.
Attack: The sound of jazz.
The city falls.

(Solitudes 8)

The falling city is, of course, both Main Street and its drugged shadow Junk City.

Kaufman felt that jazz music spoke a truth about existence that words were hard put to express. The message of the music was at odds with the daily operations of a society in which evil and oppression held the upper hand. His poem "War Memoir" opens with a clear warning: "Jazz—listen to it at your own risk." Pointing out, in a Lorcaesque image, that "Life is a saxophone played by death," Kaufman's memoir rises to a climax of thunderous irony:

What one-hundred-percent red-blooded savage
Wastes precious time listening to jazz
With so much important killing to do?
Silence the drums, that we may hear the burning
Of Japanese in atomic color-cinemascope,
And remember the stereophonic screaming.

(Solitudes 52–53)

Maybe it is because someone actually read Bob Kaufman that we now have our wars on cable television, where they look like Nintendo games and the missiles fired produce no human casualties.

"War Memoir" is not only concerned with turning around the "primitive" or "uncivilized" stereotypes so often applied to the products of African culture; Kaufman's sensibility was also carefully attuned to the universal suffering that jazz sounds express locally. In "Voyagers," he explains the meaning of these sounds in a torrent of images:

Cynical jazz, blasted from neon intestines,
Electrically had by departed saxophone maniacs,
Noisy artfully contrived screams,
Presenceless souls, trapped

On thin anonymous discs of eroded wax,
Continuous shrieks spearing through
Marbleskin earshapped antennae
Of aesthetic-soaked pincushions,
Springfoot leapers, frozen in flight,
Clinging to shallow bowled spoons

(*Solitudes* 39)

The images of heroin addiction are both specifically referential in terms of the hipster lifestyle and metaphors for a society addicted to injustice. Unlike Jack Kerouac, Kaufman knew very well that jazz was not mere ecstasy, that it was as dangerous to ordinary American illusions as every beatnik's mother said it was. Jazz was an overdose of reality.

Bob Kaufman's recitations of such poems in the Beat coffeehouses of San Francisco were able to make both white and black listeners feel a sense of solidarity in protest against the cruel complacencies of Eisenhower America, but the following decade was to bring major changes in both race relations and the use of the jazz images Kaufman created.

In his brilliant story "Will the Circle Be Unbroken?" poet Henry Dumas specified the new victims of the jazz assault. In an underground inner-city jazz club "an obviously *called* Black musician plays his rare, ancient 'afro-horn' with such pure vibrations that the sound kills three whites who had bogarded their way into the audience" (qtd. in C. Taylor 12). The hipsters of the 1940s used to get "sent" or "slayed" by particularly inventive solos. But Dumas makes the effect literal, and critic Clyde Taylor suggests that this fantastic aspect of the story might have been the result of Dumas's interest in the mystical "space-age" theories of musician-philosopher Sun Ra, who is presented in Bland's film *The Cry of Jazz*, along with discussion of antiwhite sentiments expressed by some musicians of the era (Baraka, *Daggers* 270–73). Dumas's story is indeed set in the 1960s during a period when outspoken avant-garde jazz musicians were talking about "separating" from white America, but the idea of jazz as a discourse able to visit retribution for the wrongs this society has perpetrated upon black people is equally evident in Kaufman's "Battle Report," Baraka's *Dutchman*, and other works composed in a more integrationist-minded atmosphere.

The theme of jazz stalking like an avenging Old Testament angel is indeed tinged with the fantasy of science-fiction literature and the pulp fiction that intrigued young readers in the late 1930s. But the redemptive power of the magical jazz spirit is treated with remarkable consistency by several poets. The mysterious "Afro-horn" reappears, for example, in Larry Neal's "Don't Say Goodbye to the Porkpie Hat," a poem grounded in the metaphysical concept that, just as great musicians live on in their music and the memories of their fans, "spirit lives in sound" (*Visions* 182):

> So we pick up our axes and prepare
> to blast the white dream;
> we pick up our axes
> re-create ourselves and the universe,
> sound splintering the deepest regions
> of spiritual space
> crisp and moaning voices
> leaping in the horns of destruction,
> blowing death and doom to all who have no use for the spirit.
>
> (180)

Neal's wordplay operates on two levels. While the jazz musician's use of the slang term *axe* to refer to his expensive instrument is a joke that turns on an earlier era's relegation of blacks to menial and manual rather than mental work, Neal elevates that ironic statement by imagining a labor of demolition and reconstruction on a spiritual or aesthetic rather than physical plane.

Other than Bob Kaufman, the poet who has made the most inventive use of this complex of images is Amiri Baraka. The value of jazz for Baraka is revealed in a clever story called "Answers in Progress," which includes a vignette of flying-saucer crewmen from somewhere else landing on Earth to inquire about Art Blakey's latest record. These "thin blue men" are not lost Spielberg extraterrestrials but people with a truly revolutionary mission—maintaining an alliance with black people. Baraka's point is that there is indeed communication among advanced forms of intelligent life in the universe, and those who are not hip to Art Blakey surely won't be counted in that number.

Baraka's use of the "avenging jazz spirit" motif is subtly linked with earlier popular culture elements. His poem "Black Art" draws indirectly upon the surrealist Robert Desnos's *Fantomas*, which itself was inspired by a popular French pulp fiction character. "Black Art" is directly influenced, however, by Kenneth Koch's "Fresh Air," which, Baraka says in his *Autobiography*, "sin-gle-handedly demolished the academic poets" (159). Koch's poem invokes a mysterious strangler to dispatch already "lifeless" academic poets and the editors who publish their work:

> Summer in the trees! "It is time to strangle several bad poets."
> The yellow hobbyhorse rocks to and fro, and from the chimney
> Drops the Strangler! The white and pink roses are slightly agitated by
>   the struggle
> But afterwards beside the dead "poet" they cuddle comfortingly
>   against their vase. They are safer now, no one will compare them to
>   the sea.
> Here on the railroad train, one more time, is the Strangler.
> He is going to get that one there, who is on his way to a poetry
>   reading.
> Agh! Biff! A body falls to the moving floor.
>
>   (232)

Koch's combination of disparate elements such as comic strip sound effects, his reading of Desnos, and narration similar to American adventure serials of the 1930s (which he later satirized in his 1979 novel *The Red Robins*) creates precisely the kind of poetry that would not have been acceptable to the editors he lampoons in "Fresh Air."

Baraka articulates a similar aesthetic polemic in "Black Art." Poetry for Baraka, Larry Neal has explained, "is a concrete function, an action. No more abstractions. Poems are physical entities: fists, daggers, airplane poems, and poems that shoot guns. Poems are transformed from physical objects into personal forces" (*Visions* 66). In fact, Baraka made the political thrust of his statement glowingly specific: "We want poems / like fists beating niggers out of Jocks" ("Black Art" 116). Jock's, a tavern on Harlem's Lenox Avenue, was, in the 1950s and 1960s, a favorite hangout for politicians connected to the city's Democratic Party machine; Baraka's Black Arts Repertory Theatre/School was located around the corner on 135th Street. The reference—as those who heard him read the poem on that street corner instantly under-stood—functions as idiomatic "signifying" . . . "talkin' about" pretentious community leaders . . . a purpose similar to Koch's strangler in his vendetta against those who are responsible for bad writing, but of greater political gravity. "Black Art" only makes sense when the source of its rhetorical tone is properly understood. Baraka says:

> We want poems that kill.
> Assassin poems, Poems that shoot
> guns. Poems that wrestle cops into alleys
> and take their weapons leaving them dead
> with tongues pulled out and sent to Ireland. Knockoff
> poems for dope selling wops or slick half-white
> politicians Airplane poems, rrrrrrrrrrrrrrrrrr
> rrrrrrrrrrrrrr . . . tuhtuhtuhtuhtuhtuhtuhtuhtuh
>
> (116)

This and similar poems of the period produced a general literacy panic among white critics who lacked an understanding of Baraka's rhetorical method. The temper of the times can be gauged from the transcript of Baraka's 1968 trial on a weapons charge in Newark, New Jersey, in which his poem "Black People" was cited by the judge during sentencing (Hudson, *From LeRoi Jones* 29). Critical alarm, addressed more to Baraka's perceived politics than to his poetry, was first sounded in response to the poem "Black Dada Nihilismus" by Edward Margolies (194–95).

Even though "Black Art" used overdramatized and violent images, it should be clear that the poem effectively limits itself to a call for "cleaning up" the Harlem community; further, the violent images themselves are derived from mass-cult Americana—comic books and schoolboy recess reenactments of Van Johnson "Dialing for Dollars" World War II movies.

Of course, that is not all there is to this poem. "Black Art," as Larry Neal has perceptively noted, also expresses "the will toward self-determination and nationhood, a radical reordering of the nature and function of both art and the artist" (*Visions* 66). Presenting a statement that revised Archibald MacLeish's well-known "Arts Poetica"—that is, "A poem should not mean, but be"—Baraka knows that poems must also *do* something. Like jazz, poetry must address a deep and total reality of being, and it must, somehow, perform a redemptive function.

"Black Art" is a poem written in a crisis. For the poet Baraka in Harlem, Langston Hughes's bittersweet chocolate cabarets were vanishing (as even Jock's has vanished now). In their place appeared a frustrated, deteriorating dark ghetto, elsewhere described by sociologist Kenneth Clark and by the designing politicians responsible for both the 1960s' "War on Poverty," which funded Baraka's Black Arts Repertory Theatre/School, and the inner-city upheavals that made such programs necessary.

Tracing the precursive influences on Baraka's poem in no way diminishes the work's strength, and my intention is not to footnote it to death. Rather, I wish to suggest a proper context. The immediacy and localization of Baraka's references and images, matched with the stridency of voice, clearly demand immediate improvement of the actual Harlem environment—not merely through antipoverty agencies, but through the agency of an increasingly effective poetics, by which Baraka means "consciousness." The clarities that Baraka seeks in "Black Art" swirl around the high resolutions of the comic strip, the B movie, and the simplistic solutions of frustrated everyday people to what we are all taught by professional pundits to recognize as "extremely complex problems." Baraka at first relies on the ageless "avenging jazz spirit" personified here as "Poem," but his restless and shocking juxtapositions lead us eventually to understand that our only useful clarity is, finally, black people's human recognition that reality is breath united with body:

> that they are the lovers and the sons
> of lovers and warriors and sons
> of warriors Are poems & poets &
> all the loveliness here in the world

> (117)

Ascension

Avant-Garde Jazz and the Black Arts Movement

> a love supreme.
>   for each
>   other
>   if we just
> lissssssSSSTEN
>   —Sonia Sanchez

I

If the theme of the Harlem Renaissance was racial vindication, then the Black Arts Movement can be seen as a program of reclamation. The word became popular when it appeared on picket signs of Harlem protesters who renamed a construction site on 125th Street "Reclamation Site #1." The artists and writers of the period also saw their work as a labor of reclaiming the lost souls of black folk. "The black artist," wrote Larry Neal in his 1968 essay "The Black Arts Movement," knows that "his primary duty is to speak to the spiritual and cultural needs of black people. Therefore, the main thrust of this new breed of contemporary writers is to confront the contradictions arising out of the black man's experience in the racist West" (Visions 62).

The militant attitude of writers such as Neal was reflected—and perhaps instigated—by jazz musicians, whose playing matched the intensity of an entire generation of African American intellectuals who were too young to know much about Jim Crow but old enough to see that integration was, at best, a barely hatched chicken if not a bird in the bush. One of the most interesting points of this group of young writers was an attempt to control authorship of jazz criticism and, thereby, reclaim the music itself as a central cultural expression of the black community. The story of this effort provides an instructive view of a dynamic within that community that can be traced back to the 1820s and still exerts an important influence today.

Houston A. Baker makes a distinction between that aspect of the international artistic modernist movement of the early twentieth century that was an antagonistic reaction to "replicating outmoded forms" and genteel, class-based, nineteenth-century ideals, and what he sees as the dynamic of the New Negro Movement. For Baker, the Harlem Renaissance represents an embrace of what he calls the "necessary task of employing . . . extant forms in ways that move clearly up, masterfully and re-soundingly away from slavery" (*Modernism* 101). Though Baker is eloquent, one might just as usefully suggest that his argument depends on accepting the "color line" to the extent that African American culture must be seen as essentially different from the coexistent Anglo culture. Reading Alain Locke's *The New Negro* (1925) does not necessarily offer support for this idea. Indeed, when speaking of music and the possibility that African American composers might, as did their eighteenth-century European counterparts, accomplish the "elevation" of folk forms into "high Art," Locke presents ideas that seriously challenge Baker's thesis.

Classical modernism can be seen not only as "an acknowledgement of radical uncertainty" (Baker, *Modernism* 3), but also as an attempt to redirect and revivify Western civilization through a radical reassessment of its traditions. Such a project is explicitly announced in Ezra Pound's writings in 1913, ranging from "A Few Don'ts for Imagistes" to *Patria Mia*. Insofar as Locke and W. E. B. DuBois—and even the Garveyite cultural nationalists—perceived that African Americans possessed the desire to acquire the benefits of Western civilization, they, too, could be said to have been engaged in a similarly corrective critique. Certainly, artists such as James Weldon Johnson in *God's Trombones* (1927) and Jean Toomer in *Cane* (1923) shared the stylistic agenda of other modernist writers. Baker, however, focuses on the Harlem Renaissance as a project of racial self-definition rather than on its equally important goal of using the arts to critique society and ameliorate social antagonism toward black Americans.

Amiri Baraka was certainly heir to modernist poetics and just as aware that the other modernism had failed black people, probably because it was never intended to include them. As poet, playwright, and music critic, Baraka (formerly LeRoi Jones) was a central figure of the times, both for his sometimes notorious celebrity in the "square" press and his genuine popularity among young black readers. He shared with them a somewhat alienated response to both mainstream white and African American mores. "The black poetry circuit Baraka sparked in the 60s," notes Greg Tate, "practically made John Coltrane a national hero in the black community. And if Baraka has been dubbed the Father of the Black Arts Movement it's because, as poet Mae Jackson recently related, he gave young black artists a place to go outside of white bohemia and black academia, a place more open to communion with black working-class culture" (171). It is worth noting that a good many of the black college students who found Baraka's message appealing came from working-class backgrounds. Jazz—an extraordinary edifice of intellectual-ism balanced on the working-class eloquence of the blues—was seen by this group as the perfect vehicle for expressing and exploring their social reality.

The musicians were also actively involved in the promotion of the ideas so ably expounded by Baraka. In 1965, writes Kalamu ya Salaam,

> John Coltrane consistently loaned both his name and his talents to the blossoming, racially oriented Black Arts Movement of that era.
>
> Furthermore, Coltrane was using his clout at Impulse to champion the recording of artists such as Archie Shepp, Marion Brown and oth-ers. Seemingly single-handedly John Coltrane was assaulting the barri-cades of the music world, leading a battalion of true believers into an apocalyptic and impassioned fray against the forces of traditional mu-sical taste and order. ("Man" 24)

Along with the Nigerian drummer Babatunde Olatunji, Coltrane was also ex-ploring the possibilities of launching a cooperative booking agency and record label (Salaam, "Man" 25). As the Black Arts Movement writers spoke of controlling the ideological perception of jazz, so the musicians attempted to exert more practical control over their own careers.

The period during which the Black Arts Movement flourished was full of spectacular public controversies. Beginning with a melee at the United Na-tions in 1961 when Harlem militants demonstrated to show concern about the assassination of Patrice Lumumba during the transition of the Belgian Congo to the independent nation of Zaire, the streets and television screens of the nation were filled with the clamor of a renewed African American race consciousness. There were protest marches at the 125th Street site of what is now the Adam Clayton Powell State Office Building, a project that resulted in the demolition of Lewis Michaux's famous black nationalist bookstore.

Michaux's store, established in the 1930s, was revered as a historical land-mark, and Harlem humorists acidly noted that the initials of the State Office Building accurately reflected the local taxpayers opinion of the governor and other members of what was colloquially referred to as the "white power structure." The decade of the 1960s was also marked by the shocking assas-sinations of John F. Kennedy, Malcolm X, Martin Luther King, and Robert Kennedy; a Selective Service draft system that sent poor black men to fight in Vietnam in disproportionately large numbers; often violent antiwar protests on university campuses; inner-city riots sparked by allegations of police bru-tality; and the repression of the Black Panther Party and other radical politi-cal groups by government infiltration and police gunfire.

All of this social turmoil was, naturally, reflected and analyzed in the artis-tic movements of the time, one of the most vibrant and energetic of which was the Black Art Movement. The most prominent and accessible artists in the black community were poets who expressed their reactions to such events in increasingly strident tones, which were accompanied by a music (in both jazz and rhythm-and-blues styles) that complemented the intensity of their moods. Even visual artists such as New York's Joe Overstreet and the Africobra group in Chicago produced images that consciously dismantled and defused the racial stereotypes imbricated in both mainstream and African American cultural tradition while promoting an innovative interpre-tation of African aesthetic values and racial self-respect.

Home to millions of European immigrants since the 1880s, New York's Lower East Side was still a low-rent district in 1960, and it attracted many young artists and intellectuals who could not afford to live in nearby Green-wich Village. They did, however, maintain the artistic atmosphere long asso-ciated with the Village. Baraka's work and ideas were directly influenced by other writers, painters, and especially the musicians with whom he associ-ated. Howard University classmate Marion Brown, Archie Shepp, Sun Ra, Sunny Murray, and others were close friends or artistic collaborators. It may be that their influence helped to shape Baraka's militant stance of the mid-1960s since it was widely known on the East Side that the black musicians were much more race-conscious and militant than artists in other disci-plines. Their attitude went with the territory; and it was not even a new thing. Discussing Louis Armstrong, poet Tom Dent (founder of the Umbra writers workshop) wrote:

Louis, i'm trying to understand what you were
really like
in the dark moments away from the stage.
rumors have it you were not pleasant
to be around
the shit-eating grin nowhere to be found

In the bebop era of the 1940s, that old jazzman's grin was not even found on stage. Paul Warren, a white hipster, reported Charlie Parker's 1947 North Side Chicago set at the Argyle Show Lounge in these words: "Above the silent crowd in blinding light black musicians masked themselves with insolence, separating themselves from audience by the very music they shared." A similar ambivalence might have been found at Charles Mingus's angry artist-in-residence stint at East Tenth Street's Nonagon Gallery. No grins. Miles Davis, who had played with Parker, was well known for playing with his back to the audience and walking offstage after completing his solos. The young black musicians of the 1960s appeared to be just as arrogant and temperamental as the beboppers had been. Some of them preferred not to play for white people at all. Squares or hipsters.

Baraka became closely associated with some of these young players and wrote record album liner notes and articles about them in jazz magazines. The musicians themselves were as cleverly articulate in words as they were on the bandstand; some, in fact, were poets and writers themselves. Charles Mingus and Sun Ra, both excellent poets and lyricists, spoke in vast but terse metaphors to those who took the time to listen. Sun Ra clothed his messages in the form of deeply ambiguous philosophical poems such as "The Outer Bridge":

In the half-between world
Dwell they, the sound scientists
Mathematically precise. . . .
They speak of many things
The tone scientists
Architects of planes of discipline.

(293)

He would patiently explain that black people were indeed "second-class citizens" in the United States, adding that it was nothing to be ashamed of.

"When you first went to school," he would say, "didn't you start out in the first grade? And then you went to the second, right? That's what that's about."

Mingus, for his part, bluntly and beautifully stated the resentments that are shared by all black people who have been on the receiving end of American racism. In 1962 he recorded one of his poems that eloquently expressed such feelings:

This mule ain't from Moscow
This mule ain't from the South
But this mule's had some learning
Mostly mouth to mouth

This mule could be called stubborn and lazy
But in a clever sort of way
This mule could be working, waiting and learning and planning

As he neared the conclusion of his recitation, the band sang the chorus:

Freedom for your daddy
Freedom for your momma
Freedom for your brothers and sisters
But no freedom for me

(Town Hall)

Saxophonist Archie Shepp had studied playwriting at Goddard College and published his own poems in literary magazines here and in England. His play *Junebug Graduates Tonight* was produced off-Broadway in 1965. Shepp also composed musical settings for original poems he recited in melodramatic tones at concerts and East Side loft parties. Later, he included them on his recordings. Like Mingus and Sun Ra, Shepp consciously explored the historical styles of earlier jazz in his playing, kept up to date in his reading, and was unequivocally outspoken about his social and political ideas.

After establishing the Black Arts Repertory Theatre/School in Harlem in 1965, Baraka sponsored several concerts there featuring Shepp, Albert Ayler, and Sun Ra's Arkestra. Ayler, recently returned from Europe, had a truly amazing approach to both his instrument and the jazz canon, and his playing exerted a great influence on Baraka.

Albert Ayler and other loft jazz musicians, Baraka wrote in *Black Music*, "have done away with . . . awe-inspiring popular song [that was the basis for much bebop improvisation]. When Ayler does want memory to furnish him with a fire-source, he uses coonish churchified chuckle tunes" (116). Despite his characteristic signifying irony, Baraka was both accurate and perceptive. Ayler's "Spirits Rejoice," for example, is based on a variant of the anthem "God Save the Queen," which serves as a frame for "free" improvisations bearing little formal relation to the stated theme. The connection of Ayler's approach to church music is apparent on "Angels," where his thrilling vibrato—backed by Call Cobbs, Jr., on harpsichord—recalls George Beverly Shea's "How Great Thou Art" more than it does the blue loneliness of, say, "Harlem Nocturne." Ayler's embellishments of a melody are like a gospel singer's, and his repertoire also included marches that, in their often dissonant ensembles, reflect and comment on the part that New Orleans brass bands played in the origin of jazz itself. At one point Baraka patterned his style of recitation on Ayler's yelping saxophone sound, a style that suited Baraka's allusive poetry and expressing alto voice perfectly.

Saxophonist Marion Brown, however, was probably Baraka's closest link to the young musicians. When Brown came up to New York from Howard University he was better known as a writer than as a musician. He shared a valuable cross-influence with Baraka and was a frequent visitor to the poet's Cooper Square apartment—a running buddy. As a writer and musician, Brown was able to supply a technical explanation of the importance of jazz to African American culture. "In oral societies," Brown wrote in 1973, "the ear interprets what is first perceived visually" (15). A decade earlier he had already perfected the ability to identify by ear the African tribal and African American geographical origins of specific rhythm-and-blues and jazz motifs. He gave a brilliant performance of that skill for Steve Kent and me one afternoon in the black-owned House of Jazz record store on St. Marks Place, down the block from the Five Spot. What Brown suggested in 1964 is that specific African tribal musical traditions, though distorted by Western instruments and the fickle fashions of the recording industry, can still be recognized in African American music. There is no doubt that some of Brown's ideas influenced the conclusions in Baraka's seminal *Blues People: Negro Music in Black America*, and Brown himself clearly expressed the militant race consciousness implied in his concepts: "Our having made the transition from Africa to America, without the necessary cultural institutions, was a manifestation of a superior adjustment potential and an act of societal improvisation. We brought no books. What we learned of our past was taught orally, and very often in song form" (15). And what was not encoded in the blues was probably expressed in poetic conundrums similar to Sun Ra's explanations of what it means to be a second-class citizen.

"What is seen," Brown wrote, "has little meaning until speech is used to express the emotions that arise from observation." In *Blues People* and other writings from the early 1960s, Baraka carefully weighed the effects of various approaches to the act of opening the mouth. "Speech," Baraka said, "is the effective form of a culture." In "The Myth of a 'Negro Literature,'" an address delivered to the American Society of African Culture on March 14, 1962, Baraka attempted to identify the authentic speech and culture of African people in America:

Phillis Wheatley and her pleasant imitations of 18th century English poetry are far, and finally, ludicrous departures from the huge black voices that splintered southern nights with their *hollers, chants, arwhoolies,* and *ballits.* The embarrassing and inverted paternalism of Charles Chesnutt and his "refined Afro-American" heroes are far cries from the richness and profundity of the blues. (106)

Baraka went on to present a discussion fully grounded in Marion Brown's perceptions about jazz. "Africanisms," he said,

still persist in the music, religion, and popular cultural traditions of American Negroes. However, it is not an African art American Negroes are responsible for, but an American one. The traditions of Africa must be utilized within the culture of the American Negro where they *actually* exist, and not because of a defensive rationalization about the *worth* of one's ancestors or an attempt to capitalize on the recent eminence of the "new" African nations. (111)

The notion of an American identity that cannot be understood without confronting the consequences of an essentially incomplete historical estrangement from Africa is a central feature of Baraka's writings in the early 1960s. His poem "Notes for a Speech" (1961) poignantly stated his sense of loss. "African blues," he began, "does not know me." He added:

my color
is not theirs.
Lighter, white man talk

At the end, he sounds a plaintive cry of a returned prodigal who finds that home is very difficult to reclaim:

You are as any other sad man here
American

(*Preface* 47)

The problem, of course, is that if the black man is an American in Africa, American racism will not allow him to be an American in America. The unique view of the world that results from this dilemma is what Baraka's work passionately explores.

These ideas were not merely matters of intellectual debate in sidewalk cafés in 1962 but were immediate and local. Despite the artistic energy that surrounded the Lower East Side, the young African American artists felt a sense of personal isolation. The integrated milieu had the effect of fore-grounding their racial self-consciousness. As Harold Cruse noted,

The Negro intellectual has never really been held accountable to the black world for his social role [because] the black world cannot and does not support the Negro creative intellectual. The black bourgeoisie does not publish books, does not own and operate theaters or music halls. It plays no role to speak of in Negro music, and is remote from the living realities of the jazz musician who plays out his night in the ef-fete and soulless commercial jungles of American white middle-class café culture. (454)

Unconventional musicians like Charles Mingus, not to mention younger ex-perimenters such as Albert Ayler, found themselves unwelcome even in that jungle.

Baraka cultivated a kind of nostalgia for an era when this separation of the African American artist from his community was not as extreme. "The 1940s was revolutionary," he recalled in a 1984 interview, "in terms of the music. I'm talking about Bebop. But the 1940s represents the last time for let's say forty years when the most advanced concepts of the music were worked out in the community" (Interview 8). The Lower East Side scene in the early 1960s represented integration as well as a decline in the functional role of African American communities. If there was anything beneficial about segregation, it would be that black communities enjoyed a certain amount of cultural cohesiveness. "It used to be," Baraka noted, "whether you had a million dollars or 20¢, you lived in the same community. I don't give a damn what your class was—the black bourgeoisie, the black no-wasie—you still were in the community" (8). Certainly, such feelings were personal; but Greg Tate is unfair in his judgment that Baraka had a tendency to "confuse . . . his identity complexes with those of all black people" (168). On the Lower East Side in the early 1960s, Baraka's perceptions were not based on paranoia.

The Artist as Revolutionary

Only in accordance with a Black value system will the artist be supplied with a means for a correct interpretation of the reality and relevance of the music the music makers make.
—Mtume

As an integrationist movement, the Harlem Renaissance did little to encourage the establishment of African American cultural institutions. Even so, W. E. B. Du Bois issued a "blueprint" for a Negro community theater, and Alain Locke helped to initiate a plan for an art museum in Harlem that never materialized. The fact that the lowering of racial barriers in the 1960s did not fundamentally change the status of African American artists led to a renewed call for black-controlled institutions.

The Black Arts Movement was informed by a class-based, Marxist-influenced critique of American society that did not always state its goals clearly. The Harlem Renaissance, wrote Larry Neal, "was essentially a failure. It did not address itself to the mythology and the lifestyles of the black community. It failed to take root, to link itself concretely to the struggles of that community, to become its voice and spirit" ("Black Arts Movement," *Visions* 78). These were pitfalls that the leaders of the Black Arts Movement carefully avoided. They did succeed, for a moment, in making an unheard national voice audible. They helped young African Americans open their mouths. The tools available, however, were not adequate to accomplish all of the move-ment's ambitious goals.

Because he was trying to stimulate black pride and, simultaneously, plead the African American's case to white America, Locke's discussions of jazz of-ten involved mixed signals. Employing the rhetoric of exoticism, mingled with echoes of Emerson and Frederick Jackson Turner, Locke declared in 1936 that jazz "incorporated the typical American restlessness and uncon-ventionality, embodied its revolt against the drabness of the commonplace life, put pagan force behind the revolt against Puritan restraint, and finally became the Western World's life-saving flight from boredom and over-so-phistication to the refuge of elemental emotion and primitive vigor" (*Negro and His Music* 90). Jazz musicians, however, simply felt that they were being exploited. As with any resentment, this one grew stronger with the passage of time. Locke could announce proudly in 1936 that "jazz, in its more serious form, has . . . become the characteristic musical speech of the modern age" (90). He was correct, but this development did not necessarily mean financial reward or respect for black musicians. Four decades later, singer Jon Hen-dricks noted an even more ominous development: "Even though we Afro-Americans are still impoverished, still downtrodden, still oppressed, still not yet free, our musical culture is now dominant in the entire Western world. The only thing wrong with the whole picture is that we, in our rush to inte-gration, seem to have thrown our music away" (14–15). What troubled Hen-dricks was the relative control over the music that was exerted by white crit-ics. In his view, expressed in the militant black journal *Liberator* in November 1969, neither black audiences nor the musicians themselves seemed to be able to control the aesthetic or commercial direction of the music. Here was a very specific example of the loss of a sense of community that Baraka has described.

Hendricks was particularly irked by jazz criticism, noting that "the one field of artistic endeavor where you can walk right in without credentials and become a critic is jazz. All you need is a command of the English language and a lot of opinions, plus access to musicians so they can tell you what to write" (15). Several years earlier, in an essay entitled "Jazz and the White Critic," Baraka had addressed this problem. "The irony," he wrote,

is that because the majority of jazz critics are white middle-brows, most jazz criticism tends to enforce white middle-brow standards of

excellence as criteria for performance of a music that in its most profound manifestations is completely antithetical to such standards; in
fact, quite often is in direct reaction against them. (As an analogy, sup-
pose the great majority of the critics of Western formal music were
poor, "uneducated" Negroes?) (182)

This delightful signifying was not objecting to the *race* of these critics. Baraka
carefully pointed out that many African Americans were unqualified as well:
"Jazz was collected among the numerous skeletons the middle-class black
man kept locked in the closet of his psyche, along with watermelons and gin"
(179). The issue here was *class* identification. Baraka argued that few white jazz
critics of the 1930s and 1940s had been able to either understand or identify
with "the sub-culture from which [the music] was issued" (180). In 1936 Locke
had argued that jazz was not only universal in its appeal but worthy of technical analysis for its musical sophistication. "In some important way," Locke
wrote, "jazz has become diluted and tinctured with modernism. Otherwise, as
purely a Negro dialect of emotion, it could not have become the dominant
recreational vogue of our time" (*Negro and His Music* 90). Baraka felt that, in
spite of the music's technical virtuosity, criticism should focus on the source of
the aesthetic embodied in jazz. "The catalysts and necessity of Coltrane's music must be understood as they exist even before they are expressed as music,"
he wrote. "The music is the result of the attitude, the stance. Just as Negroes
made blues and other people did not because of the Negro's peculiar way of
looking at the world" ("Jazz and the White Critic" 185).

Baraka's poetically phrased suggestion that the forms of art are derived
from preexisting social attitudes is derived from the sort of Marxist analysis,
popular in the 1930s, that is brilliantly exemplified in Christohper Caudwell's writings on poetry. Neals's essay "Ethos of the Blues" gives an even
clearer picture of this theory:

The blues are the ideology of the field slave—the ideology of a new
"proletariat" searching for a means of judging the world. Therefore,
even though the blues are cast in highly personal terms, they stand for
the collective sensibility of a people at particular stages of cultural, social, and political development. The blues singer is not an alienated
artist attempting to impose his view of the world on others. His ideas
are the reflection of an unstated general point of view. (*Visions* 113)

If Caudwell was able to correlate the styles of English verse to the economic relationships that dominated the centuries during which the poets lived, so Neal was able to suggest that the role of the blues singer in the African American community represented a surviving Africanism. The blues singer, for Neal, is an African griot in North America: "Even though he is part of the secular community, his message is often ritualistic and spiritual. Therefore, it is his spiritual role in the community which links him to the traditional priests and poets of Africa" (113). For Neal, Baraka, and the other writers of the Black Arts Movement, the avant-garde jazz musicians of the 1960s performed exactly the same role. Middle-class white jazz critics, judging performances in nightclubs or on concert stages, could not in any substantive sense employ this extended view of these artists.

"There is a story current in the Black Community," wrote Stephen Henderson in *Understanding the New Black Poetry*, "about a white critic who, after listening to some records by Coltrane and Pharoah Sanders, said with great condescension, 'It's interesting, but you can't dance to it'; whereupon a young brother said with withering scorn, '*You* can't dance to it!' " (55).

If, in fact, most white jazz critics were unqualified because of their truncated view of the music, the question of what black jazz criticism should properly address was yet to be answered. Baraka and Neal both contended that it should be based on an investigation of "socio-aesthetic" features. Among the young people who constituted the national network of what would become known as the Black Arts Movement there were a number of poets working toward a definition of just what all this meant.

Between 1960 and 1970 an outpouring of poems focused on musicians in the role of griots. As Henderson noted in *Understanding the New Black Poetry*: "This is probably the largest category of musical referents in Black poetry" (60). All of these poems issued from the idea that the blues singer or jazz saxophone player is, as Neal pointed out, the contemporary griot—a role the poets had, of course, already accepted for themselves. As a result, these poems can often be read as "praise songs" in the traditional African manner. Walter De Legall's "Psalm for Sonny Rollins" is an excellent example of this genre:

In a lifespan-while, I am
Absorbed into the womb of sound.
    I am in the sound.

The sound is in me.
I am the sound.
I am your tears that you shed for forty days
And forty nights, Theodore. I am
Your pain who you accepted as
Your bedfellow. I am your hunger and
Your thirst, which purified your
Soul, Theodore. I am your sorrow that
You won in a raffle. Pick up your axe
And let us blow down the Chicago citadels
Of convention. "You just can't play like that in here."
Let us blow down the Caucasian battlements
Of bigotry. "But we don't hire Colored musicians."
Open your tenor mouth and let
Us blow into oblivion the insensible
Strongholds of morality.
"And I'm sure he's an addict."
Blow down thunder and lightning
And White People!! Blown down moons
And stars and Christs!

> (Henderson, *Understanding* 202)

De Legall's collage of biblical language, black hipster slang, and the puritanical voices of middle-class white America is intended to translate into words the preexisting social reality that the poet imagines is expressed in Rollins's music. In fact, the saxophonist's performance is imaged as a ritual, a mass. Like Jesus, or any "brother man," Sonny Rollins has suffered. Like Joshua at Jericho, he is capable of producing a musical sound that will bring down the walls erected by the enemies of his people. De Legall conflates allusions from both the Old Testament and the book of Revelation.

De Legall's poem, like many of the period, is informed by an aesthetic that Eugene Redmond succinctly defined in his "Parapoetics":

Poetry is an applied science:
    Re-wrapped corner rap;
    Rootly-eloquented cellular, soulular sermons.

> (Henderson, *Understanding* 371)

Here, in Redmond's phrasing, one sees the poet's attempt to incorporate the entire range of African American vernacular—sacred and profane—into a poetic diction capable of accurately representing the community's history, ideology, and ("cellular") racial identity. The unspoken assumption, of course, is that such a representation is the proper function of art—whether poetry or music, verbal or nonverbal. Redmond hints that effective art is, indeed, something like a metalinguistics. How it works is suggested by his choice of the prefix *para-* rather than *meta-*; his readers or listeners would have associated that prefix more immediately with its use in words such as "paramilitary" than with "paraphrases." Indeed, for Black Arts Movement poets, poetry was capable of more than mere representation. As indicated in De Legall's poem, these writers imagined a poetry that makes thing happen.

Some poets linked their interpretations of the music to social protest in very specific terms. David Henderson's "Elvin Jones Gretsch Freak" gives us

> the man elvin behind the baptismal tubs
> that leap like cannons to the slashing sound of knives
> black elvin knows so well
> the knives the Daily News displays along with the photo
> of a grinning award-winning cop
> the kind of knives elvin talks about
> downtown by the water
> and uptown
> near the park
>
> (Henderson, *Understanding* 267)

Such a poem proceeds from the idea expressed in A. B. Spellman's "Did John's Music Kill Him?":

> trane's horn had words in it
>
> (Henderson, *Understanding* 261)

The poet had only to decipher those words. This might easily be dismissed as an irrelevant projection of the poet's moods or ideas onto music, except for the fact that many of the musicians were saying the same things. In a brief essay published in *Jazz* magazine, Archie Shepp wrote, "A piece of music is a woman in a foul dress; myriad babies howling, unfed; fat rat slick from the sewer. But what can a piece of music never be? It can never be more than Billie Holiday. But then it should strive never to be less" (24).

Again, Shepp's comments could be taken as merely a politically engaged African American's appropriation of nineteenth-century programmatic music rather than an expression of the preexisting "attitude, the stance" that Baraka sought to establish as the source of jazz music. Other musicians of the period, however, were more explicit in sounding their approval of this theory. The percussionist Mtume set forth guidelines for his peers:

> The Black musician must, as any other revolutionary artist, be a projector whose message reflects the values of the culture from which his creation owes its existence. He must be the antennae which receives the visions of a better life and time and transmits those visions into concrete realities through the use of sound and substance (each time must be a lecture via entertainment). (1)

This straightforwardly didactic approach to art was shared by the poets who contributed critical articles and reviews to Baraka's jazz journal The Cricket, published sporadically in Newark beginning in 1966. Cleveland poet Norman Jordan, for example, offered a definition of "Positive Black Music": "Black music, as well as all constructive art, must be free, and at the same time it must contain order[,] a positive harmony on the physical, mental and spiritual level" (24). Here was the other side of the movement's protest, an urge to accomplish the moral regeneration of African American people who had been victimized and damaged by racism. Taken to an extreme, this impulse led to a rigorous, almost puritanical, concern with order and moral correctness. Mwanafunzi Katibu's nonreview of an Archie Shepp record, appearing in the same issue of The Cricket, is a particularly vivid example of this tendency:

> Listening to this album. Make me tired. Its jive. Shepp hasn't, lost his, soul. Yet. But Devil Dogs can make this happen, thing abt it Archie Shepp. You shd know. The elements, you draw near are the ones you become, try to be like. If you around people who smoke, and drink all the time then thats. All you will want, to please, do.

Nothing is said about the music on this recording. Katibu, perhaps ahead of his time, aims his harshest criticism of Shepp at the saxophonist's indiscreet pose with a cigarette in hand: "Archie Shepp thinks, it's hip to take an album cover photo w/ death air flowin out his mouth. No Values" (26). At this extreme, the "critic" is not even interested in the music as an expression of the artist's attitude or stance but claims an ability to critique that attitude through a reading of the semiotics of lifestyle as revealed by personal habits. Katibu was absolutely correct about the dangers of tobacco, of course, but the fact that art is not even discussed disqualifies this article as anything more than a poison-pen letter.

Some writers were growing a bit impatient with the level of writing that was coming out of the movement. The Grackle: Improvised Music in Transition, a journal similar in purpose to The Cricket, edited by Roger Riggins, James T. Stewart, and Ron Welburn, published four issues between 1976 and 1978. In a letter to contributors, Welburn raised two sharply pointed questions:

> What level of musicological knowledge or skill should we demand of ourselves and each other [as critics]? Shouldn't we know something about music as a musician of amateur, or semi-professional, or professional ability, instead of romanticizing about cult figures and "rapping"?
>
> Isn't it time we moved away from superficial sociology to serious musicological and socio-aesthetic matters about particular artists and periods? (Letter to Lorenzo Thomas)

Welburn was not questioning the theory that jazz does, in fact, function as the artistic expression of an ideology. What he was calling for was a more rigorous standard of critical inquiry among African American jazz critics.

No movement, of course, should be judged on the basis of an extreme example of its negative potential; yet it must be noted that the Black Arts Movement, in encouraging an outspoken denunciation of racism, also encouraged the venting of a great many other resentments and the publication of a wide range of prescriptions for reform.

By 1976 the Black Arts Movement had become diffused into the general intellectual culture of black America. Baraka had redefined himself as a Marxist. Neal was directing a municipal arts council. Other young "revolutionary" poets had become university professors. Nevertheless, the movement had enjoyed an international range. The critical premises put forth by

Baraka and his colleagues in terms of discussing jazz were now eloquently phrased, in England, by Henderson Dalrymple in defense of reggae music:

Black music is too important a social agent; it fulfills too much of a social function in our lives to be left in the hands of the oppressing class. Culturally, socially and politically black music has an important role to play in the black liberation struggle. The role of our music in the struggle can only be truly revolutionary when black people are making all the decisions that will determine the music's future and direction. Only when we decide how great or how small a part our music must play in our struggle can the music be fulfilling its role as an agent of the revolutionary. (10–11)

The result of the Black Arts Movement focus on jazz was the creation of a socially conscious aesthetic standard that proved difficult for both musicians and audiences to maintain. This does not suggest that the Black Arts Movement, or earlier Afrocentric movements in fashion, failed. A useful comparison might be drawn to the surrealist movement in its *l'art pour service de la revolution* phase and the enduring impact it has had on both the fine arts and commercial design (not to mention the Black Arts Movement). It is also worth noting that the political and aesthetic problems identified by the Black Arts Movement are still being worked out today on several different fronts, including the controversy regarding rap music.

To posit critical credibility on receptive ability defined by race and culture leads logically to further distinctions. If being African American is the first qualification for a jazz critic, being a practicing musician must be next—as was hinted at by the editors of *The Grackle*. There was, of course, no means of enforcing any of these entrance requirements. Not having any institutions capable of awarding accreditation made institution-building that much more difficult. Nevertheless, the critique of the status quo voiced by Baraka, Neal, Welburn, and others offered a valuable moment of self-reflection in a critical discipline that needs more of it.

FOUR   Songs for the People

Rhythm and Blues *au service de la Revolution*

The Black Arts Movement and Popular Music

It should surprise no one to discover that most critical appreciations of black music—filled with faint praise and backhanded compliments—have also served to diminish the people who produced it. While James Weldon Johnson lauded the "black and unknown bards" whose genius surpassed the "great German master in his dream / Of harmonies" (283), most establishment music critics have tended to view the African American artist—to take a phrase from Chester Himes—as "a blind man with a pistol."

In other words, for these critics any suggestion of *intentionality*—beyond the mere desire to perform—is viewed with suspicion. The black artist is never more than a primitive. Ben Sidran noted this attitude among white audiences for black music; and critic Simon Frith is a notable example of one who has influenced others to accept this view. Indeed, even Richard Wright appears to have succumbed to it in the final days of his life in Paris.

Strangely enough, neither musicians nor genuine fans seem at all intimidated by the situation. I recall attending a concert by the Neville Brothers at Texas A & M University—which is the site of the George Bush Presidential Library and the school where right-wing Sen. Phil Gramm once taught economics. Though the audience was 95 percent white and closing in on middle age, the Nevilles performed what amounted to a Pan African cultural rally, complete with red, black, green, and gold sartorial accessories. The audience knew all the songs and sang along in delight. Similarly, Taj Mahal's repertoire of blues, rhythm and blues, reggae, and African music—performed in remarkably various venues—has borne witness to his substantial Afrocentric message for three decades.

I make these comments simply to say that the idea of political content or purpose in popular music is not at all far-fetched. But it is neither racist nor essentialist to point out that white and African American critics have characteristically seen the revolutionary potential of rhythm and blues and rock music quite differently. While white critics have seemed to focus on an individualistic style of social protest, the African American writers of the Black Arts Movement of the 1960s and 1970s proposed a collective model. These paradigmatic responses might also reflect a racial differentiation of attitudes in the United States that is still evident and fully documented in recent sociological literature.

In their attempt to redefine the ebullient and ecstatic choreography of the Apollo Theatre stage as political gestures, the Black Arts Movement critics were also trying to avoid the difficulties that had ensnared earlier leftist aestheticians. They did not seek to impose or define the parameters of a proper working-class art in the way that Simon Frith notes the Communist Party had done in the 1930s and 1940s; rather, they sought to translate into political theory what they believed was a preexisting political consciousness embodied in African American songs and folklore. Their relative lack of success was not due to naïveté about the linkage of this music to the commercial establishment but, perhaps, their underestimation of the power of that establishment to co-opt and redefine almost anything that enters its gravitational field.

It must be asked whether or not the choice of rhythm and blues as a focus for the Black Arts Movement's political reading was appropriate. The question invokes an old debate. Folklorist Francis B. Gummere, in 1894, noted that the question was often used as a way of reinforcing academic standards. "Poetry of the schools," he writes, "and poetry of the people are treated as rival claimants for the throne of excellence" (xiv). Gummere calls this a "general blunder" among literary critics, contending that

> an estimate of poetry of the people based upon the standard of the schools must lead us into error, as it led Dr. Johnson into absurdity; and when enthusiasts for the ballad like Burger, or even Jacob Grimm, attempt to judge poetry of the schools by tests which belong entirely to poetry of the people, we have confusion even more deplorable. (xv)

James Weldon Johnson's eloquent preface to The Book of American Negro Poetry, and the work of Alain Locke in the 1920s and 1930s, seems to have protected most commentators on African American poetry and music from falling into this snare. Consequently, when Black Arts Movement writers raised this issue, they did so for consciously polemical and tactical purposes (see Gabbin 140–41, 108–11).

Gummere also warns against "confusion between poetry of the people and poetry for the people, between a traditional piece of verse and a song written to please the casual crowd of an alley or a concert-hall" (xvi). As an admirer of Johann Gottfried von Herder (1744–1803), Gummere stresses collectivity—as does Larry Neal in his explication of the blues—seeking to distinguish "poetry which once came from the people as a whole, from the compact body as yet undivided by lettered or unlettered taste, and [which] represents the sentiment neither of individuals nor of a class" (*Visions* xvi; see also xlii–xlv).

It is obvious that no such cultural expression could be found in the United States in the 1960s, not even by folklorists. The focus on rhythm-and-blues music, as the nearest thing to a genuine African American demotic form, was an expedient; and the fact that its appropriation by bands from England threatened the erasure of the form's authenticity, made the critical project—at least in the eyes of Black Arts Movement critics—something of an emergency operation. This sense of emergency does not, however, explain or excuse the rhetorical excesses of some of the writing from this period; one needs to look deeper into the Black Arts Movement to find the reasons for that.

Some recent critics have dismissed this—and other aspects—of the Black Arts Movement as an instance of "allowing aesthetic judgments to be dictated by political agendas" (Van Deburg 296). Harold Cruse was much more precise and perceptive in 1967, advising artists and writers that "they must not permit themselves to come under the domination of activists and politicians who do not favor cultural front activities" (541). Black Arts Movement music criticism did not fall into the perilous zone Cruse warns about; it was, in fact, an artist-driven cultural front project.

It is a disservice to the Black Arts Movement writers and to contemporary students to ignore the important intellectual context of this particular project. A knowledge of the Black Arts Movement approach would certainly help future critics avoid such an egregious lapse as Stanley Crouch's bizarre suggestion that the plantations and sharecrop lands of Arkansas and Mississippi were somehow analogous to "cattle towns on cowboy weekends" and that Robert Johnson can be apprehended by comparing that great Delta bluesman to Davy Crockett, Daniel Boone, or Ned Buntline (Crouch ix–x).

Finally, the music criticism of these writers did succeed in spotlighting the social protest and political "self-determinative" possibilities of even a commodified popular music for both audiences and the performers themselves. Furthermore, in continuing and extending a theoretical discussion that can be traced from Herder to Alain Locke and James Weldon Johnson, the Black Arts Movement writers did not always meet but did encourage a standard for a mode of music criticism beyond mere aestheticism and press-agentry, a standard that has been capably carried forward in the 1980s and 1990s by critics such as Nelson George, Greg Tate, Tricia Rose, and Armond White.

If it is argued that the political and socioeconomic reality of African Americans is as dire today as it was in 1966, perhaps the point that must be made is that the cultural expressions of black America indeed constitute a powerful weapon of defense, self-affirmation, and resistance, but that the struggle is not merely a duel of honor. What may be required for the sane survival of African people in the United States is not "a choice of weapons" but an effective arsenal.

In his 1937 "Blueprint for Negro Writing," Richard Wright perceived African American folklore as a record of "the collective sense of Negro life in America" and a potential instrument of political awareness (196). The writer's role was the careful interpretation of this material—whether imaginatively or by informed critical evaluation—because "when a people begin to realize a meaning in their suffering, the civilization that engenders that suffering is doomed" (198). Wright later revised this view, giving even more emphasis on the folk elements. "Expression springs out of an environment," he wrote in White Man, Listen! "and events modify what is written by molding consciousness" (85). Twenty years had made him suspicious of the writer's role:

Middle-class Negroes borrowed the forms of the culture that they strove to make their own, but the migratory Negro worker improvised his cultural forms and filled those forms with a content wrung from a bleak and barren environment. (86)

Wright calls the cultural expressions of this working class "the Forms of Things Unknown" and finds examples of it in the blues, spirituals, and verses from "the dozens" (86, 88–95). For young black intellectuals at the beginning of the 1960s, Wright's view exerted a great deal of influence.

In his 1959 foreword to Paul Oliver's *The Meaning of the Blues*, however, Richard Wright buried this folk art under three levels of repression.

First of all, the blues—for Wright—originates at the very bottom of the proletarian barrel. Some Marxists have called this group the *lumpenproletariat*. It is from the field slaves, he writes,

> and their descendants that the devil songs called the blues came—that confounding triptych of the convict, the migrant, the rambler, the steel driver, the ditch digger, the roustabout, the pimp, the prostitute, the urban or rural illiterate outsider. (10)

Second, what the songs express is rather questionable:

> The most striking feature of these songs is that a submerged theme of guilt, psychological in nature, seems to run through them. Could this guilt have stemmed from the burden of renounced rebellious impulses? (9)

Finally, as if this misdirection of a possible revolutionary political expression were not bad enough, such a possibility is further subverted by the music's popular reception. "Millions in this our twentieth century," says Wright, "have danced with abandonment and sensuous joy to jigs that had their birth in suffering . . . songs created by millions of nameless and illiterate American Negroes in their confused wanderings over the American Southland and in their intrusion into the Northern American industrial cities" (7). There is little of heroism or articulate protest left in Wright's characterization of the "blues people."

Compared to his "Blueprint for Negro Writing," which finds a model for intellectuals in "a folklore which embodies the memories and hopes of [the African American's] struggle for freedom" (198); or even its early 1950s revision in *White Man, Listen!* where Wright sees the blues as a realistic admission that "their hope was hopeless" (91), the foreword to Oliver's book is an extraordinary document of bitterness and despair. Indeed, Wright sees Oliver's work as a psychological study, warning that "it would be tragic indeed that material relation to aesthetics should come under the racial or political hammer" (11). Even if this statement is a bit of calculated signifying, the general tone of the essay is bleak indeed.

In the early 1960s Wright's words came to us in cheap paperback editions, but they might just as well have been engraved on tablets of stone. Many of us took them as commandments.

Ron Karenga, for one, translated Wright's melancholy into the myopic diktat: "Black art must expose the enemy, praise the people and support the revolution." As far as the blues was concerned, Karenga announced that it was simply a backward and counterrevolutionary form (34). There the matter might have rested had it not been for the "British Invasion" of 1964.

British bands schooled in the music of Muddy Waters, Chuck Berry, and Little Richard were not content to stay on their green and ambitious isle but, in fact, began to assault the top-selling records charts in the United States. For example, Chapple and Garofalo report that in April 1964, "Beatles records were issued on five different [American] labels and they had twelve singles in Billboard's Hot 100, including the top five positions. For about three weeks the Beatles accounted for 60 percent of all singles sold" (249). Album sales were also affected, and in 1964 and 1965 only three African American artists were listed among the year's Top 50 albums (Chapple and Garofalo 249). As a matter of perspective, one may consider that only five records by white artists made the rhythm-and-blues Top 10 list before Bill Haley and the Comets appeared in 1955, paving the way for Elvis Presley and the creation of "rock and roll" as the marketing term for rhythm and blues played by white musicians (Kamin 186 n. 28, 179–80).

The British bands were direct imitators of the African American blues and rhythm-and-blues artists they had heard on records or in person (after the British immigration policies that prohibited foreign musicians from working there collapsed in 1956) and—galling to many black musicians—their success seemed to demonstrate what Chapple and Garofalo call "a racist pattern . . . whereby a style that is pioneered by black artists eventually comes to be popularized, dominated, and even defined by whites as if it were their own. That is the history of black music in American from ragtime to swing to jazz, and rock 'n' roll is no exception" (246).

Amiri Baraka, writing in Down Beat, greeted these groups with scorn, denouncing them as latter-day minstrels (Black Music 124, 205). Name-calling, of course, was not an adequate response.

In the contexts of race and money in the American music industry, imitation is more akin to theft than to flattery; but it is important to note that the advent of the British bands brought certain significant changes to the music itself.

Blues and R & B lyrics were songs about real-life situations intended for adult listeners—or, at least, those who thought they were grown. Within a decade, however, the transformation of R & B into rock and roll produced records designed for an adolescent market. As Baraka pointed out, the British bands wedded the energy of recycled blues songs "with the visual image of white American non-conformity" (*Black Music* 124). But at the point that the supposedly revolutionary potential of African American blues—no matter how repressed—becomes the stammering adolescent rage of The Who's "My Generation," Richard Wright's formulation is called seriously into question. As Nelson George perceptively noted regarding the 1965 Teenage Music Awards International (TAMI) concert, an audience that

> could cheer as Mick Jagger jiggled across the stage doing his lame funky chicken after James Brown's incredible, camel-walking, proto-moon-walking, athletically daring performance—greeting each with equal decibels—revealed a dangerous lack of discrimination. To applaud black excellence and white mediocrity with the same vigor is to view them as equals, in which case the black artist in America always loses. (George et al. 92)

That this 1965 audience of "young record buyers" was predominantly white could only be a notable fact if the observing intellectual critic proposes a difference in taste—and therefore in revolutionary potential—based on race or racial experience; and that, indeed, is what some Black Arts Movement theorists did; imagining a fuzzy neo-Marxist revolution by a proletariat that included only working-class blacks and, of course, themselves. A sort of bridge-building argument offered at the time—that the British groups represented an awakening of working-class political consciousness of their own—was problematic at best.

In a soundbite on *Anthology* (1996) Paul McCartney honestly identifies the Beatles of the early 1960s as "performers in the Liverpool dance halls." This is a band with a repertoire ranging from "Besame Mucho" done in the manner of Louis Prima to a valiant attempt to capture Little Richard's "hhhh-hoooo!" on the wonderful "I Saw Her Standing There"—probably the band's best song from that era. Indeed, *Anthology* is a CD that only a band that has already made millions—no, only a band that no longer exists—could afford to release. Nevertheless, it should be clear that the same Liverpool band represented something quite different to the habitués of the Hamburg nightclubs.

In Germany, the Beatles were dangerous and exotic. Similarly, Sonny Boy Williamson must have been apprehended differently in London in 1962 than he had been in the small towns around Helena, Arkansas, in the 1940s.

In order to make any claim that music records a specific social experience or is capable of social and political relevance, such considerations must be examined seriously.

According to Peter Wicke, the British Left saw rock music in the early 1960s as "an unappetizing expression of capitalism's ideological powers of temptation." Rather than being spokesmen for working-class youth, the Beatles—as seen by the London *Daily Worker* in 1963—were merely the most prominent victims of a system designed to "exploit job-hunting youngsters, being fed dreams of fame and money" (Wicke 102).

By way of contrast, for rhythm-and-blues entertainers such as Curtis Mayfield, Jerry Butler, Otis Redding, Joe Tex, and others, an articulate political consciousness was not something that a few overzealous critics merely overlaid on their work. Social comment—and protest—was at the center of many of their songs (see Guralnick 262–68, 315; Gilroy 140–41; and Redd 140). To those who believed such music was important, it was imperative in 1965 that they make a legitimate defense of its objectives.

Somewhat overstating his case, Michael Jarrett claims that Henry Osgood's 1926 volume, *So This Is Jazz*, provided the model for subsequent critical writing:

Instead of representing jazz as a site where experts *determine* what will and will not pass as genuine, he represented it as a site where experts accept responsibility for *distinguishing* the genuine from the counterfeit. (346)

What is useful about Jarrett's formulation, however, is that it actually describes what Black Arts Movement critics attempted to do with journals such as *The Cricket* (edited by Amiri Baraka and Larry Neal, ca. 1966–70) and *The Grackle: Improvised Music in Transition* (edited by Roger Riggins, James T. Stewart, and Ron Welburn, 1976–78). While *The Cricket* seemed to assert that critical expertise began with being black and politically astute, discussions in *The Grackle* moved steadily toward the idea that credentials for a critic of African American music should include the ability to actually play music.

The Black Arts Movement writers pursued this agenda via articles, liner notes on records, and a tremendous outpouring of poems celebrating the artists. Most interesting, perhaps, is that this campaign was an accurate reading and useful encouragement of rhythm-and-blues artists who—like Archie Shepp—had a definite political message in mind. Curtis Mayfield, James Brown, Roberta Flack, and many others were eloquent in their political statements both onstage and off—even if these statements did not always conform to the more radical views of Black Arts Movement intellectuals (see Van Deburg 212). Songs such as Curtis Mayfield's "Keep On Pushin'" and "We're A Winner," like James Brown's "I'm Black And I'm Proud," are obvious examples of what Askia Muhammad Touré was talking about. But a careful replay of records such as Brown's "It's A Man's World," Otis Redding's "Respect," and Joe Tex's humorous homilies such as "Hold On To What You Got" may be revealing. Songs like the O'Jay's "Backstabbers" are a return to the moral function of earlier African American music, including the blues that are often cautionary tales. In other words, the conversation among critics, artists, and record-buying African American audiences produced a decade of rhythm-and-blues records with a clear commitment to social commentary. The impact of the market on all of this activity might be gauged from the fact that Curtis Mayfield's "Freddie's Dead," a song intended to denounce heroin addiction, is part of the soundtrack of the 1972 movie *Superfly*, which portrays the experiences of a glamorized drug dealer (who, in Hollywood's usual and cynical equivocation, is attempting to extricate himself from the racket).

The Black Arts Movement focus on popular music was not the result of a simplistic identification but—as characteristic of most of the movement's activities—the result of an attempt to enter an ongoing intellectual conversation and challenge the dominant view. While its participants replaced the word *folk* with the Marxian vocabulary of *the people*, Black Arts Movement writers knew the history and uses of folklore study.

The eighteenth-century development of an interest in what was then called "popular antiquities" went hand in hand with the creation of the "noble savage" concept that simultaneously encrypted and distracted attention from the realities of European capitalist colonization of Asia, Africa, and the Americas. The scholars at the University of Edinburgh most actively involved in this early discussion included Henry Home, Lord Kames, and the economist Adam Smith (Whitney 338–40, 368–78).

While twentieth-century academics such as Alexander Haggerty Krappe,

acolytes of "universality," saw the folklorist's work as an attempt "to recon-
struct a spiritual history of Man, not as exemplified by the outstanding works
of poets and thinkers, but as represented by the more or less inarticulate
voices of the 'folk,'" the Harlem Renaissance writers took a much different
approach (Krappe xv, xvii; see also xx n. 2). Writing in Alain Locke's anthology *The New Negro* (1925), Charles S. Johnson explained:

> The generation in whom lingered memories of the painful degradation
> of slavery could not be expected to cherish even those pearls of song
> and poetry born of suffering. They would be expected to do just as they
> did: rule out the Sorrow Songs as the product of ignorant slaves, taboo
> dialect as incorrect English, and the priceless folk lore as the uncul-
> tured expression of illiterates. (297)

Johnson was quite aware, of course, that the Harlem Renaissance artists held
a different appreciation and, as he puts it, were "beginning to find a new
beauty in these heritages" (297). The most interesting example of this new
valuation may be Zora Neale Hurston's essay "Characteristics of Negro Expression" (1933), which celebrates the ways ordinary black people make sure
"there is an impromptu ceremony always ready for every hour of life. No little moment passes unadorned" (24).

Another rejection of the academic view of folklore came from a large
group of enthusiasts who thought that it represented the authentic record
and interpretation of political history as experienced by an oppressed proletariat. Consequently, among those involved with the promotion of American
folk music—as well as jazz and blues—were many political leftists, including members of the Communist Party USA (see Naison 211–13; Cruse
152–57). Expanding on the ideas that Alain Locke and James Weldon Johnson had popularized during the Harlem Renaissance, a writer in V. F. Calver-
ton's socialist-oriented *Modern Quarterly* stated in 1931:

> The Negro race has given this country its only pure folk music. In this
> material is good material for a national music, but not for the Cau-
> casian race to exploit as white men's music. (Qtd. in Cruse 153)

"But," notes Harold Cruse in *The Crisis of the Negro Intellectual*, "the Negro intellectuals [on the left] did not take up this issue, develop it, and fight it out

as their issue [because] cultural revolution was not the revolution the Communists were talking about" in the early 1930s (154).

By the early 1960s, Black Arts Movement writers—some of them under the personal tutelage of Harold Cruse—did, in fact, revisit this issue. Though their attempt to reconfigure the criticism of African American popular music as a political effort to be conducted by African American critics was unsuccessful, historian William L. Van Deburg has identified at least two clear lessons to be found in a study of this project. From the vantage point of the 1990s, says Van Deburg,

> However "modern" in appearance, much of black cultural expression remains grounded in traditional folkways and resonates with themes introduced by movement writers. (307)

Second, as any quick inventory of the contemporary music industry will demonstrate, the entire Black Arts Movement involvement with popular music supports the contention that "the mainstream will go to almost any length to synthesize or appropriate what Afro-America generates spontaneously within the racial soul" (Van Deburg 308).

Askia Muhammad Touré was the first writer to state quite clearly why the Black Arts Movement was so deeply involved with music. Black music, he wrote in "The Crisis in Black Culture," "is the core of our National Culture. Being the core or root, as it goes, so goes our spiritual/cultural life as a nation of people" (32). While Amiri Baraka and others were lauding the vision and accomplishments of avant-garde jazz musicians such as Sun Ra, John Coltrane, and Albert Ayler, Touré published an article in *Liberator* in 1965 that refocused critical and intellectual attention on black popular music. "Keep on Pushin': Rhythm & Blues as a Weapon" was a rhapsodic manifesto that—coupled with Touré's powers of personal persuasion and his wide-ranging lists of contacts and correspondents—resulted in a Black Arts Movement project to redefine our understanding of the art form most closely appreciated by the masses of African American people. Touré's article suggested that jazz—particularly bebop—was an authentic expression of black America's aesthetics and aspirations that had been "taken over by the racketeers and moved downtown into the clubs and bars of the middle-class pleasure seekers, away from the roots" (7). Rhythm and blues, then, was still a music that had not been misappropriated. Touré cites performers such as Johnny

Ace, Big May Belle, Little Richard, and the Orioles as authentic voices of the community:

> We didn't call it "culture" didn't call it "negro art," it was just OUR music ... OUR voice, OUR ritual, OUR understanding of those deep things far too complicated to put into words. (7)

Touré's echo of Richard Wright's term "the Forms of Things Unknown" resonated with intellectuals even as his pose of avoiding academic classification was designed to make his discourse acceptable to "just plain folks." There was, however, very little ambiguity about the reason why Touré believed that this music deserved the attention of the community's leaders and thinkers. While affectionately recalling the great performers and their songs, and noting the nascent political statements in the lyrics, Touré clearly expressed the importance of this art:

> Our main philosophical and cultural attitudes are displayed through our MUSIC, which serves as the ROOT of our culture; from which springs our art, poetry, literature, etc. Our creative artists—especially singers and musicians-function as PRIESTS, as PHILOSOPHERS of our captive nation; a holdover from our ancient past. (6)

Among the Black Arts Movement writers who further developed Touré's idea, Larry Neal was perhaps the most systematic. "Our music," he wrote in 1968, "has always been the most dominant manifestation of what we are and feel, literature was just an afterthought, the step taken by the Negro bourgeoisie who desired acceptance on the white man's terms. And that is precisely why the literature failed. It was the case of one elite addressing another elite" (*Visions* 21). The music—and, of course, Neal means the indigenous African American forms of jazz, blues, and gospel rather than the works of African American composers for symphonic presentation—surpassed this imitative literature because, he claims, "it has always operated at the core of our lives, forcing itself upon us as in a ritual. It has always, somehow, represented the collective psyche" (22).

Again, there is the clear suggestion here that Neal and Touré are carrying forward the analysis of the relation of literature and folk-based music in the African American community that is presented in Richard Wright's *White*

Man, Listen! There is ample evidence, however, that these ideas were also current among musicians at the time. In a 1965 *Liberator* interview with saxophonist Archie Shepp, Neal asked, "How can we make the art more meaningful to the people?" Shepp responds:

> I could advocate more musicians listening to rock and roll . . . we have to take advantage of a certain overview which we have that others don't have. Other people may have an intuitive working class instinct, but it takes the intelligentsia to give that order and make it meaningful.

Shepp is adamant about his desire for an explicitly political art, even in music:

> And we have to have musicians who can speak. That is important because things are too easily misconstrued. Things are too easily interpreted if left to the imagination. *Art must not be left to the imagination any longer.* (Neal, "Conversation" 24; emphasis added)

Archie Shepp's statement may, of course, give a good indication of why we are not always anxious to have the musicians speak. But his suggestion was taken seriously by the Black Arts writers who embarked upon the project of interpreting this art in the terms that artists such as Shepp intended.

Perhaps the most insightful of the Black Arts Movement music critics was Ron Welburn, a poet who was a regular contributor to *Liberator*. In "Dance and the New Black Music," Welburn not only offers the idea that African American popular music may have "revolutionary" political potential, he also gracefully interrogates the very premises of that belief. Rhythm and blues, he says, developed "as an urban by-product and extension of rural blues" just before World War II "and came into its own after bebop failed to fulfill itself as a dance music" (56). While Welburn was aware of the extramusical reasons for this—such as the configuration of jazz nightclubs during the 1950s as spaces for listening rather than dancing—he skips over the specifics to make a more generalized observation on how the music industry operates:

> Evolution in black music in the United States is actually something imposed on black expression by the conditions of Western . . . socializa-

tion and aesthetic philosophy as well as segregation and economic exploitation, all of which are foreign and distractive elements to the black experience. (56)

Welburn is concerned about a perceived opposition between highly intellectualized avant-garde jazz of the late 1960s and the popular rhythm-and-blues music of the same period. He does not dismiss the marketing categories by which the music is often defined, but suggests that the community itself can erase these artificial boundaries:

> The gap can be bridged. Junior Walker and the late Albert Ayler are illustrative cases. Despite whatever is going on in the black community, the community will respond, with a consistency that frustrates its nationhood-minded member/observers, to what it likes from audiovisual stimuli that are carefully projected into it by the cultural apparatus. It was speculated a few years ago that some wonderful black music could be created if the Junior Walker–[Albert] Ayler/[Pharaoh] Sanders styles were to merge. This they have done. (62–63)

Perhaps Maceo Parker's playing on some James Brown live performances might provide evidence for Welburn's statement. Nevertheless, he points out,

> What betrays the black community's distinctly American character is that it only responds favorably to the so-called "way-out" when packaged in a framework that is already familiar before it is made available for consumers. (62)

Welburn concludes that "no creativity in America will be recognized unless it compromises. Some artists compromise consciously; the sensibility of others with a particular feeling for the infectious makes them fair exploitation game" (64). While one may argue with that conclusion—based as it is on the complicity of the artists—it must be stated that Welburn may have been the only Black Arts Movement critic who clearly understood the extent of the music industry's powers of co-optation. In a *Liberator* article on Miles Davis, Welburn wrote, "The sad fact is that the music of a minority representation and experience in the U. S. which has subsidized the musical mainstream is still victimized by its context of presentation—i.e., it is still easy to make it a commodity with no returns" to the artists who create it ("Miles Davis" 21).

Musicians were certainly aware of the way that the market manipulated them. As his career opportunities declined in the late 1970s, Bo Diddley—acknowledged as a model by Elvis Presley, the Beatles, Rolling Stones, and others—complained, "I think one of the reasons I can't get a record deal now is that I'm not material to steal from anymore" (Tucker 20).

New and Old Gospel

The Black Arts Movement and Popular Music

If we believe the testimony of many who attended them, gatherings of poets in the 1960s were sometimes life-changing events. At Vancouver in the summer of 1963, Charles Olson read his epic Maximus poems during a conference at the University of British Columbia. According to Carol Bergé and others, that evening kicked off a decade-long battle between the energetic supporters of Olson's projective verse theories of "breath unit"–based oral poetry and the defenders of traditional English-language stanza forms and meters (Rifkin 19–20).

A few years later, in Nashville, a similar high-impact event shifted the course of African American literature.

Following a dramatic "conversion experience" at the April 1967 Fisk University Writers Conference, Gwendolyn Brooks's highly publicized—and somewhat exaggerated—adoption of a new "black sensibility" helped to legitimize the Black Arts Movement. As younger poets had been doing since about 1964, Brooks announced that she wanted her work to appeal directly to black folks in bars and barbershops, not just those in libraries or American literature classrooms.

"I want to write poetry—and it won't be Ezra Pound poetry, as you can imagine—that will be exciting to such people," she said, adding, "I don't see why it can't be 'good' poetry" (Kent 211).

It is fair to say that Brooks and the other poets envied and aspired to the central place of social acceptance and cultural importance that the black community accords to music—which is equally functional, welcome, and respected in the gospel tabernacle and the corner tavern.

The Black Arts Movement that flourished between 1965 and 1975 did not come out of a vacuum. As a direct result of the civil rights struggle of the

1950s, this artistic movement represented a further articulation of the actual desires of the African American people. As described in the *Norton Anthology of African American Literature*, "the Black Arts of the 1960s proposed to create politically engaged expression as a corollary to the new black spirit of the decade" (Gates and McKay 1796–97).

The precursors of that politically engaged arts movement are quite various, sometimes unexpected, but not difficult to identify. Peter D. Goldsmith, biographer of Folkways Records founder Moe Asch, credits musicologist Sam Charters with coining the term *social moralists* "to refer to the loose conglomeration of Americans at mid-century who supported racial equality, ethnic self-determination, and world peace" (8). This liberal, left influence certainly opened an area of public discourse that was inviting to the more impatient and intellectual youth of the late 1950s and 1960s.

It is true, however, that the question of the connection between art and politics may be more complex in regard to music than is the case with other artforms; possibly because music—unlike literature—often involves collective production and communal response. George Lipsitz has usefully pointed out that much music commentary suffers from a lack of attention to *agency*—which he defines as "the complex social interactions that create popular music" (*Time Passages* 101–2). In his book *Time Passages: Collective Memory and American Popular Culture*, Lipsitz suggests a method of examining such interactions, carefully and clearly explaining the basis of Mikhail Bakhtin's dialogic theory:

> Everyone enters a dialogue already in progress; all speech carries within it part of the social context by which it has been shaped. The dialogic model sees artistic creation as innately social and innately historical. (99–100)

We cannot approach a critical understanding of music by treating it as if it were an ancient vase in a vitrine—an artwork to be appreciated or analyzed apart from social context. In other words, Bach needs to be appreciated not only as pure sonic pleasure, but also in relationship to the composer's patrons—the Elector of Brandenberg and the subscribers to your local symphony orchestra—for those are the relationships that allow us to hear his music.

Similarly, the relationship of artists and audience, intellectual discourse and public mood regarding African American popular music in the 1960s and 1970s, represents a fascinating "call-and-response" that might teach us a great deal about the dynamics of *agency* as defined by Lipsitz.

Considering how the popularity of blues-influenced rock and roll affected white Americans in the 1950s, Lipsitz sheds light on the conundrum that faced Wright in the late 1930s. Discussing Little Richard's earliest "crossover" hit, Lipsitz writes:

> The Africanisms in "Good Golly Miss Molly" contain traces of America's most oppressive labor system—chattel slavery. But more than origins are at stake here. The musical figures and lyrical choices represented by those song forms testify to ongoing beliefs about music and society that form an important subtext of rock-and-roll music.
>
> Historically, Afro-Americans have treasured African retentions in speech, music, and art both as a means of preserving collective memory about a continent where they were free and as a way of shielding themselves against the hegemony of white racism.

Lipsitz adds, "As long as African forms contrasted with Euro-American forms, white racism was a particular and *contingent* American reality, not an inevitable or necessary feature of human existence" (*Time Passages* 111; emphasis added).

When Little Richard, Sam Phillips, and Elvis Presley, followed by the Beatles and a host of others to come, stepped through that firewall, it was as if they had actually touched the marrow of racial tradition. For theorists of the Black Arts Movement, however, the situation required careful analysis of what had happened and a plan for how to maintain control of African American cultural imperatives. Reading the literature of the day demonstrates that the situation was looked upon as a crisis. That mood is fully appreciated by Adolph Reed, Jr. when he directs attention to what he calls the irony of "the fact that the civil rights movement demanded for blacks the same 'eradication of otherness' that had been forced upon immigrant populations" ("Black Particularity" 65). On some levels, the Black Arts Movement was also a reaction to this aspect of the civil rights thrust. For Reed, this was misdirected energy:

> The nationalist elaboration of black power was naive both in that it was not sufficiently self-conscious and in that it mistook artifacts and idiosyncrasies of culture for its totality and froze them into an ahistorical rhetoric of authenticity. (68)

Reed considers what the Black Arts Movement eventually offered to be at best "an artificial particularity," an ultimately damaging "ideological construction of black uniqueness . . . projected universally in the mass market as black culture" and therefore commodified and trivialized (70). It should be remembered, of course, that the mainstream society had never had any difficulty commodifying a patently inauthentic and viciously demeaning version of black culture.

While severely criticizing its effect on American society in the 1990s, Reed is one of the few recent scholars who have made a serious effort to evaluate the historical impact of Black Power ideology and the activities—both cultural and political—of the Black Arts Movement era. But some scholars also took the matter quite seriously at the time. In 1968, sociologists Lloyd Miller and James K. Skipper, Jr., surveying the music programmed at Harlem's Black Arts Repertory Theatre/School, noted:

Without a "critical mass" of social protest of some form, few basic structural changes take place in society. The radical, yeasty element in the "new music" may be one manifestation of this "critical mass." (37)

Nor is it farfetched to imagine that young people in Harlem listening to "new music" by Albert Ayler or Sun Ra in the summer of 1965 might have later emerged as agents of significant social change.

It is important to recall that young people actually generated much social change in the decade of the 1960s. In 1969, Vincent Harding reminded *Ebony* magazine's readers that it was students who had pushed the civil rights movement

from schools to lunch counters, to buses, to beaches, to churches, to lonely struggles for registered voters and organized communities. At every level their movement was a significant challenge to the local keepers of the white way of life—and death. And the young people paid the often bloody price that such challenges always bring. (141)

Harding notes that the students did not stop there, but turned their attention as well to the curriculum they studied and the society they were being prepared to serve. This led to "a demand for a new definition of America and its institutions, a total re-evaluation from a Black perspective." This approach, says Harding, eventually widened into a skeptical examination of "America as a civilization, and by implication all of Western life and culture" (143).

The Black Arts Movement, firmly grounded in this radical critique, was an unusual avant-garde movement to the extent that it was perfectly candid and loud about its desire to *replace* the status quo, not merely challenge it. As Amiri Baraka explicitly stated in an address at the National Black Arts Festival in Atlanta in 1994, "We wanted a mass popular art" (Thomas, *Extraordinary Measures* 207). That mass popular art, they thought, would also be politically engaged; and the first place they looked for it was among jazz musicians.

Jazz, from its earliest appearance before World War I, developed simultaneously as a popular style but also as a serious and increasingly complex art form. In the 1950s, there was no question that the people who made the music—and those who loved it—shared an impressive level of sophistication. This jazz scene was the natural habitat of "the hipster." The personal flair, rapt attentiveness, and rapid response that the music seemed to require was also, for some, a model for an approach to life in general.

Burton Peretti suggests that the hard bop of the late 1950s was "presented to the public as an expression of angry black men," an expression of "militantly African-American identity" (131). Certainly, during those years, musicians such as Charles Mingus and Max Roach—though hardly representative of all hard bop players—were known for their political outspokenness on and off the bandstand.

Concerning political messages in his music, Max Roach made an interesting statement. "Two theories exist," he told Art Taylor in 1970:

> One is that art is for the sake of art, which is true; the other theory, which is also true, is that the artist is like a secretary whether he is a writer, a musician or a painter: he keeps records of his time so to speak. . . . My music tries to say how I really feel and I hope it mirrors in some way how black people feel in the United States. (112)

Roach also noted that he thought of the country itself as a work in progress because "it contains people from just about every part of the world. You'll find people of African, European, and Asiatic heritage and, of course, the people who are indigenous to the continent. But we were all thrown together to partake in this social experiment to see if human beings will be intelligent enough to live together" (Taylor 109). Interestingly, Roach's 1960 album We Insist! Freedom NOW Suite brought together musicians such as Abbey Lincoln, Coleman Hawkins, and Eric Dolphy, demonstrating that the political stance was not merely a generational characteristic. Jazz, though, was not the music that most black folks listened to.

But rhythm-and-blues music of the early 1950s was mostly about love, not social commentary; and some young people who aspired to become musical artists were unabashedly honest about what motivated them. As George Clinton, who founded the Parliaments in Newark in 1956 put it, "Frankie Ly-mon and them had the girls, man" (Mills et al. 2). Soon, Clinton and his homies were getting some attention, too. By the middle of the 1960s, how-ever, the mood of young black America had changed to the extent that even R & B had a political edge.

It is interesting to see how this happened.

A Renewed Testament

A primary source in the debates among Black Arts Movement intellectuals were the bold and important essays collected in Richard Wright's White Man, Listen! But while his discussion of what he called the "Forms of Things Un-known" seems to endorse African American folk culture as a wellspring of creativity and as potential political resistance to oppression, Wright's pref-ace to British musicologist Paul Oliver's impressive Blues Fell This Morning: The Meaning of the Blues offered a quite disturbingly different message. Reviewing the 350 songs discussed by Oliver, Wright made a peculiar observation:

> The most striking feature of these songs is that a submerged theme of guilt, psychological in nature, seems to run through them. Could this guilt have stemmed from the burden of renounced rebellious im-pulses?
>
> There is a certain degree of passivity almost masochistic in quality and seemingly allied to sex in origin that appears as part of the mean-ing of the blues. Could this emotional stance have been derived from a protracted inability to act, of a fear of acting? (Oliver ix)

A number of critics have considered Wright's ambiguous position regarding the black folk. William J. Maxwell, for instance, quotes Wright's deep expression of despair in Black Boy: "I saw that what had been taken for our emotional strength was our negative confusions, our flights, our fears, our frenzy under pressure" (Maxwell 177). From this perspective—Wright's view that "Negroes had never been allowed to catch the full spirit of Western civilization, that they lived somehow in it but not of it" (177)—it is easy to see the blues and other aspects of African American folk culture as symptoms of arrested development.

Perhaps following Wright's lead, Paul Oliver reported that he could find relatively few blues on protest themes, possibly "the result of the Negro's acceptance of the stereotypes that have been cut for him." He added:

As surely as the Southern White intends them to "keep their place" the majority of Negroes are prepared to accept it. They know that they cannot change the world but that they have to live in it. (Blues Fell 293)

As Oliver typed these words in London in 1959, listening to his antique 78s, he could not know that by the time Blues Fell This Morning hit the bookstores some of his readers would be African American college students busily engaged in sit-ins, walkouts, boycotts, and other militant manifestations of their impatience with the status quo of racial inequity.

Almost all of the pronouncements on music by Black Arts theoreticians might be seen as attempts to reconcile the contradictions raised by Wright's ambivalent position. Wright's apparent discomfort with some aspects of the blues was reflected in Ron Karenga's notoriously reductive statement, in a 1968 article in Negro Digest, that "the blues are invalid; for they teach resignation, in a word, acceptance of reality—and we have come to change reality" (36).

Musicians and other artists, of course, knew better than did the Maulana.

The rhetoric of resistance is complex and multifaceted; but it is not surprising that those who hold simplistic views of society may not recognize that fact. Musicologist Cynthia Mahabir, for instance, has pointed to Bessie Smith's recording of "'Taint Nobody's Business If I Do" and noted that the protest in the song is "mean and ironic in its humour." Mahabir also cites Baraka's play Dutchman, where the character Clay "observes the disdain and hatred he sees in Bessie Smith's music, which, he states, because it was cloaked in a race-filtered code, was not visible to Smith's white audience" (63).

Attempting to inspire an artistic movement that would attract a mass audience in the African American community, writers such as Baraka, Askia M. Touré, Larry Neal, Ron Welburn, Archie Shepp, and James Stewart proposed a role for music that would not be merely entertaining but expressive and instructive—embodying what they termed "a Black value system." Such an aesthetic had to move beyond "race-filtered" codes and bitter irony; and in order to make that move, it was necessary to reach beyond Richard Wright. It was also necessary to bring together artists working in what Black Arts Movement activists perceived as "artificially differentiated genres" such as jazz, rhythm and blues, and gospel music. In order to move beyond Wright, it was necessary to revisit the ideas articulated by Alain Locke in the 1920s and 1930s; and the work of imagining what was called "unity music" served to inoculate the aesthetic against the "elitism" some have found implied by Locke's ideas.

Sometimes it appears that the genres of popular music may be more a matter of marketing than anything else. Once established, however, the boundaries between these genres can be enforced in a number of ways—often to the detriment of talented musicians. Eric Dolphy, for example, had the reading and performance skills to play in the Los Angeles Philharmonic—a job he sought but did not get because of his color. Of course, Dolphy also had a solid foundation in bebop and R & B (Spellman, *Four Lives* 104, 126–27).

Thinking of music in terms of genre also narrowed the audience's access to joy. But these artificial categories could be difficult to overcome. There were even some advocates of "unity music" who felt—applying a standard of criticism more appropriate to the early days of *American Bandstand*—that jazz was too complex or self-consciously sophisticated to enjoy mass appeal (Scot Brown 139–44). Others thoroughly appreciated the power of R & B and wished to add it to the intellectualism of jazz. Still others took such characteristics in stride. As Scot Brown notes in *Fighting for US*, Amiri Baraka envisioned interconnections between all art forms that made the concept of "unity music" quite natural:

When describing an aesthetic blueprint for a Black nationalist societal alternative at a speech in San Francisco, Baraka did not differentiate between jazz and soul, asking the audience to "dig the idea of build-

ings that look like John Coltrane's solos or automobiles that look like
James Brown's singing." (Scot Brown 139)

Who's not going to say, "Hey, that's my car"?

It does not diminish Baraka as a critic to note that many of the ideas in his
music commentary came from the musicians themselves; he was not trying
to impose an aesthetic on the artists. And it is even possible to argue that as a
synthesis of jazz, blues, gospel, and R & B, the concept of "unity music" was
based on empirical evidence more than desire (Mackey 48). There was, perhaps, a moment when you could have heard what they had in mind.

Unity Music

There was a reason that "Green Dolphin Street" and "Laura" became bebop
standards. It is not mysterious at all. Otto Preminger's Laura (1944) and Green
Dolphin Street (1947) were hit movies. They are beautiful songs—especially so
the theme song "Laura" by David Raksin (1912–2004). The equally popular
song "Green Dolphin Street" is a wonderful example of the days when the
people who wrote background music for movies were expected to deliver
compositions of classical grandeur. The theme was actually treated like a
suite, orchestrated in many different configurations and played at different
tempi during the film it supported. Based on Ellen Goudge's best-selling romance novel, Green Dolphin Street is a two-and-a-half-hour emotional roller-
coaster starring Lana Turner. Juggling motifs of sibling rivalry along with the
trials and tribulations of being colonists in New Zealand, this movie really
might be at its best in the soundtrack by composer Bronslau Kaper
(1902–83). Across the country, for young jazz players like Arnett Cobb in
Houston or Eric Dolphy in Los Angeles, these were tunes that were often requested by customers—even as they were songs that offered great opportunities for improvisatory interpretations of melody and mood—both musical
and emotional.

About the same time that musicians were honoring requests for "Green
Dolphin Street," Charles Parker was playing a tune he called "Now's The
Time." With nonsensical dance instructions added, it became a mammoth
hit in 1948 for the Paul Williams band as "The Hucklebuck."

In fact, one old-timer told me, even in the 1960s some people knew that this was the problem with black folks period: The leaders hollered "Now's the time" and the people answered, "Yeah, to wiggle our behinds." In any event, blues and movie music were as much a part of the aural mix as classical themes were. All of this would have been in the repertoire of any jazz player who wanted to keep bread and wine on his table.

One might argue, in other words, that the visualized "unity music" had, in fact, existed more than a decade before the Black Arts Movement writers proposed their idea. In the great period, the 1940s, that marks the emergence of what is called rhythm and blues, bands like Buddy Johnson's and Louis Jordan's scored hits with all of the secular styles (Wald 195–96).

The rising artists were multitalented and musically well educated. The best young players moved easily through blues and jazz, ballads and dance tunes. Charles Brown, who had been a high school chemistry teacher in Texas, entered the Los Angeles music scene "after winning a talent contest in which he played Earl Hines's piano showcase 'Boogie on St. Louis Blues,' then encored with the 'Warsaw Concerto'" (Wald 198). Bluesman Lowell Fulson had a band in 1953 that included Ray Charles and Stanley Turrentine; and Turrentine later succeeded John Coltrane in Earl Bostic's touring group. In Los Angeles, Ornette Coleman and Eric Dolphy sometimes held the saxophone chair in Pee Wee Crayton's band. "Such artists played blues because it was in demand, and updated its style to suit the mood of the time," comments Elijah Wald (198).

There is a simple point to this long-winded story. As Eric Dolphy put it, "Music is music.'" When he was at the height of his wide popularity with black audiences, for example, Ray Charles proved that so-called genres like jazz, pop, or country and western are really meaningless labels when a genius is at the keyboard.

Black Arts Movement critics felt the same way about the arbitrary labels, stylistic divisions, and supposedly historical periodization applied to forms of African American musical expression. They envisioned art as more important than artifact and proposed a "unity music" that fully embodied the traditions of Africa as they have been reshaped in the Americas. To the fully conscious listener, spirituals, swing, gospel, or "insert-any-marketing- adjective-you-want jazz," were—as Miles Davis's tune declared—all blues. Never mind what bin it's in at the record store, they said, the music is all one music. Amiri Baraka suggested that it be called simply the music.

In a nation just as racist and even more materialistically acquisitive than the country described in DuBois's "Criteria of Negro Art," the Black Arts Movement theorists saw African American art as the *only* humane expression available. Though it was articulated rather bluntly by the young writers of the 1960s, neither DuBois, James Weldon Johnson, nor Alain Locke would have renounced this view. As early as 1897 DuBois spoke of the beauty of the spirituals and by 1925 Locke declared that "the song of the Negro is America's folk-song" and, noting brilliant concert hall performances of Paul Robeson and Roland Hayes, added:

> Negro folk song is not midway its artistic career as yet, and while the preservation of the original folk forms is for the moment the most pressing necessity, an inevitable art development awaits them, as in the past has awaited all other great folk music. (Locke, *New Negro* 208)

Locke found the spirituals flawless—words and music. "In this broken dialect and grammar," he wrote, "there is almost invariably an unerring sense of euphony." Looking at the lyrics included in Fisk University professor John W. Work's *Folk Song of the American Negro* (1915), Locke finds that "in many instances the dropped, elided, and added syllables, especially the latter, are a matter of instinctive euphonic sense" (204). There may be a hint of condescension here, but Locke's theoretical position is worth careful examination.

While Larry Neal sought to promote the Black Arts Movement as an "up from sidewalks" corrective to a failed elitist Harlem Renaissance, Ron Welburn emphasized the movement's continuation of Alain Locke's mission. Where Locke cautioned black artists against the easy popularity that might come from playing to stereotype, Welburn reads Locke's call for "a deeper jazz that is characteristically Negro" as an endorsement of the Black Arts Movement's peculiar flirtation with essentialism (Welburn, "Black Aesthetic Imperative" 149).

Again, Locke remains a moving target. It must be emphasized that his "characteristic Negro" is not an essentialist categorization. In "Legacy of the Ancestral Arts," an essay included in *The New Negro*, Locke wrote:

> What we have thought primitive in the American Negro—his naïveté, his sensationalism, his exuberance and his improvising spontaneity are then neither characteristically African nor to be explained as an ancestral heritage. They are the result of his peculiar experiences in

America and the emotional upheaval of its trials and ordeals. True, these are now very characteristic traits, and they have their artistic and perhaps even their moral compensations; but they represent essentially the working of environmental forces rather than the outcropping of a race psychology; they are really the acquired and not the original artistic temperament. (254–55)

This "made in USA" black person is precisely the figure that the Black Arts Movement was determined to replace with a more culturally aware, politically conscious, community-oriented individual.

In Locke's view, African American artists—especially in disciplines other than music—lacked a "racial idiom" based on African heritage (New Negro 262), and the Black Arts Movement theorists accepted this as their challenge. The arts would have to be made a little weightier. And "blacker." Criticism would have to be more astute. The community would need to understand that stylistic changes in black music were the result of economic and social forces—not necessarily benign—rather than a search for "aesthetic development" (Welburn, "Black Aesthetic Imperative" 134). Many writers warned against "progress" if that meant straying from the original and authentic strengths provided by an African worldview.

At the base of what we call culture, Ron Welburn posits the idea of a concept of man's place in the universe; and he is not averse to the word religion. Indeed Welburn sees African American culture as an attempt to conserve an African worldview "amidst continual harassments against religious expression" ("Black Aesthetic Imperative" 132). For Asian and African peoples, Welburn thinks, "culture does not change its aesthetic conception rapidly, if indeed at all." But European social and economic history embraced ideas of "aesthetic progress" because the "Western aesthetic sense fosters the notion of conquering the universe, not blending with it as you are, as one finds in the Eastern world" (134).

These fundamental Western intellectual positions influenced policies and actions and produced harmful results in the real world. Applying his analysis to the music business, Welburn described a critical establishment seriously at odds with the artists it reviewed. In the early 1960s—as "soul jazz" became popular, with sales edging into the zone of R & B and pop statistics—these critics "warned about the future of jazz, that the music would drift into commercialism" (138). As the music was gaining in popularity, "The critics called for 'art.' Integration was a dominant social theme at this time. Jazz, the music of the African-American, had become too black and exclusive" (139).

Welburn charges that the mainstream critics' self-serving critical disdain helped to replace "soul jazz" with bossa nova—an adaptation of Brazilian carnival music that was played in the United States primarily by white American jazzmen. The color scheme having been properly adjusted, "Bossa nova rapidly attained the commercialism jazz critics had warned about with soul jazz" (139). Naturally, those critics did not denounce this new style.

What is most impressive about Welburn's writing is his ability to conceptualize ideas and lead the reader toward an understanding of their practical impact. Like others, he also identified some problems that he was unable to solve. Grounded in the spirituals as it had to be, even the idea of "unity music" created some special difficulties. Many of the young radicals had a vision that included spirituality, but they were also hostile toward Christian heritage (Scot Brown 140–41, 199 n. 78). It became necessary to be creative. For example, Ron Karenga's seven Principles of Kawaida and the Kwanzaa holiday that ceremonialized them were intended to promote a deeper consciousness within the people. But it might also have revealed that the heritage we spent so much time talking about was more deeply seated than anyone understood. "Karenga's own oratorical style," writes historian Scot Brown, "captured the cadence of Baptist ministry and beckoned the call-and-response participation of his audience. Though dressed in African clothing, and occasionally accenting his lecture with a chant in Kiswahili, the transformed cultural nationalist leader frequently summoned the folkways of rural Parsonsburg" (36).

Dancing in the Street

If unity music was—and remains—an exciting idea, the practical question of how art forms viewed as escapist entertainment might carry important political content remains daunting. The brutally cynical cabaret of Weimar Germany offers one rather dispiriting model. Better is the socialist satire of the long-running British television comedy series *Are You Being Served*. But the question is how many in that program's huge American audience (and British viewers, too) are fully attentive to the class issues presented with such remarkable comity and wit.

John Coltrane in the 1960s was the majestic model for younger musicians (including James Brown's saxophonist Maceo Parker and rock bands such as the Doors). His album *A Love Supreme* (1964) suggested to A. B. Spellman that the saxophonist "sought a spiritual outlet in his music that would release the true universal god he sensed lurking beneath all the layers of confusion and hangups that American society stuffs all black folk with" ("Revolution" 88). While many jazz players—Pharoah Sanders with particular success—followed Coltrane toward explorations of instrumental virtuosity as well as spirituality, rhythm-and-blues artists seemed, at that same moment, to be moving toward more straightforward expressions of social commentary.

Music historian Robert Pruter has noted that "a new urgent sense of militancy and social concern was coming out of black America during the early 1970s and many rhythm-and-blues artists of the era were reflecting those feelings in their music" (*Chicago Soul* 307). There were, however, many different ways to express militant ideas. What is important also is that the audience and the artists were both in the same key. The 1970 hit "Seems Like I Gotta Do Wrong" by the Whispers, for example, is smooth, not strident—but its social commentary helped push it to the R & B Top 10 (M. Taylor 298).

Nobody saw me walking
And nobody heard me talking
Seems like I gotta do wrong, gotta do wrong, gotta do wrong
Before they notice me.

According to Suzanne E. Smith, Motown artists such as Marvin Gaye wanted to produce "songs with a social consciousness," and Gaye himself thought that Martha and the Vandellas somehow "captured a spirit that felt political" in songs like "Nowhere To Run" or "Quicksand" (170). Gaye may or may not also have intended to express something of a political spirit in "Dancing In The Street," a song he cowrote with Ivy Hunter and William "Mickey" Stevenson in 1964 (Reeves and Bego 104).

Writing in the *Liberator* magazine in October 1965, Askia Touré called "Dancing In The Street," that summer's hit by Martha and the Vandellas, "the Riot-song that symbolized Harlem, Philly, Brooklyn, Rochester, Patterson [*sic*], Elizabeth" (quoted in S. Smith 171). Touré also cited Sam Cooke's "A Change Is Gonna Come" as emblematic of the anger and righteousness of "Black revolutionary action."

Martha Reeves, of course, said she was only singing about dancing. But urban disturbances continued, and 1967 was a particularly dramatic year. For a few weeks, urban riots seemed to follow Martha and the Vandellas on tour. As she recalled, "With the Detroit riots, the Vietnam War, and the sexual revolution underway, the world was a different place, and the music that defined it changed as well" (Reeves and Bego 147, 153). Suzanne Smith points out that while Berry Gordy and his executives at Motown Records "had no interest in producing music that might evoke revolutionary sentiments or provoke radical action," they could not, of course, control how a song might be "implicated in the racial politics of its time" (171–72).

By 1970, though, Motown had established a label called Black Forum that issued poetry recordings by Langston Hughes and Margaret Danner, and albums of speeches including Stokely Carmichael's *Free Huey!* And Martin Luther King's *Why I Oppose the War in Vietnam* (S. Smith 230–31). Under the direction of Ewart Abner, former president of Chicago's Vee-Jay label (where Curtis Mayfield and the Impressions got their start), Black Forum made a small contribution to the political discourse of the Black Arts Movement with Baraka's album *It's Nation Time*, the label's most politically advanced and artistically excellent offering.

In addition to Black Forum releases—and despite what Suzanne E. Smith describes as the company's "desire to avoid conflict and maintain its commercial appeal with the widest possible audiences" (232)—by 1970 Motown joined other labels in producing records with decidedly militant political messages. An interesting conjunction of technological innovation and the nation's political mood influenced these developments. The popularity of eight-minute-long 45 rpm singles by rock groups such as the Byrds and by the militantly surrealistic Bob Dylan opened the space for Norman Whitfield to write "Ball Of Confusion" (1970) for the Temptations and provided a precedent for Curtis Mayfield's "If There's A Hell Below (We're All Gonna Go)" (1970) on his own newly launched Curtom label. As early as 1966, however, Stevie Wonder led the Motown artists in releasing serious—and very successful—records that "addressed social and political issues" directly (S. Smith 232).

There was also another important mode of militancy at work. One thrust of the Black Power political program was the black bourgeoisie's dream of establishing economic parity with their white counterparts. The very existence of black-owned companies such as Chicago's Vee-Jay Records and Detroit's Motown represents entrepreneurial expression of this desire. *Ebony* writer Alex Poinsett included such efforts under the rubric "the economics of liberation," a category that explains bandleader George Clinton's otherwise curious comments about his career motivations. At the end of the 1960s, Clinton claimed to be enamored of Jimi Hendrix's music; but his statements reveal that he was more interested in how an idiosyncratic black artist like Hendrix had attracted a white pop audience (see Mills et al. 29–33). But the music that Clinton's group began creating in 1969 was a far cry from the usual "crossover" material. As Clinton stated, "We were playing stuff in the studio that the engineer didn't even want his name on" (Mills et al. 37). It is in this context, strangely enough, that Clinton declares that the album *Chocolate City* (1975) "was straight-out commercial" (87).

James Brown and Motown inspired Clinton, not only in terms of their music but also as organizational models. "I looked at Motown as a group," he said. "Not as a company with a lot of producers, but as one big group." As a result, his own activities with Parliament and Funkadelic at one time included five interlocking groups with five separate recording contracts (Mills et al. 110–11).

At the beginning, the P-Funk was not only uncut—it was *real*, not metaphoric. In the early 1970s at Detroit's United Sound facility, Clinton and his men would actually spend days in the recording studio, rehearsing and taping around the clock, sleeping in shifts on the floor. Vocalist Dawn Silva, of the Brides of Funkenstein, recalled

> the first time I went into the studio with P-Funk. There was this horrible smell, and I remember George saying that he wasn't going to take a bath until he finished the album. And I guess the rest of the P-Funk members decided they weren't going to take one either. And after a while, you got kind of used to it. Took a while, but we got used to it. (Mills et al. 92)

These sessions were marathons of creative improvisation. The musicians would try out ideas until something sounded promising. They had lots of blank recording tape and plenty of time.

"George would usually be sitting behind the board," remembered drummer Jerome Brailey, and we'd be in the room playing and jamming—me, Bootsy [Collins], Garry Shider—and George would say, "Let's take that one," and we'd take it, you know. And then he'd come up with the lyrics. (Mills et al. 93)

Though Clinton was not immediately successful with his crossover strategies, he was not the only artist considering such questions.

Some observers thought that commercial success in music followed a predictable pattern. If success for white artists often depended upon their mastery of a watered-down black style, their black counterparts seemed tangled in a double-helix (or, more accurately, double-bind) version of this process. Pointing out how successive waves of white pop and rock acts had marginalized popular African American artists in the late 1960s, Jet magazine's Chester Higgins thought that James Brown, the Temptations, and Ray Charles had successfully "ripped off some of the white sound, strained it through the Black experience and through pure chutzpah (guts) and with some luck pushed their way into the money circles and, thus, towards a brighter, more profitable future" (60).

Higgins, an avid bebop fan, was much less appreciative of developments on the jazz scene. "Miles Davis, Julian (Cannonball) Adderley and the Ramsey Lewis Trio," he wrote, "to name a few, bending with the times, began issuing a mish-mash blend of Black jazz and white rock that keeps them in the forefront of the so-called 'New Sounds of Music' in the '70s" (60–61).

While critics such as Higgins—and from the other end of the spectrum, Askia Touré—made it appear as if the goals of "economic liberation" and "committed, revolutionary, and didactic art" might be ultimately incompatible, some marvelous musicians demonstrated that this was not so.

Julian (Cannonball) Adderley

Things look different to different people. Many of us, thinking of the period 1965 to 1975, recall our excitement about Albert Ayler and Sun Ra. Discographer Chris Sheridan, however, reminds us that this was also a period "when the whole of jazz seemed to become driven by or submerged under commercial considerations" with record companies belching out so-called jazz-rock albums and travesties such as *Basie Plays the Beatles*. On the other hand, Frank

Kofsky carefully documented the economic hardships and indignities that John Coltrane, Cecil Taylor, and Archie Shepp were forced to endure in 1965 and 1966 (142–44). While some critics extolled their artistry, the people who ran the business of nightclubs, record companies, and musical instrument factories made musicians' lives difficult. Such people, Shepp bitterly told Kofsky, "are only the lower echelon of a power structure which has never tolerated from Negroes the belief that we have in ourselves, that we are people, that we are men, that we are women, that we are human beings. That power structure would more readily dismiss me as an uppity nigger or a fresh nigger than to give me my rights" (144).

Often, the business people of jazz excused their behavior by claiming that the music lacked an audience. Anyone who needed a demonstration that jazz could indeed reach a large audience could turn to Julian "Cannonball" Adderley. In 1960, his band's recording of pianist Bobby Timmons's "Dis Here," taped live at San Francisco's Jazz Workshop nightclub, was released as a 45 rpm single on the Riverside label, enjoyed heavy jukebox attention, and sold 50,000 copies, while the entire album sold 80,000 (Sheridan xxx, 80–82; Kennedy and McNutt 118). In 1967, "Mercy Mercy Mercy," released as a single by Capitol Records, made the Top 10 pop charts with sales of 750,000 copies in six months, while the album sold 200,000 (Sheridan 174). It's probably not necessary to add that Adderley's level of success was matched by negative remarks from some critics—despite the fact that, for musical quality, *Down Beat* gave the 1967 album its top rating of four stars (Sheridan 174).

A confusing whirlwind of public acclaim and disparagement by jazz critics because of his popularity greeted Adderley's first album in 1959. Producer Orrin Keepnews was understandably annoyed when *Down Beat* reviewed the album only several months after its release with an article that "began with a negative reference to its reported sales of close to 30,000 copies" (Sheridan 227). By comparison, in 1956 Bill Doggett's now classic R & B instrumental "Honky Tonk" sold 4 million copies, while Bill Evans's 1957 debut Riverside jazz LP sold 800 (Kennedy and McNutt 67, 116).

Julian Adderley (1928–75)—like James Weldon Johnson before him—was a high school teacher in Florida before moving to New York and assuming a full-time performing career in 1955. Adderley had a pleasant demeanor but was outspoken about his beliefs and, at one time, wrote a column for the *Amsterdam News* in New York. He was also a savvy businessman and controlled much of his recording activity through his company Junat Productions (Sheridan xxxiii, 150). In a sense, Adderley's hit records matched the ideas about the black aesthetic articulated by Larry Neal. Critic Ron Welburn commended his music's "rural frame of reference" as a breath of fresh air for urbane jazz fans. "Like Jean Toomer's *Cane*," Welburn wrote, Adderley's hits "evoked a nostalgia for the South in people not even born there—a racial memory. The music re-enforced images and memories of 'the country'" ("Black Aesthetic Imperative" 131). The Adderley Quintet's crowd-pleasing "down-home" sound featured easily recognizable "soul" elements such as call-and-response and melodies borrowed from the blues and the black church.

Despite *Jet* magazine's inaccurate characterization of his music and the reason for his popularity, Adderley could not be easily dismissed. The group's work pays no attention to "jazz-rock." Adderley's own playing, and the presence in his bands of Yusef Lateef or Charles Lloyd, players with unimpeachable avant-garde bona fides, provided evidence for A. B. Spellman's assertion that one result of the 1960s "black revolution in sound is that the old rigid dichotomy between the so-called mainstream and avant garde has been diminished" ("Revolution" 89). "The secret of Cannonball's success," wrote Chris Albertson in *Down Beat*, was his use of "highly melodic material imbued with more than a hint of Gospel and blues flavoring" (12).

Interestingly enough, anyone who wanted to make a case for biology or ethnicity as cultural determinants would have had to confront the fact that soulful Adderley themes such as "Mercy Mercy Mercy" and "Country Preacher" were contributed to the band's book by Josef Zawinul, an Austrian immigrant trained at the Vienna Conservatory, who tuned his Wurlitzer electric piano to produce a sound somewhat akin to the "fuzztone" used by some rock guitarists.

Chris Sheridan describes "Country Preacher," which spent two full months on the *Cash Box* R & B charts in 1970, as "an audible sociological record" as well as a jazz recording (Sheridan 191; Albert and Hoffman 3). Introducing the composition, recorded at a Chicago church, Adderley commented on his admiration for saxophonist Ben Branch, leader of the choir and band sponsored by Reverend Jesse Jackson's Operation Breadbasket organization. Branch, an influential figure in his own right, had been with Reverend Martin Luther King, Jr. in Memphis on the day that King was assassinated (Cohodas 287). "Country Preacher" is a remarkably *live* recording with all of this talk and crowd noise almost ostentatiously included in the final product. There is a feeling of authenticity that is far from the "laugh tracks" broadcast with television situation comedies.

Other musicians understood the power of that lively ambiance. Marvin Gaye's "What's Going On" (1971) is the aural equivalent of trompe l'oeil painting. The first time I heard the record, playing on a jukebox, I walked into a dimly lit bar—attracted by the noise—and was shocked to find no one there except the bartender, a waitress, and one other lonely customer. More recently, hip-hop posses or mobs replicate call-and-response excitement by filling the stage with their own members. An actual audience is good but isn't really required. Adderley's live recording was not, however, his original plan. Riverside Records producer Orrin Keepnews had promised to record Adderley's band when it was ready, and he recalled that, due to logistical problems, he was "forced into making an on-the-job-recording that became the career-shaping blockbuster simply entitled *The Cannonball Adderley Quintet in San Francisco*" (Sheridan 165). That 1959 location recording was the precedent for *Jazz Workshop Revisited*, which generated a hit single with trumpeter Nat Adderley's "Jive Samba," an item that spent ten weeks on the Cash Box R & B chart in 1963. Beginning just before Christmas 1966, "Mercy Mercy Mercy," on the Capitol label, took Adderley back to the Cash Box charts for eighteen weeks (Albert and Hoffman 3).

Clearly, much of the effectiveness of "Country Preacher" depends upon the powerful response of the audience present when the performance was recorded. And just as clearly, Adderley's introductory remarks confirm that he was consciously striving to produce the fusion of what he himself called "jazz and other black-oriented music" that the theoreticians of the Black Arts Movement had referred to as "unity music" (Albertson 13; P. Wilson 13).

Curtis Mayfield

Perhaps the most influential example of "unity music" is the work of Chicago-based singer, guitarist, and composer Curtis Mayfield (1941–99). Like George Clinton, Mayfield's career began in the doo-wop era of the early 1950s, when he established a group called the Impressions. Writing in the British magazine *Juke Blues*, Robert Pruter attributed much of the Impressions' early success to a "three-part switch-off lead derived from the black gospel church that proved to be a fresh sound in rhythm and blues." Mayfield and the Impressions produced fifty singles that reached the R & B best-seller charts, but their unique sound was complemented by sometimes unexpectedly complex and politically resonant subject matter. Says Pruter, "With 'Keep On Pushing' (1964), which only intimated at black social concerns, and with 'We're A Winner' (1967) and 'Choice Of Colors' (1969), two overtly message songs, Mayfield was in the forefront of evoking the spirit of the times as African Americans inspired by the civil rights movement were asserting themselves as equal human beings in American society" ("Curtis Mayfield" 66).

The message, in fact, was the source of the group's appeal. As Mayfield told Michael A. Gonzales, "When the Impressions came onstage we didn't have any fancy dance steps and that's not what the audience expected. They knew that with the Impressions all they had to do was listen" (233).

But you had to listen to some strong lyrical didacticism. "Choice Of Colors," for example, questions the characteristic responses of some politically active people. Just as Reverend King protested the use of skin color to restrict the life options of African American people, Mayfield warns against adopting a similar bias:

How long have you hated your White teacher?
Who told you you love your Black preacher?

As many of the movement leaders kept repeating, what was important was deeds, not words, character, not complexion. While the music surrounding him quotes the melody of "We Shall Overcome," Mayfield promises

A better day is coming
For you and for me

if the people will trust their leaders.

"Profoundly political but never dogmatic, Mayfield's music responded to the call of the moment," writes Craig Werner (140). Mayfield's records were clearly dance music, says Werner, but the songs "entered a heated debate on the meaning of Black Power that would rage on through the seventies. Whether Black Power was a slogan, a program, an impulse or even a disaster wasn't always clear" (141).

What is certain is that Mayfield's participation in that debate was not accidental. While some might continue to emphasize the tension between political activists and some elements of the church establishment, Werner emphasizes their connections. Mayfield's powerful "Keep On Pushing," says Werner, "infused the movement with the sounds Mayfield remembered from his grandmother's Traveling Souls Spiritualist Church" (118). Werner sees the politics of the civil rights movement grounded in "the gospel vision." Mayfield's magnificent 1965 hit "People Get Ready"—like good church music—"pours a healing vision over a nation poised on the brink of chaos" (Werner 125).

In addition to his accomplishments as a singer, songwriter, and arranger, Mayfield established his own publishing firm when he was twenty and became the first African American artist to own a successful record company when he founded Curtom Records in 1968. His first solo album, *Curtis*, released on the Curtom label in 1970, remained on the R & B charts for forty-three weeks, reaching number one, and spent forty-nine weeks on the pop charts (Nathan 8). With the exception of the lovely ballad "The Makings Of You," the album was entirely devoted to "consciousness raising" lyrics. Mayfield's stark and bitterly beautiful "The Other Side Of Town" commemorates the notoriously crime-ridden Cabrini-Green district on Chicago's North Side where he grew up (Pruter, *Chicago Soul* 76). One can survive bad situations with principles intact.

"We The People Who Are Darker Than Blue," the album's best work, presents a serious, straightforward request for collective self-examination. Mayfield's lyric is delivered in the conversational tone of the blues set against lush, inventive orchestration.

> Pardon me, brother
> As you stand in your glory
> I hope you don't mind
> If I tell the whole story

An up-tempo middle section, organized around bongo drums, redirects attention toward African cultural identity, not as a treasure lost, but as a heritage retained—just as Alain Locke or Larry Neal would have it.

Deep Coda

The Black Arts Movement era was full of astonishing events. When John Coltrane appeared with Thelonious Monk in 1957, A. B. Spellman said, "It was apparent to everyone who hit the Five Spot that summer that the music would never be the same" ("Revolution" 88).

As Allen Ginsberg was fond of saying, "When the mode of the music changes, the walls of the city shake" (40).

Today you can often hear Monk's brighter moods used as "bumper music" or "buttons" between news segments on National Public Radio's *All Things Considered*. One afternoon in September you could also hear a few bars of Sun Ra's "Lights On A Satellite" used for the same purpose.

Some observers would suggest that the explosion of literary activity—and the avid response of readers—during the Black Arts Movement era certainly set the stage for today's best-selling African American writers. For example, *Not A Day Goes By*, E. Lynn Harris's saga of dazzlingly glamorous gay, bi, and confused characters, registered number two on the *New York Times* best-seller list the week of its publication (Bashir 18). Some might also draw a direct line from Gwendolyn Brooks's dream of a popular poetry to the concert stages filled with squads of swaggering and bellowing young men, baggy-pants comedians wearing garish rings and diamond-encrusted bracelets—the latest signs of make-believe insurrection thrown up by "hip-hop culture." Clearly, the meaning or ultimate value of these developments requires serious ongoing investigation.

W. E. B. DuBois bluntly asserted in 1926 that all art is propaganda; but there is no need to defend works that sink beneath an overload of didacticism. James Brown's "Don't Be A Dropout" is lame when compared to "Try Me" or the hypnotic "Papa's Got A Brand New Bag"; but the song represents Brown's understanding that the age demanded an explicit commitment to racial progress and an unequivocal stand against the forces of social dysfunction. There is also, of course, the old business of "deeds, not words." Beyond singing lyrics such as "I'm Black and I'm Proud," James Brown used his star status itself as a political statement. "Between '66 and '68," writes Cynthia Rose,

As he became a kind of folk politician, Brown's world exploded. He leased a private jet and had "Out of Sight" emblazoned along its fuselage. He endorsed the mainstream NAACP . . . onstage at the Harlem Apollo. He flew to the hospital bedside of James Meredith when that Civil Rights integrationist was shot on his March For Freedom in Mississippi. He played shows which benefited SNCC—Stokely Carmichael's radical Student Non-Violent Co-Ordinating Committee—as well as Dr. King's more moderate Southern Christian Leadership Convention [sic].

James Brown in the 1960s, says Rose, "was a one-man demonstration of how deep the codes and meaning of music run in black America, how they evoke an historic continuum, how they can move to unite" (55–56).

The era of the Black Arts Movement was a period when the African American music and art matched the mood of the people. It is sufficient to note that the best songs of the era demonstrated that the lyrics of popular music can be about more than an obsessive focus on the condition of our hearts, pocketbooks, or buttocks.

How You Like Me Now?

Rap and the Legacy of the Black Arts Movement

"Which is more threatening to America," asks novelist John Edgar Wideman in response to the most recent conservative attack on rap music, "the violence, obscenity, sexism and racism of movies and records, or the stark reality these movies and music reflect?" ("Tough Talk" 32). Some years earlier, Time Warner chairman Gerald Levin "described rap as a legitimate expression of street culture which deserves an outlet" (Zoglin 37). Both of these views are, of course, legitimate; but there is another side to the issue.

Rap is a unique adaptation of older African American folk forms such as the once all-male narrative entertainments called "toasts" and the topical "signfyin'" allusive style that informs much of the performance-oriented poetry of the Black Arts Movement of the 1960s and 1970s. The element of signifyin' always, of course, produces an ambiguous "double voiced" discourse. That fact, however, is not an adequate defense for those whose works promote destructive behavior.

In the past few years there has been a heated public controversy in the United States about rap music, particularly the genre known as gangsta rap, with accusations that it promotes antisocial behavior. Certainly, the debate itself has promoted the visibility of many political figures in their election campaigns. Nevertheless, the national controversy about rap mirrors a similar conflict in the African American community and is not entirely cant. The so-called culture wars in the United States must also be viewed in the context of a very high urban crime rate and horrifying statistics of juvenile homicide.

It is just as important to consider rap and its development within the context of African American cultural transmission.

In his poem "Subtitles," the brilliant young poet Paul Beatty subtly addresses how adolescent bravado, Japanese action movies, the Santa Ana wind (known to cause damaging wildfires in California and, according to folk wisdom and Johnny Carson monologues, short-tempered or foolish behavior), and easy access to real semiautomatic guns have combined to make the Los Angeles ghetto a dangerous place:

living the project credo

bushido walks
loaded gals talk
a moviemakin' ghetto akira kurosawa
waits patiently for the santa anas
to blow in the heros direction

(38)

Many feel that, in addition to vividly expressing the views of Paul Beatty's generation, rap is—like the items included in his poetic montage—just one more element that promotes violence and real deaths.

A further complication in this debate, for both scholars and citizens, is the fact that a cultural manifestation such as gangsta rap has been promoted (hyped by both the media and the academy) as a genuine oppositional force, the self-proclaimed artistic voice of the black community but—naturally—is also marketed to "mainstream" youth (though there seems to be little inquiry regarding its effect, injurious or otherwise, on that demographic group). When this is taken into account it becomes clear that the issue of gangsta rap in the black community has little to do with whether or not "rap is one *of* the most important shapers of popular styles globally" (Baker, *Black Studies* 63). The issue is who, or what institutions, determine, influence, or ultimately control what is to be perceived as the normative voice *of* the African American community. Are black youth socialized by churches or record companies? Intellectuals or ersatz artists? Teachers or truant officers? Are the community's values and traditions transmitted by its elders or by marketing executives at corporations?

In the late 1930s sociologist Ruth A. Inglis noted that the question regarding the relationship between art and society usually is answered either by what she called the *reflection theory* or the *social control theory*. The first view is that art reflects the norms, values, and ideology of its society; the second is that art shapes society. "Unlike the Reflection Theory," she wrote, "the Social

Control Theory vests in literature an active role of leadership. Proverbially, the pen is mightier that the sword" (528). Those who would censor art that they don't like usually claim to believe the social control theory, while the artist, defending her work, stands behind the statement that it merely reflects "reality." The recent controversies about rap and heavy metal music are classic examples of this scenario.

Important in both theories, of course, is the idea that the artist is not entirely autonomous; that art is always involved in a proactive or reactive, visionary or documentary relationship with other nonnative structures and is, therefore, an important "socializing code." For the artists of the Harlem Renaissance and the Black Arts Movement—both efforts to utilize the arts in the service of political advancement for African Americans as a group as opposed to the mere advancement of artistic careers—this relationship was a central concern. "The force of what we have to say," wrote Black Arts Movement spokesman Larry Neal, "can only be realized in action" (Visions 20).

Alain Locke would have agreed. The Harlem Renaissance artists worked with "the consciousness of acting as the advance guard of the African peoples in their contact with Twentieth Century civilization; [and] the sense of a mission of rehabilitating the race in world esteem" (Locke, New Negro 14). The Black Arts Movement accepted and modified this mission but focused it closer to home. "The poet," Neal wrote, "is a key bearer of culture. Through myth, he is the manipulator of both . . . the collective conscious and unconscious." He added a comment that is often overlooked, but is of great importance in understanding the Black Arts Movement's unique combination of political activism and avant-garde aesthetics:

> The suppression of art, whether it occurs in the West or in the East, whether it occurs under capitalism or socialism, is detrimental to man's spiritual survival. Without spirit, the substance of all his material accomplishments means essentially nothing. (Visions 54–55)

The art of the Black Arts Movement posited a moral advantage; poets acknowledge that the African American community was—and remains—impoverished, while denouncing affluent white America for its soullessness. If the civil rights marches demonstrated innate courage and dignity, then the Black Arts Movement sought to instill pride in black America through a program of rigorous self-criticism. Unlike the leaders of the Harlem Renaissance, participants in the Black Arts Movement were less concerned with how others viewed African Americans than what we thought of ourselves.

After the Deluge

> Ain't nobody really influenced me, you know what
> I'm saying; just tired of being on the streets. You
> know what I'm saying?
> —Biggie Smalls

The dance floor of an inner-city or suburban nightclub is not a frivolously chosen site for a discussion of normative issues in art. In fact, as far as African American cultural imperatives are concerned, there is no site more perfect. Hands going this way, feet moving, your hips inscribing an eccentric orbit within this circle of motion, ears alive, the beat pounding against your chest—more than your mind is engaged. You will understand, more clearly than from any historical lecture or teleological exegesis, exactly what George Clinton means:

> Here's the chance
> to dance
> my way
> out of this constriction
>
> Feet, don't fail me now!

("Loopzilla")

Metaphor aside, as far back as slavery, dances paralleled religious services as a normative institution in the African American community (Hazzard-Gordon 64). Dance and music also represent the most communal forms of art and, as such, became an important focus for an artistic movement explicitly concerned with shaping the community's self-image.

In spite of their preoccupation with race, it is apparent when reading the theoretical essays of the Black Arts Movement writers that they generally accepted the definition of culture offered by Michel Leiris:

Whereas race is strictly a question of heredity, culture is essentially one of tradition in the broadest sense, which includes the formal training of the young in a body of knowledge or a creed, the inheriting of customs or attitudes from previous generations, the borrowing of techniques or fashions from other countries, the spread of opinions through propaganda or conversation. (21)

"Music," wrote poet Askia Muhammad Touré in 1969, "is the core of our National Culture. Being the core or root, as it goes, so goes our spiritual/cultural life as a nation of people" ("Crisis" 32). Amiri Baraka eloquently reiterated that idea in a poem:

The nation is like our selves, together
seen in our various scenes, sets where ever we are
what ever we are doing, is what the nation
is
doing
or
not doing

("The Nation Is Like Ourselves" 265)

Touré developed the idea into a strategy for communicating the ideas of the Black Arts Movement to the community. In an article in Liberator he suggested that the economics of the music business in the 1950s had alienated jazz musicians from the black community with the result that "Rhythm and Blues was the only music left to sing out the aspirations and soul stirrings of Black folks uptown" ("Keep On Pushin'" 7). He attempts to show how popular R & B and even Motown songs reflect a note of social protest and "revolutionary" consciousness. While many young African Americans in the late 1960s were reading Frantz Fanon and the Muhammad Speaks newspaper, many others were not. Thus Touré's purpose—and that of many other Black Arts Movement poets—was to reveal that a revolutionary message already was present in the songs that the masses were listening to. A logical next step, which did not take long in coming, was to produce a type of poetry that shared the same medium. By the 1970s local collaborations of Black Arts Movement poets, actors, and musicians across the country had spawned a national market for poetry recordings. The LPs of the Last Poets were probably the best-selling examples of this surprising development, but Amiri Baraka's own Motown Records release, *It's Nation Time*, was undoubtedly the best. Certainly, there is a direct connection between the popularity of these records and the emergence of rap at the beginning of the 1980s.

Though his name is frequently included in lists of supposed influences on contemporary rap artists, poet Gil Scott-Heron's recordings are almost sui generis. He did not always recite his poems, he also sang them; but Scott-Heron's lyrics are literary, a far cry from the standard love odes of pop songs or even the more complex situations of Broadway musicals. "Pieces Of A Man," for example, describes the depression of a man whose unemployment makes it impossible to provide for his family. Scott-Heron's performance style is reminiscent of Latin jazz vocalists such as Willie Torres or Ismael Quintana, and his musical colleagues included Ron Carter, Hubert Laws, Brian Jackson and other top jazz instrumentalists.

Scott-Heron's well-known "The Revolution Will Not Be Televised" is a complex text. It is not so much antitechnology as it is a critique of the media attention that produced success for the civil rights movement's moral indictment of racism and widespread public disgust with the war in Vietnam. Scott-Heron was also aware that, after the establishment had mastered the medium, it could also be used to trivialize political issues. The Black Arts Movement was not, however, antagonistic toward all media. There was a great deal of excitement regarding Marshall McLuhan's unconventional book *The Medium Is the Message,* which (to underscore McLuhan's theoretical position—and make more money) had also been issued as a CBS record album. The Black Students Union at San Francisco State College, in fact, composed an ambitious plan calling for the movement to progress beyond pamphlets and poetry broadsides to film and other media. The poet's phonograph records were, however, the only successful realization of this proposal.

Poets who recorded in a more traditionally literary style than Gil Scott-Heron—though they also used musical settings—included Sarah Webster Fabio, whose album *Boss Soul* includes "Work It Out," a poem presenting a catalog of popular dances as a means of criticizing political apathy in the black community.

The Last Poets produced extraordinary works that appealed as both performances and poetry. Suliaman El Hadi's rhythmic "Before The White Man Came" and "Blessed Are Those Who Struggle" are effective political statements; and Jalal Nuriddin's talent ranged from the dramatically cautionary "O. D." to an amazing interpretation of the iconography of the United States currency. "E Pluribus Unum" utilizes both historical fact and creative etymology to create a type of signifyin' political rhetoric popularly received in the community:

> Thirteen stripes in the original flag!
> Thirteen demons from the Devil's bag!
> Thirteen berries and thirteen leaves!
> Thirteen colonies of land-grabbing thieves!

(Last Poets 58)

Although the Last Poets were politically astute and sophisticated in their analysis, they were not always paragons of good taste. "This Is Madness" by Omar Ben Hassen, for example, attacks political ignorance in the African American community by vilifying a number of civil rights leaders while praising Malcolm X and John Coltrane. Much of the satire, however, is vulgar and off-color.

Gylan Kain, on his album *The Blue Guerilla* (1971), showed no concern at all for good taste even if he reinforced the fact that the black church in the South is the matrix of African American culture and art. "Clouds" is a nonsensical parody of the Gospel according to John delivered in the style of a country preacher—but without the nostalgic respect that informs James Weldon Johnson's *God's Trombones*. "Loose Here" also draws upon Kain's childhood church experiences but segues into an imitation James Brown vamp that is actually a "collage" of Brown's song titles and expressions—verbally "sampled" and surrealistically garbled.

Baraka's *It's Nation Time*, performances of poems published in *Spirit Reach* and *In Our Terribleness*, was the best work to emerge from the poetry and music collaborations of the period. "Answers In Progress," originally published in *Tales*, is recited here, set to beautiful jazz with African drum choir. "All In The Street" begins with the familiar inner-city ghetto landscape and, like a luminous John Biggers painting, transforms the expected scene into a grand and magical vision:

> Imagine these streets
> along which walk some people

some evolved humans
look like *you*
maybe walk, stroll
rap like you

What Baraka conjures then is the vision of the black community in-formed, and thereby transformed, by the Black Arts Movement's revitalization of self-knowledge and pride in a heritage that antedates and will survive racism and economic oppression:

Look at
the clothes on the women the
beautiful sisters clothed in supernew
silk looking spun diamond lace
the geles and bubas of a future generation

But future generations would not wear geles or bubas. The mood of African American youth in the 1990s was cogently expressed by poet Kevin Powell: "All i want is the opportunity to have an opportunity/where does one run to when stuck in the promised land?" (263).

Rap, Amiri Baraka told Henry Louis Gates, Jr., "was a continuation of the Black Arts Movement. But since the corporations have co-opted it they have substituted gangster thuggery for political defiance. This is always the form used in low commercialism—the substitution of titillation for political content" (Gates, "Sudden Def" 40).

Whether rap is a direct descendant of the Black Arts poets who made records in the early 1970s or not, it is a fact that by the end of the decade the cry of the masses changed from "What do we want? FREEDOM!" to "We want the Funk!"

It is useful to analyze the record that began the rap movement in 1979. The Sugar Hill Gang, considered by "authentic" hip-hop pioneers to have been impostors, produced an interesting dramatic novelty in "Rapper's Delight" (T. Rose, *Black Noise* 55–57, 195 n. 78). The three rappers, like professional wrestlers, are clearly performing stereotyped roles: Master Gee, "the baddest rapper there ever could be," is a ladies' man; Big Bank Hank, lacking Master Gee's matinee idol handsomeness, flaunts his wealth ("I got bodyguards, I got two big cars"), advertising for gold diggers. But he also promises to mistreat any greedy girl who applies. Wonder Mike, the interlocutor, only adds a silly scatological story about poverty. This record became an instant hit because it was clearly a risqué entertainment, a "party record" in the tradition of Redd Foxx's X-rated comedy albums of the 1950s. Though widely criticized on the street as lacking in originality and authenticity, the Sugar Hill Gang offered an excellent performance of the rhythmic rap style of oration; indeed, their recording is something like a classic anthology of street corner rhymes (George et al. 14). The question of whether the rappers were extemporizing these rhymes or presenting a memorized text is as irrelevant in this context as it would be in terms of Illinois Jacquet's solo on "Flying Home" on any given night. The audience knows that initially it was an improvisation and demands only that it be delivered now with the same intensity.

If "Rapper's Delight" established rap as novelty, "The Message" (1982) by Grandmaster Flash and the Furious Five is a somewhat different story. Here was a brilliant performance of a text with a clear and unequivocal political statement; a protest of social conditions in the urban ghetto and also an unflinching indictment of the culpability of some residents. If anything deserves to be seen as a continuation of the aesthetic of Black Arts Movement poetry, it is this recording. But this direction—and this level of political clarity—was soon quite overwhelmed by the grittier subgenre called gangsta rap.

In 1985, critic Nelson George saw rap as positive social commentary, "a challenge to the pop music mainstream to realize that life is about a lot more than silly love songs" (George et al. 26). But a bunch of ruffians were waiting in the wings, ready to bum rush the show. Soon the "pep rally" started by the Bronx disc jockeys in the 1970s began to sound like a locker room.

The issue of profanity in lyrics is important but ultimately of secondary concern; what is critical is the *value system* that is communicated in songs and poems. One difficult aspect of the development of gangsta rap is the shift from the Sugar Hill Gang's obvious satire to a pretense of factual documentary.

Ice T, an eloquent member of the Los Angeles street gang the Crips, got his first show business opportunity in a low-budget film called *Breakin'*.

I tried to rap like New York rappers. I was trying to rap about house parties. "I'll rock the mic, I'll rock the mic, I'll rock the mic." My buddies were all laughing. They would say to me, "Ice, how are you gonna rap about rocking the house parties? We rob parties, man. We're the niggers who come in and say, 'Throw your hands in the air, and leave 'em there.'" (Ice T and Siegmund 96–97)

Ice T responded by writing a song about a gangbanger pursued by the police, "Six In The Morning." "This song," he writes, "was the beginning of what is now called Gangsta Rap. I call it reality-based rap, because I used real situations and brought them onto the records" (97). Willie D of Houston's Geto Boys reports a similar viewpoint:

We can't candycoat an unsweetened world. . . . We got to be true to ourselves. We cant talk about this shit and then go home and go to Fifth Ward and hang with our buddies and think everything's supposed to be fine. Cuz we'd get our ass kicked, cuz we wouldn't be real anymore. (Criss 10–11)

What counts, of course, is what an artist actually has to *say* about this "unsweetened world."

There is a difference between the use of bellicose metaphors to boast of one's prowess and cleverness as a rapper and the "praise songs" glorifying armed robbery and murder presented by the Notorious B.I.G., whose CD *Ready to Die* (1994) is equally remarkable as an aural drama (something like a movie without pictures) and as an example of degradation set to music. Certainly the world was a rougher place in the 1990s, in some respects and in some places, than it used to be; and, of course, young people always believe that the stakes are higher than ever. Yet it makes sense to attempt comparative judgments.

Grand Puba's dialogue with Mary J. Blige on "What's The 411?" recalls the much more light-hearted banter of Otis Redding and Carla Thomas on "Tramp," a 1960s rendition of bluesman Lowell Fulsom's warning about materialism and deception. Similarly, Salt 'N' Pepa's catty challenge on "I'll Take Your Man" parallels Naughty By Nature's celebratory "O.P.P.," and each song adds a competitive edge to the type of sexual play earlier extolled in the Isley Brothers's "Love the One You're With"—an energized R & B cover of Stephen Stills's hippie "free love" anthem. But MéShell N'degé Ocello's advice, "If you think he's your boyfriend, well, he wasn't last night," is more complex, a more clearly "double voiced" instigation. Is it a complaint about male duplicity, or a caution against female naïveté? Or, again, yet another testimony to the age-old game of sexual and status competition that thrives in all classes, climes, and cultures?

The point is that one must be quite careful in deciphering many rap performances, as with any poetry. Even the violent encounters on the streets described in the Geto Boys's "My Mind's Playing Tricks On Me" (1993) can be interpreted as metaphoric since the song is essentially a dream narrative:

I live by the sword
I take my boys with me everywhere I go
Because I'm paranoid
I'm looking over my shoulder,
Peeping 'round corners
My mind's playing tricks on me

Or maybe not.

Contending Forces

Maybe one day, when I'm old, people will finally realize that rap is here to stay, just the same way people are beginning to realize—thirty years later—that James Brown is a genius.
—Kurtis Blow

No one, in all of human history, has ever learned anything from someone else's mistakes. Nevertheless, the alarm expressed about rap in some sectors of the African American community is justified if one accepts the idea that, in addition to the pure profit motive, "there is the agreement—or at least the determination—of all executive authorities [in the culture industry] not to produce or sanction anything that in any way differs from their own rules, their own ideas about consumers, or above all themselves" (Horkheimer and Adorno 122).

This amounts to something much less than a "conspiracy theory"; rather, it raises the question of how a community of consumers can exercise a similar authority according to its own values. It is not merely a matter of the reality that "the audience will not watch what it does not want to see" (Twitchell

24), it is a matter of contending forces and competing interests focused here on taste in music but implying more far-reaching normative issues within and beyond the community. Tricia Rose has noted the complexity of some rap lyrics and deplored the fact that "attacks on rap music offer profoundly shallow readings of its use of violent and sexist imagery" ("Rap Music" 154). James B. Twitchell has also argued convincingly that the use of violence in popular culture is not only often ritualistic but serves as one of our "socializing codes"; that while literary and "contemporary televised displays of preposterous violence seem subversive, they are ultimately dramatizations of moral order" (31–32, 262). Aggressive reenactments, like the grim world depicted in gangsta rap videos, are seen by Twitchell as therapeutic ways to "pantomime what is too traumatic to learn by actual experience." In effect, "Such fables all reiterate the more—get back in line" (262).

Certainly this effect might be operative for most of the millions of consumers of gangsta rap records; there are, after all, only one million people in prison in the United States. But it is not a very comforting thought when measured against recent statistics of violent acts involving automatic weapons in black urban neighborhoods. Beyond that, the question remains regarding who controls the socializing codes that affect African American youth. Does the community take its cues from its elders, or are youth socialized by their peers under the direction of record and video producers?

There really are three considerations here. One is economic, another is political, and the third concerns cultural heritage and its transmission—but none of these is quite as simple as first appears. In *Afro-Blue: Improvisation in African American Poetry and Culture*, Tony Bolden reminds us of Louis Althusser's statement that "the class that controls the wealth in society also exercises power over the distribution of cultural production" (19).

Bakari Kitwana, who served a stint as editor of *The Source: The Magazine of Hip-Hop Music, Culture & Politics*, a glossy monthly journal popular with young African American readers, was not a gangsta rap fan even though many of the artists responsible for it are profiled in the magazine's pages. In Kitwana's opinion, the dominance of gangsta rap and its meretricious worldview serves to "reinforce the white economic elite's agenda for Blacks, demonstrating the depth of Black economic and political powerlessness." Beyond that, it suggests to him that "Black Americans as a people, regardless of their economic status, are not respected by the collective white economic elite" (*Rap* 58). Kitwana has pointed out that several years ago Time Warner,

MCA Records, Capitol-EMI, Polygram, Sony Music, and BMG bought out or became distributors for the independent American labels that initiated rap, and these international corporations, as Horkheimer and Adorno predicted in the 1940s, effectively decide what becomes available to the consumer (20–21). In other words, black youngsters in schoolyards might make up poems about what they consider important, but corporate executives decide which of those poems will be impressed into millions of CDs or widely advertised via video interpretations treated to "heavy rotation" on MTV.

This economic situation also has a direct effect on whatever the potential of rap music might be to make political statements. Rap artists committed to exploring that potential have found an intelligent and energetic critic in Tricia Rose. Her *Black Noise: Rap Music and Black Culture in Contemporary America* is a lucid and serious discussion of the music. "Rap," says Rose, "is a technologically sophisticated project in African-American recuperation and revision" (185). Even a black nationalist writer such as Del Jones notes, "The ignorant have said for years that we can't deal with the English language. Rap slaps that lie down. The masters of Hip-Hop turn the English language inside out, upside down and spit life into it" (116). There are indeed rap artists such as Public Enemy, A Tribe Called Quest, KRS-1, Arrested Development, and the Watts Prophets who attempt to provide the social critique that was a goal of the Black Arts Movement. In New York, Last Poets member Omar Ben Hassan serves as mentor to Cutthroat, a rap group that attempts to redirect the gangsta scenario into a more "positive" cautionary mode. None of these artists, however, seem to have achieved the level of political analysis exemplified by the Last Poets, let alone Amiri Baraka in his "nationalist period." Furthermore, Paul Gilroy's assertion that even the most dedicated cultural critic "cannot keep up with the sheer volume of hip-hop product anymore" (200) becomes ominous when one notes that most of this volume is not promoting political activism or even the elevation of consciousness beyond a disgruntled "consumerism by any means necessary."

The plethora of records and videos that exploit and glorify guns and easy money, does, in fact, reflect a disturbing reality. As the Notorious B.I.G. puts it on "Things Done Changed":

Back in the days
The parents used to take care of us

Look at 'em now
They even fucking scared of us

And, in an article in *The Source*, Kitwana noted:

Never before in Black American history have Blacks been involved in inflicting such an extraordinary amount of lethal violence on one another and never have Black youth wreaked so much havoc on the psyche of older adults in the Black community to the point where they fear young people. It is a fear . . . which is contributing greatly to a generation gap that seriously interrupts the flow of cultural knowledge from one generation to the next. ("Are You Ready" 57)

Kitwana's point is precisely what is most vexing about the emergence of the latest gangsta rap style.

"Our music," wrote Larry Neal, "has always been the most dominant manifestation of what we are and feel" (*Visions* 20). Indeed, if the poets of the Black Arts Movement offered a prototype for a performance-oriented poetry that addressed the real life, social, political, and economic issues faced by the African American community, then it can be said that the emergence of gangsta rap—a perversion of the impulse to positive social criticism—demonstrates the interruption of cultural transmission noted by Bakari Kitwana.

Askia Muhammad Touré would remind us that Larry Neal saw art as "the harbinger of future possibilities." In 1968 Neal stated, "Afro-American life and history is full of creative possibilities, and the movement is just beginning to perceive them" (*Visions* 20, 78).

"The Black Arts Movement," says Touré, "was intended to be a *spiritual* path. The misogyny and violence in Rap is disturbing. This is *not* our tradition; it may be the tradition of the *lumpen*, perhaps, but not the Black working-class or middle-class."

Touré is aware that commercial interests have helped to determine not only what rap product gets the most attention, but also how the literature of the Black Arts Movement itself has been interpreted. "Political hacks messing over literature," he said in a recent interview, "got more mainstream attention than the poets who were serious about what we were doing."

It should be clearly understood that, for Touré and others, the serious business of the Black Arts Movement had much less to do with rhetorical attacks on the white American capitalist "power structure" than with the attempt to take control of the means of cultural transmission in the African American community; to be able to determine which images would function as the "socializing code" in that community. If anything, the current controversy regarding rap demonstrates that the Black Arts Movement did not succeed in that campaign.

Askia Muhammad Touré is not, however, discouraged. "We have to support that which is supportable and critique that which is abominable," he says. "But it's up to us to straighten this mess out."

APPENDIX

Don't Deny My Introduction

An Unfinished Essay by Lorenzo Thomas

[At the time of his death, Lorenzo Thomas had just
begun a preface to this volume. Though he was not
able to complete it, the following lines belong here
and are offered as Lorenzo left them.
—Aldon Lynn Nielsen]

The day John Handy III came to town, he was featured on television. But if
you were down you had a chance to meet him at the Dom on St. Marks Place,
the truly happening place those days on New York's Lower East Side. Everyone was excited by the advance word; and, when it hit, the new LP from Columbia Records delivered a knockout punch.

It was a Sunday afternoon and in the Dom's cool, dark basement lounge
Handy and cellist Calo Scott sat up on the bar and played some thoughtful,
beautiful music. Intricate and soulful. These were artists with total mastery
of their instruments and men completely delighted with the opportunity to
share their gift with each other. They stopped just in time for everybody in the
place, a couple of dozen folk, to help John watch himself on TV. It was a family affair.

So, too, was Slug's in the Far East, with sawdust on the floor and the lingering perfume of stale beer and whiskey. Slug's was a dump—a neighbor-
hood dive on tenement-lined East Third Street that had somehow been transformed into a major venue for the most exciting new jazz in New York City.
The sounds were big but the place was small. When Sun Ra's Arkestra played
there, musicians and their arsenal of instruments filled the tiny stage and
much of the audience space, too. But Slug's was still the best place to be on
that night in October when the clocks changed back from daylight savings
time and you got an extra set with the cats blowing like madmen.

It was also the place where, on a less auspicious night, an angry woman
shot Lee Morgan down. This, too, though tragic, was a family affair. The bril-

liant and beautiful trumpeter was the demented woman's husband and what went down that night had long before been recorded in ancient song.

Slug's was nothing if not authentic. So tragedy might come by one night . . . just as on other nights one could sit at the end of the bar and still be close enough to watch what exactly Rahsaan Roland Kirk was doing with his unique reed instruments, just as one could watch "a bad new white boy" named Eddie Daniels accepted into the fraternity of the militant New York jazz players based strictly on his ability to play the music—tested this very night onstage at Slug's before your ears.

Greil Marcus's *Invisible Republic* and works by Bill Barlow and Elijah Wald have suggested that musicians come in more than simple varieties of amateur and professional—one picking and singing on the front porch, the other surrounded by an entourage on a private jet en route to a one-night stand in a football stadium in New Guinea. This can get tricky. Blues is indeed music of the people, but Elijah Wald has argued that "the main purveyors of blues music were professional musicians" who "worked in all sorts of settings from formal concert halls to street corners, to places that few of us would think of as performance venues. A good example is the local barbershop" (43).

In an isolated rural area, the only musicians who could devote themselves full time entirely to their art would be those who were physically unfit for other types of labor. Music for most would be an avocation. Local celebrity would be awarded those with great talent—but the audience would know about their shortcomings and character flaws, too.

We are told that in traditional African societies there was no strict line drawn between secular and religious music; that this distinction was made in what is now the United States with the emergence of blues and jazz. As Tony Bolden puts it,

> The glaring contradictions between the brutal realities of sharecropping and the angelic images of the hereafter become too explosive to be housed inside the church; so the blues packed a box lunch, as it were, and left. (48)

The didacticism of the Black Arts Movement was not new. Nor did it simply vanish as the movement lost energy in the 1980s.

Richard "Dimples" Fields scored a hit with a record that seemed to in-

clude all of the new required elements: social commentary, rhythmic recitation, street slang, as well as Fields's magnificently pure high tenor singing.
"If It Ain't One Thing It's Another" (1982) presents a poetic inventory of a
working-class young man's hardships, not least of which is "an ugly woman
named Sadie / claiming that she's having my baby." But the list of social
problems and personal shortcomings provokes a recollection of Grandma's
words of wisdom, and suddenly the audience must absorb a full-scale ser-
mon with texts drawn from Matthew 20, Daniel 2, and Revelation 21. "Keep
on dreaming a big dream," says Fields; but his proposal for making that
dream come true is based on prayer, not political action or even conscious-
ness-raising beyond the scope of being "brought up the right way." Nevertheless, the shape of the work clearly demonstrates how widespread the idea
of social commentary in African American popular music had become.

It might also be said that the didactic mode in African American art has
sometimes appeared in the guise of political comment, sometimes as social
directive, sometimes as religious exhortation—always however, an important element of the artistic motive.

How then do we account for the authenticity of the folk? Sterling Brown,
speaking of blues songs written by professional poets and musicians, offers
clarity. Regarding the phonograph album *Southern Exposure* (1941), Brown
writes: "Blues composed by Waring Cuney and Josh White on poverty, hard-
ship, poor housing, and jim crow military service, come from conscious pro-
pagandists, not truly folk. They make use of the folk idiom in both text and
music, however, and the folk listen and applaud" (*Son's Return* 262). This is
tricky business.

Recognizing the importance of African American art does not—and
should not—mean merely recasting it in European trappings. Recently, for
example, Bucknell University professor Rick Benjamin has argued that Gunther Schuller and others erred in orchestrating Scott Joplin's *Treemonisha*
(1911) for the symphonic ensemble used in European grand opera. According to Benjamin, Joplin's innovation included "stripping opera of its
grandiosity" by featuring music intended to be played by the standard the-
atrical pit orchestra of the 1890s touring circuit. In Benjamin's view, Joplin's
Treemonisha is valued for invention, not hybridity.

"Although the score is deeply rooted throughout in the syncopated
rhythms, harmonies and instrumental sonorities of ragtime," wrote *San
Francisco Chronicle* reviewer Joshua Kosman, Joplin "uses those elements to

create set pieces that go far beyond the conventions of the [popular] style." But Joplin clearly is not attempting to copy or parody his European contemporaries writing in the operatic mode.

It is obvious today that the popular music of the entire planet is based on American music. But this is not necessarily what Alain Locke and others envisioned at the beginning of the twentieth century when they compared black folk forms and the magisterial symphonies of Bach, Brahms, and Beethoven.

"Integration of African music into Western music was not an additive process," writes Stephen Brown:

> it was nothing at all like nineteenth-century composers making use of folk tunes—nothing at all like Dvořák's symphony "From the New World." It involved instead a reordering of musical priorities and a reimagining of how rhythm works. (13)

It is also to be noted that the existence of a term such as "the popular music of the world" depends upon economic and political relationships that have made music a commodity, a product of culture—or perhaps "cultural product"—controlled by a few corporations with international marketing capability.

Peering through a socialist lens, Paul Laurence Dunbar, W. E. B. DuBois, and James Weldon Johnson might have seen something like this coming, but if they did, they might not have been happy about it.

Black Arts activists seemed unaware that they had inherited the very didacticism they denounced in their elders. This was complicated by the fact that, as self-styled bohemians, the artists were anxious to denounce the socioeconomic status quo along with bourgeois concepts of life. Many of these artists, of course, were drawn from the ranks of future Sunday school teachers who have always been attracted by rhetorical conceits, poetry, and the arts. Thanks to McCarthyism they had at best a smattering of Marx.

Works Cited

Adorno, Theodor W. "On Jazz." 1936. Trans. Jamie Owen Daniel. *Discourse* 12 (Fall–Winter 1989): 45–69.

Adorno, Theodor W. "Perennial Fashion—Jazz." 1953. *Prisms*. Trans. Samuel and Shierry Weber. Cambridge: MIT Press, 1983. 119–32.

Albert, George, and Frank Hoffman, comps. *The Cash Box Black Contemporary Single Charts, 1960–1984*. Metuchen, N.J.: Scarecrow Press, 1986.

Albertson, Chris. "Cannonball the Communicator." *Down Beat*, January 8, 1970, 12–13.

Allen, Norm R., Jr., ed. *African-American Humanism: An Anthology*. Buffalo, N.Y.: Prometheus, 1991.

Armstrong, Louis. *Satchmo: My Life in New Orleans*. New York: New American Library, 1954.

Aschoff, Peter R. Rev. of *Blues off the Record: Thirty Years of Blues Commentary*. By Paul Oliver. *Living Blues* 69 (1986): 40–41.

Ayler, Albert. "To Mr. Jones—I Had a Vision." *Cricket* (1969): 27–30.

Baker, Houston A., Jr. *Black Studies, Rap, and the Academy*. Chicago: University of Chicago Press, 1993.

Baker, Houston A., Jr. "Handling 'Crisis': Great Books, Rap Music, and the End of Western Homogeneity (Reflections on the Humanities in America)." *Callaloo* 13 (Spring 1990): 173–94.

Baker, Houston A., Jr. *Modernism and the Harlem Renaissance*. Chicago: University of Chicago Press, 1987.

Baker, Ray Stannard. *Following the Color Line: An Account of Negro Citizenship in the American Democracy*. 1908. Williamstown: Corner House, 1973.

Balliett, Whitney. *Jelly Roll, Jabbo, and Fats: 19 Portraits in Jazz*. New York: Oxford University Press, 1983.

Baraka, Amiri. "Answers in Progress." *Tales*. New York: Grove, 1967. 118–21.

Baraka, Amiri. *The Autobiography of LeRoi Jones/Amiri Baraka*. New York: Freundlich, 1984.

Baraka, Amiri. "Black Art." *Black Magic: Collected Poetry 1961–67*. Indianapolis: Bobbs-Merrill, 1969. 116–17.

Baraka, Amiri [LeRoi Jones]. *Black Music*. New York: William Morrow, 1967.

Baraka, Amiri [LeRoi Jones]. *Blues People: Negro Music in White America*. New York: Morrow, 1963.

Baraka, Amiri. *Daggers and Javelins: Essays 1974–1979*. New York: Quill, 1984.

Baraka, Amiri. "Expressive Language." The Poetics of the New American Poetry. Ed. Donald M. Allen and George Butterick. New York: Grove, 1975. 373–77.

Baraka, Amiri. Interview by Michel Oren and Lorenzo Thomas. Houston, June 21, 1984.

Baraka, Amiri. It's Nation Time. Motown/Black Forum B457L.

Baraka, Amiri. "Jazz and the White Critic." 1963. The LeRoi Jones/Amiri Baraka Reader. Ed. William J. Harris. New York: Thunder's Mouth Press, 1991. 179–86.

Baraka, Amiri. [LeRoi Jones]. "The Jazz Avant Garde." Metronome, September 1961, 9–12, 39.

Baraka, Amiri. The Music. New York: William Morrow and Company, 1987.

Baraka, Amiri [LeRoi Jones]. "The Myth of a 'Negro Literature.'" Home: Social Essays. New York: Morrow, 1966.

Baraka, Amiri. "The Nation Is Like Ourselves." 1970. Postmodern American Poetry. Ed. Paul Hoover. New York: W. W. Norton, 1994. 265–67.

Baraka, Amiri [LeRoi Jones]. Preface to a Twenty Volume Suicide Note. New York: Totem/Corinth, 1961.

Baraka, Amiri. Spirit Reach. Newark, N.J.: Jihad Productions, 1972.

Baraka, Amiri. "State/meant." 1965. The Le Roi Jones/Amiri Baraka Reader. Ed. William J. Harris. New York: Thunder's Mouth Press, 1991. 169–70.

Baraka, Amiri, and Fundi [Billy Abernathy]. In Our Terribleness: Some Elements and Meaning in Black Style. Indianapolis: Bobbs-Merrill, 1970.

Barlow, William. "Looking Up at Down": The Emergence of Blues Culture. Philadelphia: Temple University Press, 1989.

Bashir, Samiya A. "On the Shelf." Black Issues Book Review 2 (September–October 2000): 18.

Basie, Count, as told to Albert Murray. Good Morning Blues: The Autobiography of Count Basie. New York: Random House, 1985.

Bastin, Bruce. Red River Blues: The Blues Tradition in the Southeast. Urbana: University of Illinois Press, 1986.

Beatty, Paul. Big Bank Take Little Bank. New York: Nuyorican Poets Cafe, 1991.

Beeth, Howard, and Cary D. Wintz, eds. Black Dixie: Afro-Texan History and Culture in Houston. College Station: Texas A & M University Press, 1992.

Berger, Morroe, Edward Berger, and James Patrick. Benny Carter: A Life in American Music. 2 vols. Metuchen, N.J.: Scarecrow Press, 1982.

Beverley, John, and Marc Zimmerman. Literature and Politics in the Central American Revolutions. Austin: University of Texas Press, 1990.

Bodenheim, Maxwell. "Jazz Kaleidoscope." Bringing Jazz! New York: Liveright, 1930. 35–42.

Boggs, Vernon W. "Musical Transculturation: From Afro-Cuban to Afro-Cubanization." Popular Music and Society 15 (Winter 1991): 71–83.

Bolden, Tony. Afro-Blue: Improvisation in African American Poetry and Culture. Urbana: University of Illinois Press, 2004.

Botkin, B. A. "Self-Portraiture and Social Criticism in Negro Folk-Song." 1927. The Politics and Aesthetics of "New Negro" Literature. Ed. Cary D. Wintz. New York: Garland, 1996. 230–34.

Bratton, William. "A Note on Doc Pomus." Antaeus 71–72 (Autumn 1993): 149–52.

Brewer, J. Mason. "The Mother's Last Works to Her Son in the Country." Encyclopedia of Black Folklore and Humor. Ed. Henry D. Spalding. Middle Village, N.Y.: Johnathan David, 1978. 150.

Brown, Marion. "Improvisation and the Aural Tradition in Afro-American Music." *Black World*, November 1973, 15.

Brown, Scot. *Fighting for US: Maulana Karenga, the US Organization, and Black Cultural Nationalism.* New York: New York University Press, 2003.

Brown, Stephen. "Third Sound of the African Empire." *Times Literary Supplement*, August 6, 2004. http://www.timesonline.co.uk/tol/incomingFeeds/article748524.ece

Brown, Sterling A. "The Approach of the Creative Artist." *Journal of American Folklore* 59 (October–December 1946): 506–7.

Brown, Sterling A. "The Blues." *Phylon* 13 (1952): 286–92.

Brown, Sterling A. "The Blues as Folk Poetry." *Folk-Say: A Regional Miscellany*. Ed. B. A. Botkin. 1930. *The Book of Negro Folklore.* Ed. Langston Hughes and Arna Bontemps. New York: Dodd, Mead, 1959. 371–86.

Brown, Sterling A. *Collected Poems.* Ed. Michael S. Harper. 1980. Chicago: Tri-Quarterly Press, 1989.

Brown, Sterling A. "Lonesome Valley" [9 poems]. *Folk-Say: A Regional Miscellany.* Ed. B. A. Botkin. Norman: University of Oklahoma Press, 1931. 113–23.

Brown, Sterling A. "Negro Folk Expression: Spirituals, Seculars, Ballads and Work Songs." *Phylon* 14 (1953): 45–61.

Brown, Sterling A. *Negro Poetry and Drama.* 1937. New York: Arno Press, 1969.

Brown, Sterling A. "Our Literary Audience." *Opportunity* 8 (February 1930): 42–46, 61.

Brown, Sterling A. *A Son's Return: Selected Essays.* Ed. Mark A. Sanders. Boston: Northeastern University Press, 1996.

Brown, Sterling A. "Weep Some More My Ladie." *Opportunity* 10 (March 1932): 87.

Brown, Sterling A., Arthur P. Davis, and Ulysses Lee, eds. *The Negro Caravan.* 1941. Salem: Ayer, 1987.

Brown, W. O. "The Nature of Race Consciousness." *Social Forces* 10 (October 1931): 90–97.

Brown, William Wells. *The Rising Son: Or, the Antecedents and Advancement of the Colored Race.* 1873. New York: Negro Universities Press, 1970.

Bruce, Janet. *The Kansas City Monarchs: Champions of Black Baseball.* Lawrence: University Press of Kansas, 1985.

Bruynoghe, Yannick. "In Chicago with Big Bill and Friends." *Living Blues* 55 (Winter 1982–83): 6–21.

Budds, Michael J. *Jazz in the Sixties: The Expansion of Musical Resources and Techniques.* Iowa City: University of Iowa Press, 1990.

Burgett, Paul. "Vindication as a Thematic Principle in the Writings of Alain Locke on the Music of Black Americans." *Black Music in the Harlem Renaissance.* Ed. Samuel A. Floyd, Jr. New York: Greenwood Press, 1990. 29–54.

Chambers, Iain. *Urban Rhythms: Pop Music and Popular Culture.* London: Macmillan, 1985.

Chapple, Steve, and Reebee Garofalo. *Rock 'n' Roll Is Here to Pay: The History and Politics of the Music Industry.* Chicago: Nelson-Hall, 1977.

Charters, Samuel. *The Legacy of the Blues: A Glimpse into the Art and the Lives of Twelve Great Bluesmen: An Informal Study.* London: Calder and Boyars, 1975.

Cohodas, Nadine. *Spinning Blues into Gold: The Chess Brothers and the Legendary Chess Records.* New York: St. Martin's Press, 2000.

Cole, Bill. *John Coltrane.* New York: Schirmer Books, 1976.

Coleman, Janet, and Al Young. *Mingus/Mingus: Two Memoirs.* New York: Limelight Editions, 1991.

Conover, Willis. "Jazz Mailbag." *Jazz*, November 1965, 6–8.

"A Conversation with Paul Oliver." *Living Blues* 54 (Autumn–Winter 1982): 24–30.

Cooper, Harry. "On Uber-Jazz: Replaying Adorno with the Grain." *October* 75 (Winter 1996): 99–133.

Coral, Gus, David Hinckley. and Debra Rodman. *The Rolling Stones: Black and White Blues.* 1963. Atlanta: Turner, 1995.

Coss, Bill. "Caught in the Act." Rev. of Eric Dolphy Quintet and Ree Dragonette at Town Hall. *Down Beat,* January 17, 1963, 42–43.

Costello, Donald P. "Black Man as Victim." *Commonweal* 28 (June 1968): 436–40.

Criss, Catherine. "For Houston's Geto Boys, Anything Goes in the World of Gangsta Rap." *Texas Magazine (Houston Chronicle),* April 5, 1992, 10–14.

Crouch, Stanley. "Introduction." *Love in Vain: The Life and Legend of Robert Johnson.* By Alan Greenberg. Garden City, N.Y.: Doubleday, 1983. vii–xii.

Cruse, Harold. *The Crisis of the Negro Intellectual.* New York: William Morrow, 1967.

Cunard, Nancy, ed. *Negro: An Anthology.* 1934. New York: Ungar, 1970.

Cunningham, Carl. "Symphony, Rice, UH to Offer Minority Internships." *Houston Post,* January 29, 1992, D2.

Dalrymple, Henderson. *Bob Marley: Music, Myth, and Rastas.* Sudbury, Middlesex: Carib-Arawak, 1976.

Dance, Helen Oakley. *Stormy Monday: The T-Bone Walker Story.* Baton Rouge: Louisiana State University Press, 1987.

De Man, George. *Helena: The Bridge, the River, the Romance.* Little Rock, Ark.: Phillips County Historical Society, 1978.

DeMichael, Don. "John Coltrane and Eric Dolphy Answer the Jazz Critics." *Down Beat,* April 12, 1962, 20–23.

Denselow, Robin. *When the Music's Over: The Story of Political Pop.* London: Faber and Faber, 1990.

Dent, Tom. "For Lil Louis." *Black World,* September 1975, 65.

Dolphy, Eric. Worksheet. August–December 1962. In the author's possession.

Dolphy, Eric. Letter to Reverend John Doherty. Kwangju, Korea, February 2, 1963. In the author's possession.

Dolphy, Sadie. Draft of letter to Vladimir Simosko, Princeton, New Jersey. Undated manuscript [ca. 1972]. In the author's possession.

Dougherty, Steven. "From 'Race Music' to Heavy Metal: A Fiery History of Protests." *Rock Music in America.* Ed. Janet Podell. New York: H. W. Wilson, 1987. 143–46.

Douglas, Ann. *Terrible Honesty: Mongrel Manhattan in the 1920s.* New York: Farrar, Straus and Giroux, 1995.

DuBois, W. E. B. "Criteria for Negro Art." *Crisis,* October 1926, 290–97.

DuBois, W. E. B. *The Souls of Black Folk. The Norton Anthology of African American Literature.* Ed. Henry Louis Gates, Jr., and Nellie McKay. New York: Norton, 1997. 613–740.

Dumas, Henry. "Will the Circle Be Unbroken?" 1965. *Goodbye, Sweetwater: New and Selected Stories.* Ed. Eugene Redmond. New York: Thunder's Mouth Press, 1988. 85–91.

Dunbar, Paul Laurence. *The Sport of the Gods.* New York: Dodd, Mead and Company, 1902.

Eliot, T. S. "Tradition and the Individual Talent." *The Sacred Wood: Essays on Poetry and Criticism.* 1930. New York: Barnes and Noble, 1960. 47–59.

"Eric Dolphy Quintet and Ree Dragonette, Poet in *Reflections and Entrances.*" Program. Town Hall, New York, November 20, 1962.

Evans, Martin C. "Memories Set to Music: His." *New York Newsday,* July 30, 2004, A17.

Fauset, Arthur Huff. "American Negro Folk Literature." *The New Negro*. Ed. Alain Locke. 1925. New York: Atheneum, 1992. 238–44.

Fernett, Gene. *Swing Out: Great Negro Dance Bands*. 1970. New York: Da Capo Press, 1993.

Ferris, William H. "Negro Composers and Negro Music—Is There Race in Music? Is There Race in Art?" 1922. *African Fundamentalism: A Literary and Cultural Anthology of Garvey's Harlem Renaissance*. Ed. Tony Martin. Dover: Majority Press, 1991. 299–302.

Finkelstein, Sidney. *Jazz: A People's Music*. 1948. New York: International, 1988.

Fisher, Miles Mark. *Negro Slave Songs of the United States*. Ithaca, N.Y.: Russell and Russell, 1968.

Fisher, Rudolph. "Miss Cynthie." *Best Short Stories by Negro Writers*. Ed. Langston Hughes. Boston: Little, Brown, 1967. 35–47.

"Folksongs and the Top 40: A Symposium." *Sing Out!* February–March 1966, 12–21.

Frankenstein, Alfred V. *Syncopating Saxophones*. Chicago: Robert O. Ballou, 1925.

Franklin, H. Bruce. *Prison Literature in America: The Victim as Criminal and Artist*. New York: Oxford University Press, 1989.

Frith, Simon. *Sound Effects: Youth, Leisure, and the Politics of Rock*. London: Constable, 1983.

Fullinwider, S. P. *The Mind and Mood of Black America: 20th Century Thought*. Homewood, Ill.: Dorsey Press, 1969.

Gabbin, Joanne V. *Sterling A. Brown: Building the Black Aesthetic Tradition*. 1985. Charlottesville: University Press of Virginia, 1994.

Garofalo, Reebee. "Crossing Over: 1939–1989." *Split Image: African Americans in the Mass Media*. Ed. Jannette L. Dates and William Barlow. Washington, D.C.: Howard University Press, 1990. 57–121.

Gates, Henry Louis, Jr. "Sudden Def." *New Yorker*, June 19, 1995, 34–42.

Gates, Henry Louis, Jr., and Nellie Y. McKay, eds. *Norton Anthology of African American Literature*. New York: W. W. Norton, 1977.

Gellert, Lawrence. "Negro Songs of Protest." *Negro: An Anthology*. Ed. Nancy Cunard. 1934. New York: Ungar, 1970. 226–37.

Gellert, Lawrence. "Remembering Nancy Cunard." *Nancy Cunard: Brave Poet, Indomitable Rebel, 1896–1965*. Ed. Hugh Ford. Philadelphia: Chilton, 1968. 141–44.

Gennari, John. "Jazz and the Cultural Canon." *Reconstruction* 1 (1991): 25–32.

George, Nelson. *The Death of Rhythm & Blues*. New York: Pantheon, 1988.

George, Nelson, et al. *Fresh: Hip Hop Don't Stop*. New York: Random House, 1985.

Gilbert, Andrew. "Tailored Ragtime." *San Jose Mercury News*, June 20, 2003, 29, 33.

Gilroy, Paul. *Small Acts: Thoughts on the Politics of Black Culture*. London: Serpent's Tail Press, 1993.

Ginsberg, Allen. "When the Mode of the Music Changes, the Walls of the City Shake." *Second Coming* 1.2 (1961): 40–42.

Gioia, Ted. *The Imperfect Art: Reflections on Jazz and Modern Culture*. New York: Oxford University Press, 1988.

Glover, Tony. "R&B." *Sing Out!* May 1965, 7–13.

Goldberg, Stephen E. *George Gershwin: A Study in American Music*. 1931. New York: Ungar, 1958.

Goldsmith, Peter D. *Making People's Music: Moe Asch and Folkways Records*. Washington, D.C.: Smithsonian Institution Press, 1998.

Gonzales, Michael A. "The Legend of Soul: Long Live Curtis Mayfield!" *Soul: Black Power, Politics, and Pleasure*. Ed. Monique Guillory and Richard C. Green. New York: New York University Press, 1998. 227–35.

Grandmaster Flash and the Furious Five. "The Message." *Rap: The Lyrics*. Ed. Lawrence A. Stanley. New York: Penguin, 1992. 150–54.

Grant, Robert B. *The Black Man Comes to the City: A Documentary Account from the Great Migration to the Great Depression, 1915–1930*. Chicago: Nelson-Hall, 1972.

Greene, Lorenzo J., Gary R. Kremer, and Anthony F. Holland. *Missouri's Black Heritage*. St. Louis: Forum Press, 1980.

Grothaus, Larry. "Kansas City Blacks, Harry Truman, and the Pendergast Machine." *Missouri Historical Review* 69 (October 1974): 65–82.

Gummere, Francis B. *Old English Ballads*. 1894. New York: Russell and Russell, 1967.

Guralnick, Peter. *Sweet Soul Music: Rhythm and Blues and the Southern Dream of Freedom*. New York: Harper and Row, 1986.

Guterl, Matthew Pratt. *The Color of Race in America, 1900–1940*. Cambridge: Harvard University Press, 2001.

Hales, Douglas. *A Southern Family in White and Black: The Cuneys of Texas*. College Station: Texas A & M University Press, 2003.

Hampton, Lionel, with James Haskins. *Hamp: An Autobiography*. New York: Warner Books, 1989.

Hampton, Wayne. *Guerilla Minstrels*. Knoxville: University of Tennessee Press, 1986.

Handy, W. C. *Blues: An Anthology*. New York: Albert and Charles Boni, 1926.

Handy, W. C. *Father of the Blues: An Autobiography*. New York: Macmillan, 1955.

Harding, Vincent. "Black Students and the 'Impossible' Revolution." *Ebony*, August 1969, 141–48.

Hare, Maud Cuney. *Negro Musicians and Their Music*. Washington, D.C.: Associated Publishers, 1936.

Hare, Maud Cuney. *Norris Wright Cuney: A Tribune of the Black People*. New York: Crisis Publishing Company, 1913.

Harper, Phillip Brian. "Nationalism and Social Division in Black Arts Poetry of the 1960s." *Critical Inquiry* 19 (Winter 1993): 234–55.

Harris, Sheldon. "Roy Brown, 1925–1981." *Living Blues* 52 (Spring 1982): 54.

Harris, William J., ed. *The LeRoi Jones/Amiri Baraka Reader*. New York: Thunder's Mouth Press, 1991.

Harrison, Paul Carter. *The Drama of Nommo*. New York: Grove Press, 1972.

Hart, Philip. *Orpheus in the New World: The Symphony Orchestra as an American Cultural Institution*. New York: W. W. Norton, 1973.

Hawes, Hampton, and Don Asher. *Raise Up Off Me*. New York: Coward, McCann and Geoghegan, 1974.

Hazzard-Gordon, Katrina. *Jookin': The Rise of Social Dance Formations in African-American Culture*. Philadelphia: Temple University Press, 1990.

Henderson, David. "Keep On Pushing." 1965. *The Poetry of Black America*. Ed. Arnold Adoff. New York: HarperCollins, 1973. 408–12.

Henderson, Stephen E. "The Heavy Blues of Sterling Brown: A Study of Craft and Tradition." *Black American Literature Forum* 14 (Spring 1980): 32–44.

Henderson, Stephen E. *Understanding the New Black Poetry: Black Speech and Black Music as Poetic References*. New York: Morrow, 1972.

Hendricks, Jon. "Jazz and Its Critics." *Liberator*, November 1969, 14–17.

Hentoff, Nat. Liner notes. Archie Shepp. *On This Night*. ABC/Impulse A-97. 1965.

Higgins, Chester. "What's Ahead for Blacks in Music?" *Jet*, April 22, 1971, 57–61.

Hinckley, David. "A Little Movement in Your Sacroiliac." *New York Daily News*, September 16, 2004. http://www.nydailynews.com/archives/news/2004/09/16/2004-09-16_a_little_movement_in_your_sac.html

Hirsch, Jerrold. "Folklore in the Making: B. A. Botkin." *Journal of American Folklore* 100 (January–March 1987): 3–38.

Hoffmann, Frank W. "Popular Music and Its Relationship to Black Social Consciousness." *Popular Music and Society* 8 (1982): 55–61.

Horkheimer, Max, and Theodor W. Adorno. "The Culture Industry: Enlightenment as Mass Deception." *Dialectic of Enlightenment.* 1944. Trans. John Cumming. New York: Continuum, 1990. 120–67.

Horricks, Raymond. *The Importance of Being Eric Dolphy.* Turnbridge Wells, Kent: D. J. Costello, 1989.

Howard, Aaron. "Illinois Jacquet Remembers: Houston's Music Legends a Half-Century Back." *Houston Public News*, October 16, 1996, 14–15.

Hudson, Theodore R. *From LeRoi Jones to Amiri Baraka: The Literary Works.* Durham, N.C.: Duke University Press, 1973.

Hudson, Theodore R. "The Trial of LeRoi Jones." *Imamu Amiri Baraka (LeRoi Jones): A Collection of Critical Essays.* Ed. Kimberly W. Benston. Englewood Cliffs, N.J.: Prentice-Hall, 1978. 48–53.

Hughes, Langston. *The Collected Poems of Langston Hughes.* Ed. Arnold Rampersad and David Roessel. New York: Knopf, 1994.

Hughes, Langston, and Arna Bontemps, eds. *The Book of Negro Folklore.* New York: Dodd, Mead, 1959.

Hurston, Zora Neale. "Characteristics of Negro Expression." 1934. *The Sanctified Church.* Berkeley, Calif.: Turtle Island, 1981. 49–68.

Hurston, Zora Neale. "Characteristics of Negro Expression." *Negro: An Anthology.* Ed. Nancy Cunard. 1934. New York: Frederick Ungar, 1970. 24–31.

Hutchinson, George. *The Harlem Renaissance in Black and White.* Cambridge: Harvard University Press, 1995.

Ice T and Heidi Siegmund. *The Ice Opinion: Who Gives A Fuck?* New York: St. Martin's Press, 1994.

Inglis, Ruth A. "An Objective Approach to the Relationship between Fiction and Society." *American Sociological Review* 3 (August 1938): 526–33.

Jackson, Richard L. *Black Literature and Humanism in Latin America.* Athens: University of Georgia Press, 1988.

James, Etta, and David Ritz. *Rage to Survive: The Etta James Story.* New York: Villard Books, 1995.

Jarrett, Michael. "Four Choruses on the Tropes of Jazz Writing." *American Literary History* 6 (Summer 1994): 336–53.

"Jazz and Revolutionary Black Nationalism (Part 3)." *Jazz*, June 1966, 28–30.

"Jazz and Revolutionary Black Nationalism (Part 10)." *Jazz*, January 1967, 38.

"Jazz Compositions by Gunther Schuller." Program. Circle in the Square, New York, May 16, 1960.

"Jazz Loses a Great One: Dolphy Dies in Berlin." *Overture* 44 (July 1964): 3, 15.

Johnson, Charles S. "The New Frontage on American Life." *The New Negro.* Ed. Alain Locke. 1925. New York: Atheneum, 1992. 278–98.

Johnson, James Weldon. "O Black and Unknown Bards." 1908. *The Portable Harlem Renaissance Reader.* Ed. David Levering Lewis. New York: Viking, 1994. 282–83.

Johnson, James Weldon, and J. Rosamond Johnson. *The Book of American Negro Spirituals.* 1926. New York: Da Capo Press, 1981.

Jones, Del. *Culture Bandits.* Vol. 1: *Cultural Genocide in AmeriKKKa.* Philadelphia: Hikeka Press, 1990.

Jordan, Norman. "Positive Black Music." *Cricket* (1969): 24–25.

Kallen, Horace M. *The Liberal Spirit.* Ithaca, N.Y.: Cornell University Press, 1948.

Kamin, Jonathan. "The White R&B Audience and the Music Industry, 1952–1956." *Popular Music and Society* 4 (1975): 170–87.

Karenga, Ron. "Black Cultural Nationalism." 1968. *The Black Aesthetic.* Ed. Addison Gayle, Jr. Garden City, N.Y.: Anchor Books, 1971. 31–37.

Karenga, Ron. "Black Cultural Nationalism." 1968. *The Black Aesthetic Movement.* Ed. Jeffrey Louis Decker. Dictionary of Literary Biography Documentary Series, vol. 8. Detroit: Gale Research, 1991. 32–36.

Katibu, Mwanafunzi. "Archie Shepp, As-9162, Three for a Quarter, One for a Dime." *Cricket* (1969): 26.

Katznelson, Ira. *Black Men, White Cities: Race, Politics, and Migration in the United States, 1900–30, and Britain, 1948–68.* Chicago: University of Chicago Press, 1976.

Kaufman, Bob. *The Ancient Rain: Poems 1956–1978.* New York: New Directions, 1981.

Kaufman, Bob. *Solitudes Crowded with Loneliness.* New York: New Directions, 1965.

Keller, David. "Eric Dolphy: The Los Angeles Years." *Jazz Times,* November 1981, 13–14.

Kennedy, Rick, and Randy McNutt. *Little Labels—Big Sound: Small Record Companies and the Rise of American Music.* Bloomington: Indiana University Press, 1999.

Kent, George E. *A Life of Gwendolyn Brooks.* Lexington: University Press of Kentucky, 1990.

King, B. B., with David Ritz. *Blues All Around Me: The Autobiography of B. B. King.* New York: Avon, 1996.

Kitwana, Bakari. "Are You Ready to Die? Gun Violence and the Hip-Hop Generation." *Source,* August 1995, 56–57.

Kitwana, Bakari. *The Rap on Gangsta Rap.* Chicago: Third World, 1994.

Koch, Kenneth. "Fresh Air." 1958. *The New American Poetry.* Ed. Donald M. Allen. New York: Grove, 1960. 229–36.

Kochman, Thomas. "The Kinetic Element in Black Idiom." *Rappin' and Stylin' Out: Communication in Black America.* Ed. Thomas Kochmand. Urbana: University of Illinois Press, 1972. 160–69.

Kofsky, Frank. *Black Nationalism and the Revolution in Music.* New York: Pathfinder Press, 1970.

Kosman, Joshua. "Scott Joplin Opera Leaps Back to Life." *San Francisco Chronicle,* June 24, 2003, D1, D2.

Kouwenhoven, John A. *The Arts in Modern American Civilization.* 1948. New York: W. W. Norton, 1967.

Krappe, Alexander H. *The Science of Folklore.* 1930. New York: W. W. Norton, 1964.

Lang, David. "Archie Shepp—Jazz Playwright." *Jazz,* January 1966, 26.

Larrey, Inge. "Remembering Milt Larkin: A Photo in Words." *Houston Jazz Scene,* October 1996, 1, 5–6.

The Last Poets. *Vibes from the Scribes: Selected Poems.* London: Pluto Press, 1985.

Leiris, Michel. *Race and Culture*. Paris: UNESCO, 1958.

Lester, Julius. "Len Chandler." *Sing Out!* April–May 1966, 9.

Lester, Julius. "Le Roi Jones." Rev. of *Blues People*. By Le Roi Jones. *Sing Out!* September 1965, 77–78.

Levine, Lawrence W. *Black Culture and Black Consciousness: Afro-American Folk Thought from Slavery to Freedom*. New York: Oxford University Press, 1978.

Lewis, David Levering. *W. E. B. DuBois: Biography of a Race, 1868–1919*. New York: Henry Holt, 1993.

Lhamon, W. T., Jr. *Deliberate Speed: The Origins of a Cultural Style in the American 1950s*. Washington, D.C.: Smithsonian Institutional Press, 1990.

Lindsay, Vachel. *The Art of the Moving Picture*. 1922. New York: Liveright, 1970.

Linnemann, Russell J. "Alain Locke's Theory of the Origins and Nature of Jazz." *Alain Locke: Reflections on a Modern Renaissance Man*. Ed. Russell J. Linnemann. Baton Rouge: Louisiana University Press, 1982. 109–21.

Lipscomb, Mance, and Glen Alyn. *I Say Me for a Parable: The Oral Autobiography of Mance Lipscomb, Texas Bluesman*. New York: Da Capo Press, 1994.

Lipsitz, George. *Class and Culture in Cold War America: "A Rainbow at Midnight."* South Hadley, Mass.: Bergin and Garvey, 1982.

Lipsitz, George. *Time Passages: Collective Memory and American Popular Culture*. Minneapolis: Minnesota University Press, 1990.

Lock, Graham. *Forces in Motion: Anthony Braxton and the Meta-reality of Creative Music*. London: Quartet Books, 1988.

Locke, Alain. *The Negro and His Music*. 1936. New York: Arno Press and New York Times, 1969.

Locke, Alain. "Negro Music Goes to Par." 1939. *The Critical Temper of Alain Locke: A Selection of His Essays on Art and Culture*. Ed. Jeffrey C. Stewart. New York: Garland, 1993. 117–21.

Locke, Alain, ed. *The New Negro: An Interpretation*. 1925. New York: Atheneum, 1992.

Locke, Alain. "Toward a Critique of Negro Music." 1934. *The Critical Temper of Alain Locke: A Selection of His Essays on Art and Culture*. Ed. Jeffrey C. Stewart. New York: Garland, 1993. 109–15.

Lomax, Alan. "Zora Neale Hurston: A Life of Negro Folklore." *Sing Out!* October–November 1960, 12–13.

Lomax, John A. "Self-Pity in Negro Folk-Songs." *Nation* 9 (August 1917): 141–45.

Lomax, Joseph F. "Zydeco—Must Live On!" *What's Goin On?* (in *Modern Texas Folklore*). Ed. Francis Edward Abernathy. Austin: Encino Press, 1976. 216.

Long, Richard A. "Interactions between Writers and Music during the Harlem Renaissance." *Black Music in the Harlem Renaissance*. Ed. Samuel A. Floyd, Jr. New York: Greenwood Press, 1990. 129–37.

Mackey, Nathaniel. *Discrepant Engagement: Dissonance, Cross-Culturality, and Experimental Writing*. Cambridge, U.K.: Cambridge University Press, 1993.

Mahabir, Cynthia. "Wit and Popular Music: The Calypso and the Blues." *Popular Music* 15 (January 1996): 55–81.

Margolies, Edward. *Native Sons: A Critical Study of Twentieth Century Black American Authors*. Philadelphia: Lippincott, 1968.

Marian Anderson. PBS documentary, April 1992. Broadcast April 18, 1992, KUHT-TV, Houston.

Marks, Anthony. "Young, Gifted and Black: Afro-American and Afro-Caribbean Music in Britain 1963–88." *Black Music in Britain: Essays on the Afro-Asian Contribution to Popular Music.* Ed. Paul Oliver. Philadelphia: Open University Press: 1990. 102–17.

Martin, Asa E. *Our Negro Population: A Sociological Study of the Negroes of Kansas City, Missouri.* 1913. New York: Negro Universities Press, 1969.

Maxwell, William J. *New Negro, Old Left: African-American Writing and Communism between the Wars.* New York: Columbia University Press, 1999.

Melly, George. *Revolt Into Style: The Pop Arts.* Garden City, N.Y.: Anchor Books, 1971.

Miller, Lloyd, and James K. Skipper, Jr. "Sounds of Black Protest in Avant-Garde Jazz."1968. *The Sounds of Social Change: Studies in Popular Culture.* Ed. R. Serge Denisoff and Richard A. Peterson. Chicago: Rand McNally, 1972. 26–37.

Miller, Paul Eduard. "Roots of Hot White Jazz Are Negroid." *Down Beat,* April 1937, 5.

Mills, David, et al. *George Clinton and P-Funk: An Oral History.* New York: Avon, 1998.

Mingus, Charles. *Town Hall Concert.* Solid Sate Records, SS 18024. 1962.

Mordecai, Joyce. Telephone interview. January 19, 1992.

Morris, Ronald L. *Wait until Dark: Jazz and the Underworld, 1880–1940.* Bowling Green, Ohio: Bowling Green University Popular Press, 1980.

Mtume. "Trippin'—a Need for Change." *Cricket* (1969): 1–2.

Munro, C. Lynn. "LeRoi Jones: A Man in Transition." *CLA Journal* 17 (1973): 57–78.

Naison, Mark. *Communists in Harlem during the Depression.* New York: Grove Press, 1985.

Nathan, David. Liner notes. *Curtis Mayfield: Curtis.* Rhino Records CD R 79932, 2000.

Neal, Larry. "Any Day Now: Black Art and Black Liberation." *Ebony,* August 1969, 54–62.

Neal, Larry. "New Grass/Albert Ayler." *Cricket* (1969): 37–40.

Neal, Larry. *Visions of a Liberated Future: Black Arts Movement Writings.* Ed. Michael Schwartz. New York: Thunder's Mouth Press, 1989.

Neal, Larry. "A Conversation with Archie Shepp." *Liberator,* November 1965, 24–25.

Niles, Abbe. "Introduction." *Blues: An Anthology.* By W. C. Handy. New York: Albert and Charles Boni, 1926. 12–45.

Norman, Philip. *Shout! The Beatles in Their Generation.* New York: Simon and Schuster, 1981.

Ogren, Kathy J. *The Jazz Revolution: Twenties America and the Meaning of Jazz.* New York: Oxford University Press, 1989.

Oliver, Paul. *Aspects of the Blues Tradition.* New York: Oak Publications, 1970.

Oliver, Paul. *Blues Fell This Morning: The Meaning of the Blues.* New York: Horizon Press, 1961.

Oliver, Paul. *The Meaning of the Blues.* New York: Collier Books, 1963.

Ortiz, Fernando. *Los Negros Brujos.* 1906. Miami: Ediciones Universal, 1973.

Ossman, David. *The Sullen Art: Interviews with Modern American Poets.* New York: Corinth, 1963.

Ostendorf, Berndt. *Black Literature in White America.* Totowa, N.J.: Barnes and Noble, 1982.

Ostransky, Leroy. *Jazz City: The Impact of Our Cities on the Development of Jazz.* Englewood Cliffs, N.J.: Prentice-Hall, 1978.

Owens, Calvin, and Sara Owens. Interview. Houston, January 5, 1992.

Pearson, Nathan W., Jr. *Goin' to Kansas City.* Urbana: University of Illinois Press, 1987.

Peretti, Burton W. *The Creation of Jazz: Music, Race, and Culture in Urban America.* Urbana and Chicago: University of Illinois Press, 1992.

Peretti, Burton W. *Jazz in American Culture.* Chicago: Ivan R. Dee, 1997.

Poindexter, Ray. *Arkansas Airwaves.* North Little Rock, Ark.: n.p., 1974.

Poinsett, Alex. "The Economics of Liberation." *Ebony,* August 1969, 150–55.

Pomus, Doc. "Doc Pomus Remembers." *Living Blues* 69 (1986): 12–13.

Pomus, Doc. "The Journals of Doc Pomus (1978–91)." *Antaeus* 71–72 (Autumn 1993): 157–84.

Porter, Roy, with David Keller. *There and Back: The Roy Porter Story.* Baton Rouge: Louisiana State University Press, 1991.

Powell, Kevin. "Mental Terrorism." *In the Tradition: An Anthology of Young Black Writers.* Ed. Kevin Powell and Ras Baraka. New York: Harlem River Press, 1992. 261–64.

Pratt, Ray. "The Politics of Authenticity in Popular Music: The Case of the Blues." *Popular Music and Society* 10 (1986): 55–78.

Pruter, Robert. *Chicago Soul.* Urbana: University of Illinois Press, 1991.

Pruter, Robert. "Curtis Mayfield." *Juke Blues* 46 (Spring 2000): 65–66.

Ra, Sun. *The Immeasurable Equation: The Colleted Poetry and Prose.* Ed. James L. Wolf and Hartmut Geerken. Norderstedt, Germany: Waitawhile, 2005.

Redd, Lawrence N. *Rock Is Rhythm and Blues: The Impact of Mass Media.* East Lansing: Michigan State University Press, 1974.

Reed, Adolph L., Jr. "Black Particularity Reconsidered." *Telos* 39 (Spring 1979): 71–93.

Reed, Adolph L., Jr. *Stirrings in the Jug: Black Politics in the Post-segregation Era.* Minneapolis: Minnesota University Press, 1999.

Reeves, Martha, and Mark Bego. *Dancing in the Street: Confessions of a Motown Diva.* New York: Hyperion, 1994.

"Remembering Eric: An Interview with Mr. and Mrs. Eric Allan Dolphy, Sr." *Jazz Heritage Foundation* 3 (June 1982): 9–13.

Rifkin, Libbie. *Career Moves: Olson, Creeley, Zukofsky, Berrigan, and the American Avant Garde.* Madison: University of Wisconsin Press, 2000.

Robertson, Stanley G. "The Modern Touch: We Remember Eric Dolphy." *Los Angeles Sentinel,* July 9, 1964, 6B.

Robinson, Leroy. "West Coast Record Date." *Jazz,* November 1965, 18–21.

Rogers, J. A. "Jazz at Home." *The New Negro.* Ed. Alain Locke. 1925. New York: Atheneum, 1992. 216–24.

Romney, Hugh. "Altar Piece." *Beat Coast East: An Anthology of Rebellion.* Ed. Stanley Fisher. New York: Excelsior, 1960. 53–54.

Rose, Cynthia. *Living in America: The Soul Saga of James Brown.* London: Serpent's Tail Press, 1990.

Rose, Tricia. *Black Noise: Rap Music and Black Culture in Contemporary America.* Hanover, N.H.: Wesleyan University Press, 1994.

Rose, Tricia. "Rap Music and the Demonization of Black Males." *Black Male: Representations of Masculinity in Contemporary American Art.* Ed Thelma Golden. New York: Whitney Museum of Art and Henry N. Abrams, 1994. 149–55.

Rowell, Charles H. "Sterling A. Brown and the Afro-American Folk Tradition." *Studies in the Literary Imagination* 7 (Fall 1974): 131–52.

Russell, Ross. *Jazz Style in Kansas City and the Southwest.* Berkeley and Los Angeles: University of California Press, 1971.

Rutter, Larry. "The Animal Loves You, Wear It in Your Eyes." *Jazz*, January 1967, 26–29.

Salaam, Kalamu ya. "The Magic of Juju: An Appreciation of the Sixties Black Arts Movement." Unpublished typescript, 1996.

Salaam, Kalamu ya. "The Man Who Walked in Balance." *Coda*, September–October 1992, 20–26.

Sales, Grover. *Jazz: America's Classical Music*. Englewood Cliffs, N.J.: Prentice-Hall, 1984.

Savaglio, Paula. "Polka Bands and Choral Groups: The Musical Self-Representation of Polish-Americans in Detroit." *Ethnomusicology* 40 (Winter 1996): 35–47.

Schuller, Gunther. "In Tribute: Eric Dolphy, 1928–1964." *Down Beat*, August 27, 1964, 12.

Schuller, Gunther. *The Swing Era: The Development of Jazz, 1930–1945*. New York: Oxford University Press, 1989.

Seagrave, Kerry. *Payola in the Music Industry: A History, 1880–1991*. Jefferson, N.C.: McFarland, 1994.

Shanet, Howard. *Philharmonic: A History of New York's Orchestra*. Garden City, N.Y.: Doubleday, 1975.

Shaw, Arnold. *Honkers and Shouters: The Golden Years of Rhythm and Blues*. New York: Macmillan, 1978.

Shepp, Archie. "On Jazz." *Jazz*, August–September 1965, 24.

Sheridan, Chris, comp. *Dis Here: A Bio-Discography of Julian "Cannonball" Adderley*. Westport, Conn.: Greenwood Press, 2000.

Sidran, Ben. *Black Talk*. 1971. New York: DaCapo Press, 1981.

Siegel, Dorothy Schainman. *The Glory Road: The Story of Josh White*. White Hall, Va.: Shoe Tree Press, 1991.

Silber, Irwin. "Fan the Flames." *Sing Out!* May 1965, 63–65.

Simosko, Vladimir, and Barry Tepperman. *Eric Dolphy: A Musical Biography and Discography*. 1974. New York: Da Capo Press, 1979.

Sinclair, Upton. *The Jungle*. 1906. New York: New American Library, 1980.

Slavens, George Everett. "The Missouri Negro Press, 1875–1920." *Missouri Historical Review* 64 (July 1970): 413–31.

Smallwood, James M. *Time of Hope, Time of Despair: Black Texans during Reconstruction*. Port Washington, N.Y.: Kennikat Press, 1981.

Smith, David Lionel. "Amiri Baraka and the Politics of Popular Culture." *Politics and the Muse: Studies in the Politics of Recent American Literature*. Ed. Adam Sorkin. Bowling Green, Ohio: Bowling Green University Popular Press, 1989. 222–38.

Smith, David Lionel. "The Black Arts Movement and Its Critics." *American Literary History* 3 (Spring 1991): 93–110.

Smith, Henry Nash. "Culture." *Southwest Review*, January 1928, 249–55.

Smith, Suzanne E. *Dancing in the Street: Motown and the Cultural Politics of Detroit*. Cambridge: Harvard University Press, 1999.

Smith, W. O. *Sideman: The Long Gig*. Nashville: Rutledge Hill Press, 1991.

Snellings, Rolland [Askia Muhammad Touré]. "Keep on Pushin': Rhythm & Blues as a Weapon." *Liberator*, October 1965, 6–8.

Snitzer, Herb. "The Realities of Cultural Prestige: A Reply to Gennari." *Reconstruction* 1 (1991): 33–34.

Songha, Wanyandey. "Marxism and the Black Revolution." *Liberator*, September 1969, 16–17.

Spady, James G. *Larry Neal: Liberated Black Philly Poet with a Blues Streak of Mellow Wisdom.* Philadelphia: PC International Press and Black History Museum Umum, 1989.

Spaeth, Sigmund. *The Facts of Life in Popular Song.* New York: Whittlesey House / McGraw Hill, 1934.

Spellman, A. B. *Four Lives in the Bebop Business.* New York: Pantheon, 1966.

Spellman, A. B. "Revolution in Sound." *Ebony,* August 1969, 84–89.

Spivak, John L. "Flashes from Georgia Chain Gangs." *Negro: An Anthology.* Ed. Nancy Cunard. 1934. New York: Frederick Ungar, 1970. 124–30.

Stewart, Jeffrey C., ed. *The Critical Temper of Alain Locke: A Selection of His Essays on Art and Culture.* New York: Garland, 1993.

Stewart, Jimmy. "Introduction to Black Aesthetics in Music." *The Black Aesthetic.* Ed. Addison Gayle, Jr. Garden City, N.Y.: Anchor Books, 1972. 77–91.

Stowe, David W. "Jazz in the West." *Western Historical Quarterly* 23 (February 1992): 53–73.

Sugar Hill Gang. "Rapper's Delight." *Rap: The Lyrics.* Ed. Lawrence A. Stanley. New York: Penguin, 1992. 319–27.

Tate, Greg. "Growing Up in Public: Amiri Baraka Changes His Mind." *Flyboy in the Buttermilk: Essays on Contemporary America.* New York: Simon, 1992: 168–77.

Taylor, Art. *Notes and Tones: Musician to Musician Interviews.* New York: Da Capo Press, 1993.

Taylor, Clyde. "Henry Dumas: Legacy of a Long-Breath Singer." *Black World,* September 1975, 4–16.

Taylor, Marc. *A Touch of Classic Soul: Soul Singers of the Early 1970s.* Jamaica, N.Y.: Aloiv, 1996.

Thomas. J. C. *Chasin' the Trane: The Music and Mystique of John Coltrane.* New York: Da Capo Press, 1976.

Thomas, Lorenzo. "Askia Muhammad Touré: Crying Out the Goodness." *Obsidian* 1.1 (1975): 31–49.

Thomas, Lorenzo. *Extraordinary Measures: Afrocentric Modernism and Twentieth-Century American Poetry.* Tuscaloosa: University of Alabama Press, 2000.

Thomas, Lorenzo. "Jazz Angel." *Houston Metropolitan Magazine,* October 1990, 52–55, 105–6.

Thomas, Will H. *Some Current Folk-Songs of the Negro.* 1912. Austin: Texas Folklore Society, 1936.

"Tough Talk on Entertainment." *Time,* June 12, 1995, 32–35.

Touré, Askia Muhammad. "The Crisis in Black Culture." *Black Arts: An Anthology of Black Creations.* Ed. Ahmed Alhamisi and Harun Kofi Wangara. Detroit: Black Arts Publications, 1969. 29–39.

Touré, Askia Muhammad. *JuJu.* Chicago: Third World, 1970.

Touré, Askia Muhammad [Rolland Snellings]. "Keep On Pushin': Rhythm and Blues as a Weapon." *Liberator,* October 1965, 6–8.

Touré, Askia Muhammad. "The Sound of Allah's Horn." *Black Arts: An Anthology of Black Creations.* Ed. Ahmed Alhamisi and Harun Kofi Wangara. Detroit: Black Arts Publications, 1969. 135–39.

Touré, Askia Muhammad. Telephone interview. Atlanta, July 13, 1995.

Tucker, Neely. "Bo Diddley." *Living Blues* 77 (December 1987): 17–20.

Twitchell, James B. *Preposterous Violence: Fables of Aggression in Modern Culture.* New York: Oxford University Press, 1989.

Van Deburg, William L. *New Day in Babylon: The Black Power Movement and American Culture, 1965–1975.* Chicago: University of Chicago Press, 1992.

Vincent, Ted. *Keep Cool: The Black Activists Who Built the Jazz Age.* London: Pluto Press, 1995.

Wald, Elijah. *Escaping the Delta: Robert Johnson and the Invention of the Blues.* New York: Amistad Books, 2004.

Walrond, Eric D. "The Negro Exodus from the South." *Current History*, September 1923, 942–44.

Walton, Ortiz M. *Music: Black, White and Blue.* New York: William Morrow, 1972.

Warren, Paul. "Holding Up All Sorrow for Heaven to See." *Village Voice*, July 6, 1972, 32.

Washington, Forrester B. "The Detroit Newcomers' Greeting." *The Survey*, July 14, 1917, 333–35.

Watkins, Mel. "The Lyrics of James Brown: Ain't It Funky Now, or Money Won't Change Your Licking Stick." *Amistad 2.* Ed. John A. Williams and Charles F. Harris. New York: Vintage, 1971. 21–42.

Watson, Ian. *Song and Democratic Culture in Britain: An Approach to Popular Culture in Social Movements.* New York: St. Martin's Press, 1983.

Watts, Daniel H. "Editorial: The Carmichael/Cleaver Debate." *Liberator*, September 1969, 3, 5.

Welburn, Ron. "The Black Aesthetic Imperative." *The Black Aesthetic.* Ed. Addison Gayle, Jr. Garden City, N.Y.: Doubleday, 1972. 126–42.

Welburn, Ron. "Dance and the New Black Music." *Black Review 2.* Ed. Mel Watkins. New York: William Morrow, 1972. 55–65.

Welburn, Ron. Letter to Lorenzo Thomas. January 2, 1978.

Welburn, Ron. "Miles Davis and Black Music in the Seventies." *Liberator*, October 1970, 21, 23.

Welburn, Ron. "Record Review: The Last Poets." *Liberator*, November 1970, 20, 23.

Wells, John D. "Me and the Devil Blues: A Study of Robert Johnson and the Music of the Rolling Stones." *Popular Music and Society* 9 (1983): 17–24.

Werner, Craig. *Higher Ground: Stevie Wonder, Aretha Franklin, Curtis Mayfield, and the Rise and Fall of American Soul.* New York: Crown, 2004.

Westminster Presbyterian Church. Program. Los Angeles, March 17, 1946.

Wexler, Jerry, and David Ritz. *Rhythm and the Blues: A Life in American Music.* New York: Alfred A. Knopf, 1993.

"What's Happening: Newport 1965." *Sing Out!* November 1965, 3–8.

The Whispers. "Seems Like I Gotta Do Wrong." *The Best of the Whispers.* BMG Records, 2002.

White, Josh, with Robert Shelton and Walter Raim. *The Josh White Songbook.* Chicago: Quadrangle, 1963.

"White Man's Music Started Jazz—Says Nick." *Down Beat*, March 1937, 1.

Whiteman, Paul, and Mary Margaret McBride. *Jazz.* 1926. New York: Arno Press, 1974.

Whitney, Lois. "English Primitivistic Theories of Epic Origins." *Modern Philology* 21 (May 1924): 337–78.

Wicke, Peter. *Rock Music: Culture, Aesthetics, and Sociology.* Trans. Rachel Fogg. Cambridge: Cambridge University Press, 1990.

Wilkins, Roy, with Tom Mathews. *Standing Fast: The Autobiography of Roy Wilkins*. 1982. New York: Da Capo Press, 1994.

Williams, Doris. *Lonesome Traveler: The Life of Lee Hays*. 1988. Lincoln: University of Nebraska Press, 1993.

Williams, Martin. "Introducing Eric Dolphy." *Jazz Review* 3 (June 1960): 16–17.

Wilson, Pat. "Conversing with Cannonball." *Down Beat*, June 22, 1972, 12–13.

Wilson, Thomas D. "Chester A. Franklin and Harry S. Truman: An African-American Conservative and the 'Conversion' of the Future President." *Missouri Historical Review* 88 (October 1993): 48–77.

Winslow, Pete. "Beautiful Wreckage: An Essay on the Poetry of Bob Kaufman." *St. Andrews Review* 3.1 (1974): 21–35.

Work, John W. *American Negro Songs*. New York: Howell, Soskin, 1940.

Wright, Richard. "Big Boy Leaves Home." *Black Writers of America: A Comprehensive Anthology*. Ed. Richard Barksdale and Kenneth Kinnamon. New York: Macmillan, 1972. 548–64.

Wright, Richard. "Blueprint for Negro Writing." 1937. *The Portable Harlem Renaissance Reader*. Ed. David Levering Lewis. New York: Viking, 1994. 194–205.

Wright, Richard. "Foreword." *The Meaning of the Blues*. By Paul Oliver. New York: Collier Books, 1963. 7–12.

Wright, Richard. *White Man, Listen!* 1957. New York: Harper Perennial, 1995.

Zoglin, Richard. "A Company under Fire: Targeted as the Chief Cultural Offender, Time Warner Struggles to Defend Itself." *Time*, June 12, 1995, 37–39.

Index